40 QUESTIONS ABOUT
Typology and Allegory

Mitchell L. Chase

Benjamin L. Merkle, Series Editor

KREGEL
ACADEMIC

40 Questions About Typology and Allegory
© 2020 Mitchell L. Chase

Published by Kregel Academic, an imprint of Kregel Publications, 2450 Oak Industrial Dr. NE, Grand Rapids, MI 49505-6020.

This book is a title in the 40 Questions Series edited by Benjamin L. Merkle.

ISBN 978-0-8254-4638-2, print
ISBN 978-0-8254-6919-0, Kindle
ISBN 978-0-8254-7766-9, epub

Printed in the United States of America

22 23 24 25 26 27 28 / 8 7 6 5 4 3 2

"Typology and allegory are confusing concepts for many Christians, sometimes to the point that they are avoided altogether. Mitchell Chase clears away the fog surrounding these ancient Christian interpretive practices and helps us understand their relevance. But this isn't just a good book on typology and allegory; it's a practical primer on Christian biblical interpretation. I cannot recommend it highly enough!"
— Matthew Y. Emerson, Professor of Religion, Oklahoma Baptist University, and Dean of Hobbs College of Theology and Ministry; author of *"He Descended to the Dead": An Evangelical Theology of Holy Saturday*

"Somehow I grew up being taught the Bible and studying the Bible in college and through various serious Bible study organizations without ever learning about typology. And I know that I am not alone. Over and over again, I hear those who have loved and studied the Bible for a lifetime, but are newly discovering these things, ask, 'How come I never saw this before?' *40 Questions About Typology and Allegory* is a book I will be recommending to those who are new to biblical theology to help them grow in seeing that God has used types and shadows in history and in the Bible to help us see the person and work of Christ more clearly. This book's simplicity, clarity, and specificity will not only deepen understanding; it will also generate wonder and proper awe at the revelation of Jesus Christ."
— Nancy Guthrie, author of *Even Better Than Eden*; Bible teacher for Biblical Theology Workshops for Women

"Mitch Chase deftly shows how the Old Testament, through prefigurings, promises, and patterns, leans forward to anticipate the coming Messiah. With clear structure and short chapters, this is a handy resource to consult as you prepare to teach the Scriptures, all of which center on Christ. The Old Testament may be a room dimly lit, but there are stores of treasure to be seen."
— Matt Smethurst, managing editor, The Gospel Coalition; author of *Before You Open Your Bible*

"You need to read this book! There is a revolution afoot in biblical interpretation and the road to the future runs through the past. The recovery of premodern exegesis is reinvigorating preaching and inspiring theologians to make the Bible their primary source again. You may have wondered what all the fuss is about and wished for a sure-footed guide to introduce you to the landscape. Look no further. This is a useful book because it takes a large number of very important ideas that scholars have been discussing for a while now and puts them into an accessible, clear, and concise format that students, pastors, and professors will find engaging and helpful. There are important differences between typology and allegory, but there are much bigger differences between the way that orthodox, premodern interpreters make use of them and the way they function in the hands of modern, historical critics. It is a matter of perspective and this book will help you gain a better perspective on how to go about interpreting the Bible as divine revelation."
— Craig A. Carter, Professor of Theology, Tyndale University; author of *Interpreting Scripture with the Great Tradition: Recovering the Genius of Premodern Exegesis*

"Typology and (especially) allegory are sometimes viewed as swear words in modern biblical interpretation. These interpretive strategies are seen as the *reductio ad absurdum* of premodern hermeneutics—flights of fancy made possible only because the ancients had no awareness of modern critical methodologies. But in this extraordinarily helpful book, Mitchell Chase rehabilitates these important interpretive tools for an evangelical audience, not only by exploring how they work in practice, but also by demonstrating the theological vision of Scripture and history that renders them intelligible."
— Luke Stamps, Associate Professor of Theology, Anderson University; author of *Thy Will Be Done: A Contemporary Defense of Two-Wills Christology*

"I love thinking about typology and allegory because these methods are so ingrained in how the Scriptures are to be read. The Bible keeps building on its metaphors and images till they are bursting with life and meaning. Mitch Chase recognizes this and offers a wise, careful, and comprehensive survey of these reading strategies. He covers definitions, how they were employed in church history, and identifies types and allegories in the Scriptures. Readers now have a great starting point for thinking well about these important topics."
— Patrick Schreiner, Associate Professor of New Testament and Biblical Theology, Midwestern Baptist Theological Seminary; author of *The Ascension of Christ*

"Mitchell Chase has written a book that will profit God's people—church members, theological students, pastors, and teachers. Of the many qualities of this book, the first is that it is well written. Chase discusses issues that are often fuzzy in the minds of God's people—typology and allegory—in a very accessible manner. A second quality of this book is that it is scripturally based. This is the case not simply because Chase quotes Scripture but because he bases his arguments on the entailments of Scripture. He is not afraid to think contemplatively about what Scripture means by what it says and how its meaning ought to affect interpretation. A third quality of this book is that its argument is canonical. Chase argues his case based on the Old and New Testaments, and on how Scripture interprets Scripture. A fourth quality of the book is that it is historically rooted. Chase's book displays a wholesome and necessary respect for the thoughts of great minds who have gone before us. Since presuppositions are both inevitable and determinative, why not come to Scripture with time-proven assumptions? Chase's book helps us at this very point. A fifth quality of this book is that it is practically relevant. It will help God's people understand the written Word of God in order to love, worship, and serve God better. I thank Mitchell Chase for writing this book. It will, with careful study, provide great help to the church of God. It will inform all, challenge many to rethink issues related to typology and allegory, and confirm the hunches of others."
— Richard C. Barcellos, pastor of Grace Reformed Baptist Church, Palmdale, CA; Associate Professor of Exegetical Theology, IRBS Theological Seminary; author of *Getting the Garden Right: Adam's Work and God's Rest in Light of Christ*

For Jim Hamilton,
a dear Christian brother,
whose love for the Bible and joy in Christ
have impacted and shaped me,
to the glory of God.

Contents

Acknowledgments / 9

Introduction / 11

Part 1: The Bible's Big Story

1. What Story Is the Bible Telling? / 17
2. How Does the Bible Tell Its Story? / 25

Part 2: Questioning Typology

Section A: Understanding Typology

3. What Is Typology? / 35
4. What Are the Theological Assumptions of Typology? / 41
5. Should We Identify Types the New Testament Does Not Identify? / 47
6. Do All Types Lead to Christ? / 53
7. Are Types Only Recognizable in Hindsight? / 59
8. Are All Types Historical? / 65
9. Is Typology the Result of Exegesis or Something Else? / 71

Section B: Typology in Church History

10. How Was Typology Practiced in the Early Church? / 79
11. How Was Typology Practiced in the Middle Ages? / 87
12. How Was Typology Practiced in the Early Modern Era? / 95
13. How Was Typology Practiced in the Enlightenment? / 101
14. How Was Typology Practiced in the Late Modern Era? / 107
15. How Was Typology Practiced in the Postmodern Era? / 111

Section C: Identifying Types

16. How Do We Identify Types? / 119
17. What Types Are in Genesis? / 123
18. What Types Are in Exodus? / 137
19. What Types Are in Leviticus through Deuteronomy? / 145
20. What Types Are in Joshua through Ruth? / 153
21. What Types Are in 1 Samuel through 2 Chronicles? / 159
22. What Types Are in Ezra through Esther? / 167
23. What Types Are in Job through Song of Solomon? / 173
24. What Types Are in Isaiah through Malachi? / 181

Part 3: Questioning Allegory

Section A: Understanding Allegory

25. What Is Allegory and Allegorical Interpretation? / 193
26. What Are the Theological Assumptions of Allegory? / 199

Section B: Allegory in Church History

27. How Was Allegory Practiced in the Early Church? / 207
28. How Was Allegory Practiced in the Middle Ages? / 215
29. How Was Allegory Practiced in the Early Modern Era? / 221
30. How Was Allegory Practiced in the Enlightenment? / 229
31. How Was Allegory Practiced in the Late Modern Era? / 235
32. How Was Allegory Practiced in the Postmodern Era? / 241

Section C: Identifying Allegories

33. How Should We Practice Allegorical Interpretation? / 249
34. Are There Allegories in Genesis through Deuteronomy? / 255
35. Are There Allegories in Joshua through Esther? / 261
36. Are There Allegories in Job through Song of Solomon? / 267
37. Are There Allegories in Isaiah through Malachi? / 273
38. Are There Allegories in Matthew through Acts? / 279
39. Are There Allegories in Romans through Revelation? / 287

Part 4: Reflecting on Typology and Allegory

40. Why Should Interpreters Care about Typology and Allegory? / 295

Select Bibliography / 301
Scripture Index / 305

Acknowledgments

Joy is the word that comes to mind when I reflect on writing about typology and allegory. These subjects required the use of many articles and books in the history of interpretation, as well as many primary sources. I'm grateful for the treasure trove of sources in the library at The Southern Baptist Theological Seminary, which allowed me to use many books over many months.

My wife Stacie read through the manuscript, offering helpful comments and suggestions that strengthened the content. Her support and encouragement are life-giving.

I'm thankful for Ben Merkle, the editor for the excellent 40 Questions series, who gave timely feedback and edits. He has been supportive of this book from start to finish! It's been a blessing to work with him.

With great appreciation, I want to acknowledge Chad Ashby, Matt Emerson, Josh Philpot, and Patrick Schreiner, who all devoted time to engage this material and who responded with suggestions to help my arguments be clearer and more compelling.

My gratitude abounds for Kosmosdale Baptist Church, where I have the privilege of being the preaching pastor. My dear brothers and sisters, I thought of you again and again as I wrote this book, praying that you, as well as all the saints who read it, will see the glory of Christ in the Word of God.

Introduction

In chapter 10 of *The Magician's Nephew*, Uncle Andrew lacked the eyes to see—to *really* see—the wonder of what Aslan had sung into being. Wonderful sights and sounds filled scenes around the characters as Narnia woke to life. But C. S. Lewis explains why Uncle Andrew was frightened: "For what you see and hear depends a good deal on where you are standing: it also depends on what sort of person you are."[1] That statement is true for Bible readers too.

Whenever we approach the Bible, we're standing somewhere. Let's look around. First, we're standing in the twenty-first century AD, with two millennia of Christian interpretive tradition behind us. Second, we're standing in a skeptical age where the Bible is viewed, in many cases, with disdain, condescension, confusion, and rejection.

But where are you standing personally? This question matters because the Bible is not like any other book, and so we shouldn't approach it like any other book. We need eyes to see the wonder of what Aslan has sung into being: sixty-six God-breathed books, written over fourteen hundred years by more than forty authors, in multiple languages and on multiple continents, together telling one grand story, an epic rivaling all others and summoning us to allegiance. As Erich Auerbach writes,

> The world of the Scripture stories is not satisfied with claiming to be a historically true reality—it insists that it is the only real world, is destined for autocracy. All other scenes, issues, and ordinances have no right to appear independently of it, and it is promised that all of them, the history of all mankind, will be given their due place within its frame, will be subordinated to it. The Scripture stories do not, like Homer's, court our favor, they do not flatter us that they may please us and enchant us—they seek to subject us, and if we refuse to be subjected we are rebels.[2]

1. C. S. Lewis, *The Magician's Nephew* (New York: HarperTrophy, 1955), 148.
2. Erich Auerbach, *Mimesis: The Representation of Reality in Western Literature* (Princeton, NJ: Princeton University Press, 1953), 14–15.

Some Bible readers are rebels, and this affects how they read and what they see. They may wholly reject the Bible's authority, inspiration, and unity. Other readers may affirm its inspiration and submit to its authority, and yet struggle to grasp its unity. They read a Bible that has been too compartmentalized in their minds, so they don't see or enjoy its coherence and continuity. We should affirm the Bible's authority, inspiration, and unity, and we should press on to understand the implications of these affirmations for interpretation. We should prayerfully depend on the Spirit for faith, humility, and illumination. Why do such pursuits and prayers matter in reading the Bible? Because what we see is influenced by where we stand and by the kind of people we are.

My aim in this book is to orient Bible readers to the subjects of typology and allegory, that we might be more faithful readers of Scripture as we behold more fully the glory of its story. We'll make our journey by asking forty questions along the way. I aim to persuade you that, rightly considered, the tools of typology and allegory are useful and—dare I say—*vital* for reading Scripture. I'm aware that you may not agree with every conclusion or be persuaded by every argument, but the pervasive use of typology and allegory by the Christian church throughout history should beckon us to the table to listen and discuss. After all, this is the Bible we're talking about! Should we not give ourselves diligently to study it? Should we not look to and learn from the cloud of witnesses who have gone before us during these past two thousand years?

Part 1 focuses on the Bible's big story. As you would expect from opening chapters, these are foundational for everything that follows. Parts 2 and 3 treat typology and allegory, respectively. We will seek to understand what typology and allegory are, we will explore how they have been used in church history, and we will identify where they are used in the Bible. Part 4 offers closing reflections. Certainly not every conceivable question will have been asked about typology and allegory, though I hope to have posed, among these forty, the most relevant and important questions.

Maybe you never imagined reading a book about typology and allegory, yet here you are. But what if I told you that these subjects can profoundly affect the way you understand the Bible? What if you knew that a christological understanding of the Psalms would affect the way you pray? What if grasping typology and allegory deepened your confidence in the Bible's authority and inspiration? What if these ways of reading led to more delightful times of devotion and study? What if this kind of reading meant you would be standing with the saints of old? What if studying typology and allegory impacted the way you prepared sermons and preached the Scripture?

This book is an invitation to a kind of reading—a kind of *seeing*. But I must warn you: once you see the beauty of typological and allegorical readings in the Old and New Testaments, you can't unsee it. And you wouldn't want to, even if you could.

I've dedicated this book to James M. Hamilton Jr. In the Lord's kind providence, I have known Jim since 2005, and his love for the Lord and for the Word of God is inspiring. In 2013, I completed my PhD under Jim's supervision at The Southern Baptist Theological Seminary, becoming his first doctoral student to graduate. Through his faithful teaching and preaching and writing, he has exemplified how to hold the whole Bible together and proclaim the riches of Christ from its pages.

PART 1

The Bible's Big Story

What Story Is the Bible Telling?

The first time I read the *Harry Potter* series, I did not know where the story was heading. And not until all seven books are read does the fullness of the epic become clear. If the reader knows only the first book, the grasp of the larger story is limited and ultimately deficient. But with each successive book, the reader's understanding grows, as well as his or her appreciation for previous adventures. If you want to enjoy the books even more, read them again. A secret for greater joy in reading is to reread great stories.

Slowly but Surely

Rereading great stories leads not to a duller experience but to a deeper one. The same is true for the Bible. The more time we spend in the pages of Scripture, the more we will see its treasures. But the Bible does not tell its story quickly. We must be patient readers, wrapping our minds around many books and expecting to miss all sorts of connections the first time—or tenth time—through its pages.

Slowly but surely, the message of Scripture unfolds from Genesis to Revelation. Have you considered how much time passes between these two books? After God tells Abraham that his descendants will enter the land of promise (Gen. 12:1–3), the Israelites do not inherit the land until at least five centuries later. After Jacob tells Judah that the scepter will not depart from Judah's tribe (Gen. 49:10), the first king from that tribe does not rule in the Promised Land until almost a millennium later. After Malachi indicts his listeners for their neglect and violations of the Mosaic law, four centuries of prophetic silence pass before John the Baptist comes on the scene.

The timeline is longer in the Old Testament than in the New. Even though the dates of events in Genesis 1–11 are uncertain, the stories from Genesis to Malachi unfold over thousands of years. Contrast this timespan with the New Testament: the ministry, death, and resurrection of Jesus, as well as the preaching and writing of the apostles, took place within the first century AD.

Leaning Forward and Looking Ahead

Genesis

One reason for the timespan of the Old Testament era is its anticipatory purpose. The whole Old Testament is leaning forward. God's good and ordered world (Gen. 1–2) was disrupted by rebellion and sin (Gen. 3), and the rest of the story tells us what God is going to do about it. He intends to make his blessings flow as far as the curse is found. Adam and Eve, and everyone who comes after them, will no longer live in the sacred dwelling place of Eden, for sin brings exile and death. But God promises a serpent-crushing seed of the woman (Gen. 3:15), and from that point onward in the storyline, the reader is on the lookout for that son.

As humankind multiplies, so does sin. Cain kills Abel (Gen. 4), and eventually everyone's heart is only evil all the time (Gen. 6:5). God floods his creation, sparing only Noah's family out of all humankind (Gen. 6–8). But after surviving the flood, Noah sins and thus shows he is not the righteous deliverer who would reverse the curse (Gen. 9). The problem of sin persists from generation to generation. Noah's descendants unite to make a name for themselves and build a tower reaching the heavens (Gen. 11). The Lord confuses their speech and disperses the people. But as the people spread, so does sin.

At age seventy-five, a man named Abram encounters the true and living God. He and his family will be a blessing, somehow, to all the families of the earth (Gen. 12:2–3). This future blessing will overcome the curse of sin. God promises land and offspring to Abram (Gen. 12), and he puts these promises into a covenant (Gen. 15). God changes Abram's name to Abraham (Gen. 17:5), and at age one hundred, Abraham becomes the father of Isaac (Gen. 21). Isaac fathers Jacob (Gen. 25), and Jacob fathers twelve sons (Gen. 29–30). The line of Abraham is increasing, and the Bible continues to devote attention to selected stories about these figures. But the prophesied deliverer of Genesis 3:15 has not yet come.

Jacob is renamed Israel (Gen. 32:28), and his descendants become the Israelites. Jacob's sons conspire against Joseph and sell him into slavery (Gen. 37), but God superintends the tragedy of Joseph's downfall and raises him up in due course. A famine strikes the land of Canaan—which is the land promised to Abraham's offspring—and Jacob's children sojourn to Egypt for food. Eventually they learn that their brother Joseph is alive (Gen. 45). The brother they rejected becomes the brother whom God uses to sustain their families in Egypt (Gen. 46–47). Later, Joseph dies in hope that God will one day lead the Israelites out of Egypt (Gen. 50).

Exodus–Deuteronomy

The Israelites remain in Egypt for hundreds of years, at some point becoming slaves to a paranoid and harsh pharaoh (Exod. 1). Then Moses is born

(Exod. 2). When Moses is eighty years old, he encounters the true and living God in a blazing bush, and God declares that the time has come to free the Israelites from Egyptian captivity and bring them into the Promised Land (Exod. 3). Through a series of signs and wonders, God debilitates the land of Egypt, humiliates the pharaoh, and ensures the release of the Israelites (Exod. 7–12). When obstacles arise, God overcomes them and cares for his people. He leads the Israelites through the Red Sea on dry ground and then crashes the walls of water onto the pursuing Egyptian army (Exod. 14). He gives the Israelites water when they're thirsty (Exod. 15), food when they're hungry (Exod. 16), and victory over enemies when they're attacked (Exod. 17).

On the way to the Promised Land, the Israelites follow God's guidance to Mount Sinai, where Moses receives the law of God (Exod. 19–23). The people agree to keep God's law and enter into a covenant with the Lord (Exod. 24). Following specific instructions, the people construct a portable dwelling place for the Lord—called the tabernacle—that they will carry with them through the wilderness and into the Promised Land (Exod. 25–40). This glory-filled tabernacle will be the place for the system of sacrifices (Lev. 1–7). Outside of Eden, God is making a way for sinners to relate to him, for he is holy and they are not. Sinners come to God through sacrifice.

After a little less than a year at Mount Sinai, the Israelites pick up camp and begin to move at the direction of the Lord (Num. 10). They're heading to the Promised Land! Spies enter the land ahead of the rest of the people, in order to scope out the inhabitants and any strongholds, but the spies return with a mixed report of excitement and fear (Num. 13). The Israelites rebel against Moses and the Lord, demonstrating evil hearts and unbelief, so God pronounces a judgment of forty years in the wilderness until the older generation of Israelites is dead (Num. 14).

In the last year of Moses's life, at age 120, he readies the second generation of Israelites to enter the Promised Land. He reminds the listeners of their history (Deut. 1–3). He calls them to obedience and to fear the Lord (Deut. 4–6). He preaches about laws, idolatry, feasts, foods, warfare, tithes, and worship (Deut. 13–26). If the Israelites will keep the law, there will be blessing, but curses will come if they refuse to keep the law (Deut. 28–30).

Joshua–2 Samuel

After Moses dies, Joshua becomes his successor (Josh. 1). Joshua leads the Israelites across the Jordan River (Josh. 3), and at last the people are in the land promised to their forefathers, the patriarchs. The conquest of the land begins with Jericho (Josh. 6), and the dominion of the Israelites spreads throughout the territories of Canaan (Josh. 7–12). Boundaries in the land are established, and the tribes of Israel are ready to receive their promised inheritance (Josh. 13–22). With the Israelites now in the land, they are poised to be a holy nation mediating the knowledge of Yahweh and living as a light to the unholy nations. The Mosaic covenant is renewed, and the Israelites are eager to devote themselves to the service and will of the Lord (Josh. 23–24).

The deliverer of Genesis 3:15 still does not come. The Israelites may be in the Promised Land, but not all is well in this new sacred space. Sin abounds; the curse abides. The Israelites are unfaithful to the law, so God brings consequences that prompt the people's repentance, and in response to their repentance God raises up a military leader—called a judge—to save them (Judg. 1–2). Yet the cycle continues: sin, judgment, repentance, deliverance. Israel has no king, and in those days everyone was doing what seemed right in their own eyes (Judg. 21:25).

During the dark period of the judges, God prepares a king for the people. In the providential story of Ruth and Boaz, their marriage begins a family that leads to David (Ruth 4:18–22). And when David is thirty years old, he becomes king over the whole land of Israel (2 Sam. 5). The scepter is wielded from Judah's tribe, and the effects are substantial. David takes control of the city of Jerusalem and orders the ark of the covenant to be brought there (2 Sam. 5–6). God makes a covenant with David, promising to raise up an offspring from David's line, a son who would rule forever (2 Sam. 7:12–13). Since the Bible reader has been on the lookout for the victorious son foretold in Genesis 3:15, God's covenant with David not only confirms that earlier promise but also clarifies that the serpent-crushing seed of the woman will be a *son of David*.

1 Kings–2 Chronicles

The first son of David is Solomon, though he is not the one who will reign forever. Solomon receives surpassing wisdom and reigns for forty years over a golden age of Israel's history. During Solomon's reign, the temple is constructed and solidifies the importance of Jerusalem (1 Kings 5–8). The dwelling place of God is in Zion, the chosen city. Tragedy, however, is on the horizon. When Solomon's son Rehoboam becomes king, he provokes a rebellion from the people in approximately 930 BC (1 Kings 12). Some of them follow Rehoboam, and some follow a man named Jeroboam. The united land of Israel divides into northern and southern kingdoms.

The rest of 1–2 Kings and 1–2 Chronicles reports the dynasties resulting from the split. The northern kingdom (known as Israel) lasts until the Assyrians conquer it in 722 BC, and the southern kingdom (known as Judah) lasts until the Babylonians conquer it in 586 BC. Though these centuries involve unfaithfulness to the Mosaic covenant and a litany of unrighteous kings, God is not silent. He sends a host of prophets, some to the north and others to the south, to proclaim God's word to the people and to call for repentance.

But the people will not repent, and God will not relent. Judgment comes to the north and south by foreign armies. The destruction by Babylon is particularly horrific, because the Israelites are taken into exile, the walls around

Jerusalem are wrecked, the king from David's line is removed, homes—including the palace—are destroyed, and the temple is laid in ruins. Israel experiences national death. During this downfall, the longed-for deliverer does not arise. Where is the one from David's line who will overcome God's enemies and reverse the curse of sin and death?

The prophets who warn of God's judgment also prophesy the people's restoration. And in 539 BC, after decades of captivity, the Persians conquer Babylon and a year later allow exiles to return to Jerusalem. The returning exiles resume life in the Promised Land, planning to rebuild the temple and their homes. But not everything will return to the way it was. The Persian king is now king of the Promised Land too. There will be no son of David ruling on the throne in Jerusalem.

Ezra–Esther

Thousands of exiles return to the land, but not everyone does. Chronologically, the events in Esther occur before those of Ezra and Nehemiah, and Esther's story takes place from 483 to 473 BC outside the Promised Land and during the reign of the Persian Empire. In God's providence, Esther becomes the wife of Ahasuerus (Esther 2) and thwarts a plot to destroy the Jewish people (Esther 4–5).

In 458 BC, Ezra comes to Jerusalem and teaches the people (Ezra 7). Back in the land for eighty years now, the people need more than rebuilt homes and a rebuilt temple. The people themselves need to be rebuilt! They need edification and instruction, and the Lord uses Ezra to provide it. A decade later, Nehemiah comes to Jerusalem and leads in the rebuilding of the walls around Jerusalem, which the people complete in 444 BC after fifty-two days (Neh. 6:15). The people need reformation, and the books of Ezra and Nehemiah report responses of confession and repentance.

Job–Malachi

The books of Genesis through Esther unfold the storyline of the Old Testament in chronological order. The books of Job through Malachi were written during this time period. The books of Job through Song of Solomon are typically considered wisdom literature, consisting of instruction, lessons, and truths for people who seek to flourish in a fallen world. The books of Isaiah through Malachi are typically considered prophetic literature, consisting of those prophets whom God set apart to enforce the law of Moses and the covenant thereof.

All these books sustain and advance the hope that God will send a redeemer to deliver sinners and establish justice. But when the Old Testament period closes with the prophetic voice of Malachi, the promised Messiah has not yet come. After many centuries of waiting, the readers are still leaning forward and looking ahead.

Promise and Fulfillment

Matthew–John

Four centuries of prophetic silence are broken by the coming of the Messiah and his forerunner John the Baptist. Matthew opens his Gospel by telling us, in verse 1, that this is the story of the Son of David (Matt. 1:1). The Old Testament left readers with great expectations, and those expectations will be met in the person and work of Jesus. In concert together, Matthew, Mark, Luke, and John report the extraordinary conception, humble birth, sinless life, authoritative teaching, miraculous power, atoning death, victorious resurrection, and triumphant ascension of Jesus the Christ. He is the seed of the woman who crushes the serpent and brings blessing to a world under the curse of sin and death.

Acts

The good news about Jesus is a global gospel, so the book of Acts tells how the early church eventually spread from Jerusalem to the ends of the earth (Acts 1:8). They proclaim the gospel of Christ to Jews and Gentiles, calling for faith and repentance. The apostles suffer for this news, enduring persecution, imprisonment, and ostracism. But God pours out his Spirit upon all flesh and empowers his witnesses by this same Spirit. In their speeches, the apostles herald God's appointed purpose and the fulfillment of Old Testament promises through the life, death, and resurrection of Christ.

Romans–Jude

Twenty-one of the New Testament books are letters. Most are written by Paul, and the others are from James, Peter, John, Jude, and whoever wrote Hebrews. Some letters have a wide audience in multiple locations, other letters are to specific individuals, and still others are to particular churches. These six letter-writers address their audience(s) in the authority of Christ and by the inspiration of the Spirit. All the New Testament letters are penned after the resurrection and ascension of Jesus, so they are dispatched in the era of the new covenant. They explain the gospel, interpret the Old Testament, exhort the saints, expose false teachings, promise the return of Christ, warn of future judgment, and hope for the resurrection of the dead.

Revelation

While John is on the isle of Patmos, God grants him a vision of Christ (Rev. 1). John records Christ's words for the churches of Asia (Rev. 2–3). The remainder of the Apocalypse involves heavenly scenes of glory as well as depictions of earthly judgments. The idols of the age will win the allegiance of unbelievers, but believers will worship the Lord Jesus Christ and endure to the end. The wicked will face the just wrath of God, and the saints will be vindicated. All God's elect will be kept and raised. Death and the evil one will be overthrown and condemned (Rev. 20). The victory over the serpent will be eternal in duration and cosmic in scope. Better than the garden of Eden, the glorious city of God will be a new heaven and earth where the old order of things has passed away and all things have become new (Rev. 21). The beginning of Genesis is aiming at the end of Revelation.

Summary

The Bible is the story about Jesus Christ. The Old Testament is a long story that predicts and prepares for his coming, and the New Testament is the explosive announcement of his arrival and what that means for the world. If the Old Testament is about the promise, the New Testament heralds the fulfillment. We need the whole Bible to tell the story about Jesus. The opening chapters of Genesis tell us about God's good world, what went wrong, and what God planned to do about it. As the epic of Scripture unfolds, God sets apart the family of Abraham, which leads eventually to the nation of Israel. And through that family and nation, God blesses the families of the earth with the seed of Abraham and son of David—the Lord Jesus Christ. O come let us adore him!

REFLECTION QUESTIONS

1. How often do you read the Bible? Are there parts of the Bible you've never read thoughtfully?

2. Have you studied the storyline of Scripture? Are there big pieces of the story that remain puzzling to you?

3. What parts of Old Testament history should you study more carefully, so that your understanding of the storyline will increase?

4. How is God's promise of a deliverer in Genesis 3:15 fulfilled in the rest of Scripture?

5. If someone asked you to summarize the storyline of Scripture in five minutes, which people and events would you include?

How Does the Bible Tell Its Story?

When someone paints a landscape onto a canvas, more than one color is necessary. Every color plays a part so that, together, a beautiful picture emerges. The beautiful story of the Bible is told in various ways, too. Sometimes a biblical author uses simple historical narration, other times a genealogy, song, prophecy, or parable is used. When all the genres of Scripture come together on the canonical canvas, the redemptive picture is bold and compelling. In this chapter, I want to reflect on ways the Bible tells its story that deserve careful consideration in light of the remainder of this book.

If colors on a canvas can illustrate the Bible's genres, I want to think about how the colors got there. The strokes matter, every move and turn. The author starts up here instead of down there. The brush is dragged to make this shape, but only dabbed to make that one. The painter's moves—not just the colors chosen—help explain why the picture looks the way it does.

Careful Selection

As you read through the Bible, questions may naturally arise about unreported events. What were Adam and Eve's first days like outside Eden? What kinds of things did Noah and his family do inside the ark for the months they were aboard? What was Abraham doing before God appeared to him at age seventy-five? What was life like for Moses growing up in Pharaoh's household?

The Bible doesn't answer every question we bring to it, because the content of the Bible is selective. Inspired by the Holy Spirit, the biblical authors tell the story carefully and selectively. This process will inevitably mean that many details about certain characters and stories are not given to us. Furthermore, sometimes we may be surprised by what *is* included. For instance, in Genesis 23 there is a whole narrative devoted to Abraham's purchase of a place to bury his wife Sarah. And in Exodus 25–40, large amounts of text describe the materials for, instructions for, and construction of the tabernacle.

Interpreted History

While the biblical authors do record history, they also interpret it. We learn not only what happened but why it matters. Therefore, the authors are not disinterested storytellers. The biblical storyline has a theological agenda, and the authors do not apologize for it. The world's true Lord has made himself known and is directing history toward his ordained purposes. We learn not just that the Israelites left the oppressive nation of Egypt; we learn why. We learn not just that the Israelites entered the land of Canaan; we learn why. We learn not just that a child named Jesus was born in Bethlehem; we learn why. We learn not just that Jesus died on the cross; we learn why.

In short, the Bible is *interpreted* history. The aim of Holy Scripture is the same aim that God himself has in all he does: the exaltation of his name. The heart that truly worships the Lord is a heart that believes God's revealed Word and, most specifically, trusts in Jesus the Son of God. Take John's Gospel, for example. John is fully transparent about the purpose for which he recorded the miracles: "Now Jesus did many other signs in the presence of the disciples, which are not written in this book; but these are written so that you may believe that Jesus is the Christ, the Son of God, and that by believing you may have life in his name" (John 20:30–31). John was selective, and his selections served a greater agenda: that the reader might believe in Christ unto life.

We must not divorce the history recorded in the Bible from the lens of the Bible's authors. By interpreting what takes place, the biblical authors are giving us spectacles to wear, and their lenses are the only ones through which we will see the Bible clearly.

Organic Development

Across the timespan of the Bible's storyline, there is a discernible organic development. The books of the Bible connect together, like puzzle pieces snapping into place. The story begins with the "beginning." In order to bring blessing to the cursed world, God sets apart the family of Abraham. Abraham's descendants become the Israelites, and the rest of the Old Testament tells the story of those Israelites: how they are enslaved in Egypt and then delivered from it, how they enter the Promised Land yet eventually face the ruin and devastation of exile, and how they return to the Promised Land by the mercy and favor of the Lord. Matthew, Mark, Luke, and John connect to the Old Testament hopes and prophecies as they herald the arrival of God's redeemer and kingdom. And in the remainder of the New Testament, readers see the mission of and messages to Christ's church.

In order to grasp the Bible's story, perseverance as a reader is necessary. The Pentateuch (Genesis through Deuteronomy) is the soil from which the story of Israel stems and continues. And the wisdom authors and writing prophets contribute to the storyline by laying before their readers how to love

God and neighbor, how to flourish as God's people in God's place for God's glory, lest judgment fall. Authors in the wisdom and prophetic literature also direct the reader's eyes to ultimate judgment and vindication, themes that are taken up and developed further in the New Testament.

As we persevere in reading the Bible, and as we recognize the organic development of its grand story, we will see the indispensability of its parts. Whether we're reading a list of "begats" or the narration of a miracle or the cubit-measurements of the tabernacle, all of the Bible matters, because all of the Bible was inspired by God for his people. And because the Bible reveals the God who is, the organic development and connectedness of the Bible matters, for there is nothing more important than knowing God.

Scripture Using Scripture

As the biblical authors write the revelation of God's will and ways, it is common practice for later Scripture to use earlier Scripture. And the nature of this use varies.

Quotation, Allusion, and Echo

The categories proposed by Richard Hays are helpful: biblical authors may engage in quotation, allusion, or echo.[1]

Quotations of Scripture may have different lengths. For instance, in Hebrews 8:8–12 the author quotes Jeremiah 31:31–34, whereas in 1 Corinthians 9:9 Paul quotes Deuteronomy 25:4. And a quotation may or may not be preceded by an introductory formula such as, "It is written."

Allusions to the Old Testament may occur in simply a few words or an expression. In Mark 1:6, John is wearing a garment of hair and a leather belt, which alludes to Elijah's garment and belt in 2 Kings 1:8. Allusions are more subtle than quotations and require a sensitivity that is cultivated over a period of time through immersion in the Old Testament. Since an author usually intends for readers to recognize allusions in his material, allusions must be overt enough for audiences to detect them.[2]

The distinction between an allusion and an echo is blurry.[3] If a distinction must be made between them, then length and intentionality may be the difference. An echo may be shorter than an allusion, even just a single word. In Luke 9:31, Moses and Elijah have appeared on a mountain with Jesus, who is transfigured before them, and they speak of his imminent "exodus." The term

---

1. Richard B. Hays, *Echoes of Scripture in the Letters of Paul* (New Haven, CT: Yale University Press, 1989), 18–31. See also his book *Echoes of Scripture in the Gospels* (Waco, TX: Baylor University Press, 2016), 10.
2. Bryan D. Estelle, *Echoes of Exodus: Tracing a Biblical Motif* (Downers Grove, IL: IVP Academic, 2018), 33.
3. G. K. Beale, *Handbook on the New Testament Use of the Old Testament: Exegesis and Interpretation* (Grand Rapids: Baker Academic, 2012), 32.

"exodus" is an obvious echo of Israel's deliverance from Egypt. With the factor of intentionality, an echo may reflect something not consciously intended by the human author, whereas an allusion would reflect a more conscious intent. Still, a sharp distinction between allusion and echo may be unnecessary and ultimately unhelpful. After all, when the author uses "exodus" in Luke 9:31, surely the selection of that one word reveals an intent by the author to evoke that ancient deliverance.

Metalepsis

In using an earlier Old Testament passage, the biblical author may intend to evoke a larger matrix of Old Testament context. The quotation or allusion or echo, then, would function more like a hook to transport the reader into far more than an earlier verse. This technique is known as metalepsis.[4]

Consider Luke 9:31, which I referenced in the previous section. Moses and Elijah spoke with Jesus about his upcoming "exodus." This important word does not connect to a particular Old Testament verse but to a larger scheme of narratives that involve Israel getting out of Egypt. As Moses brought deliverance from slavery through an exodus, Jesus would bring deliverance from sin through a new and greater exodus. And through the use of the word "exodus," the reader can accurately frame and interpret the upcoming death of Jesus.

Cluster of Texts

Sometimes a biblical author uses a cluster of Old Testament texts. Matthew reports the Father's words spoken at the baptism of Jesus: "This is my beloved Son, with whom I am well pleased" (Matt. 3:17). The first phrase alludes to Psalm 2:7 ("You are my Son"), and the last phrase alludes to Isaiah 42:1 ("Behold my servant, whom I uphold, my chosen, in whom my soul delights"). The significance of these texts is clear when you see the larger context of each verse. Psalm 2 describes the installation of the Son of David who will rule forever, and Isaiah 42 is about the Servant of the Lord who would have the Spirit and bring justice. Jesus is the promised Son of David and the prophesied Servant.

Matthew 3:17 uses Old Testament texts that were neither quoted nor signaled by a phrase invoking Scripture. And, yet, there at a baptism in the Jordan River comes a heavenly announcement about the identity of Jesus. We will grow in our awareness of text-clusters only to the degree that we deepen our immersion in the Old Testament. The biblical authors were soaked in the Old Testament worldview and text, and so we should expect that their writings would be soaked with the same.

---

4. Hays, *Echoes of Scripture in the Letters of Paul*, 20.

The Old Testament in the Old Testament

Thus far I have given examples of the New Testament's use of the Old. But we find Scripture's use of Scripture long before the New Testament was written. In Ecclesiastes 3:20, the claim that everyone is "from the dust, and to dust all return" is allusion to Genesis 3:19. In Ezekiel 14:14 there is a reference to the man Job. Isaiah 1:10 mentions Sodom and Gomorrah from Genesis 18–19. In Psalm 106:7–12, the psalmist sings about the deliverance through the Red Sea and the subsequent hymn in Exodus 14–15. The writing prophets decried the idolatry of Israel and warned of coming judgments that had been promised in Leviticus 26 and Deuteronomy 28.

The Old Testament uses the Old Testament. This truth should not be taken for granted; we must state it and ponder its implications. The unfolding of the biblical story involved the use and reuse of earlier Scripture. The biblical authors employed this practice, and so their strategies for using earlier Scripture should be very interesting to us.[5] In fact, the way biblical authors use earlier texts is the banner under which this book is written.

Narrative Recapitulation

In analyzing blocks of Scripture, the interpreter will notice the recasting, or recapitulation, of earlier narratives in later narratives. This way of writing establishes continuity within God's Word and across the biblical covenants, and it testifies to God's providence throughout history. Narrative capitulation is rooted in the overall unity of Scripture. When aspects of a biblical story are reminiscent of an earlier account in multiple ways, interpreters should consider whether narrative recapitulation has been used.

After Abraham goes to the Promised Land, he faces a famine and so departs for Egypt (Gen. 12:10). There in Egypt, Abraham's wife is taken from him and into Pharaoh's house (12:15). But God poured out plagues upon Pharaoh's house, and eventually Pharaoh sent away Abraham's wife (12:17–19). When Sarah and Abraham left Egypt, they had more possessions than when they first arrived there (12:16, 20). These events in Abraham's and Sarah's lives are recapitulated on a national scale in the experience of Israel. At the end of Genesis, the Israelites face famine in the Promised Land and head to Egypt (Gen. 41–47). But as time passes, a pharaoh subjects the Israelites (Exod. 1:8–14). God pours out plagues on the house of this pharaoh (Exod. 7–12), and eventually the Israelites go free, leaving with plunder and possessions (12:35–41).

---

5. It is beyond the scope of this chapter to explore the various methods used by the biblical authors in their treatment of earlier Scripture. But books abound that explore this subject. See Sidney Greidanus, *Preaching Christ from the Old Testament: A Contemporary Hermeneutical Model* (Grand Rapids: Eerdmans, 1999); G. K. Beale and D. A. Carson, eds., *Commentary on the New Testament Use of the Old Testament* (Grand Rapids: Baker Academic, 2007).

Figures of Speech

The biblical authors employ multiple literary devices as they write. I have already discussed metalepsis and allusions, so I will not revisit them here. But we should consider other ways the biblical authors embed their messages. They frequently use figures of speech such as metaphor, simile, hyperbole, personification, metonymy, and symbolism.[6]

Metaphor and Simile

A writer uses a metaphor in order to compare two things by equating them. For example, "God is light" (1 John 1:5) invites the reader to ponder how God is like light. Or, "The Lord is my shepherd" (Ps. 23:1) invites the reader to consider the ways that God is a shepherd for his people.

A simile also compares two things but uses "like" or "as." The psalmist compares his longing to the thirsting deer: "As a deer pants for flowing streams, so pants my soul for you, O God" (Ps. 42:1). Jesus speaks about the kingdom he has inaugurated: "The kingdom of heaven is like treasure hidden in a field" (Matt. 13:44).

Hyperbole

A writer may exaggerate a point, using hyperbole. In the fifth plague upon Egypt, "All the livestock of the Egyptians died" (Exod. 9:6). Yet during the sixth plague, boils broke out in sores "on man and beast throughout all the land of Egypt" (Exod. 9:9). There were beasts during the sixth plague which did not die during the fifth plague, even though the narrator had said, "All the livestock of the Egyptians died." The narrator used hyperbole in the fifth plague to express how widespread the devastation was.

In Luke's Gospel, Jesus teaches, "If anyone comes to me and does not hate his own father and mother and wife and children and brothers and sisters, yes, and even his own life, he cannot be my disciple" (Luke 14:26). Jesus is forcing us to see that ultimate allegiance is due him alone. He does not want us to hate our family. Yet his radical call to a Christ-centered life is clear.

Personification

A writer uses personification when something inanimate is portrayed in an animate way. The Lord warns Cain, "And if you do not do well, sin is crouching at the door. Its desire is for you, but you must rule over it" (Gen. 4:7). Sin crouches; in other words, Cain must beware the snares of sin.

In Proverbs, Wisdom has a voice. "How long, O simple ones, will you love being simple? How long will scoffers delight in their scoffing and fools hate knowledge?" (Prov. 1:22). By giving a voice to Wisdom, the biblical author

---

6. There are other figures of speech in the Bible. See Leland Ryken, *Words of Delight: A Literary Introduction to the Bible*, 2nd ed. (Grand Rapids: Baker Academic, 1992).

hopes to woo the listener with the soundness of a life that fears the Lord and shuns evil. Folly also has a voice: "Stolen water is sweet, and bread eaten in secret is pleasant" (Prov. 9:17). Through personification, the writer highlights the danger and absurdity of foolish living.

Metonymy

When a word (or group of words) is substituted by something else, metonymy has occurred. As Jesus talks about John's practice of baptism, he asks, "The baptism of John, from where did it come? From heaven or from man?" (Matt. 21:25). By "heaven," Jesus could just as well have said "God," and that is clearly what is meant.

Jesus criticizes those who take their oaths less seriously by substituting other words for God's name, such as "heaven" or "earth" or "Jerusalem" (Matt. 5:34–35). Since heaven is God's throne and earth his footstool and Jerusalem the king's city, swearing with such words is just a roundabout way of invoking God's name. The oaths are binding even though the oath-takers are using metonymy.

Symbolism

The biblical authors sometimes use symbols to communicate their point. A symbol could be a number, an object, or an image that signifies or represents something else. The use of symbols may be rooted in something tangible that, over time, develops a symbolic import. The power of symbols is effective when readers share the author's framework or worldview, which makes such symbols understandable and meaningful.

In Genesis 49:10, Jacob tells his sons, "The scepter shall not depart from Judah, nor the ruler's staff from between his feet." A scepter symbolized a king's authority. By using this symbol, Jacob associated the tribe of Judah with royalty. As another example, the account in Exodus 12 is about lambs slain on the first Passover (Exod. 12:21–22). The symbolism of this lamb is clear when the apostle Paul writes that "Christ, our Passover lamb, has been sacrificed" (1 Cor. 5:7).

Summary

Bible readers must think about what story the Bible is telling as well as how its story is told. The biblical authors, by the Spirit's inspiration, both report and interpret the historical accounts they have selected. The narrative of the Bible's storyline unfolds in an organic way, with later texts using earlier texts and thus creating an interconnected record of redemption. Through different genres and figures of speech, the biblical authors tell the epic of God's written revelation.

REFLECTION QUESTIONS

1. How might the interconnectedness of Scripture be an argument for its trustworthiness and inspiration?

2. In addition to the ones discussed in this chapter, what other figures of speech do the biblical authors use?

3. Can you think of a few places in the New Testament that quote the Old Testament?

4. Can you think of stories in the Old Testament that seem to echo earlier Old Testament stories?

5. Are there parts of Scripture you tend to overlook or skip? Think about how they contribute to the overall story and unity of Scripture.

PART 2

Questioning Typology

Understanding Typology

What Is Typology?

Despite the miracles that the religious leaders had seen Jesus perform, they say, "Teacher, we wish to see a sign from you" (Matt. 12:38). Jesus promises the sign of the prophet Jonah: "For just as Jonah was three days and three nights in the belly of the great fish, so will the Son of Man be three days and nights in the heart of the earth" (12:40). The contemporaries of Jesus were more accountable to what they heard than even the Ninevites were in Jonah's day: "The men of Nineveh will rise up at the judgment with this generation and condemn it, for they repented at the preaching of Jonah, and behold, something greater than Jonah is here" (12:41).

How is Jesus using the story and example of Jonah? He speaks with comparison ("For just as Jonah was . . . so will the Son of Man be") and with language that heightens the significance of the comparison ("something greater than Jonah is here").

Jesus is using something known as typology.

The Occurrences of "Type" (*Tupos*)

The Greek term *tupos* occurs fifteen times in the New Testament.[1] It refers to an impression, image, example, or pattern.[2] In at least four instances, biblical authors use *tupos* to connect to an earlier part of Scripture.

- First, Paul calls Adam a "type" of Christ. He writes, "Yet death reigned from Adam to Moses, even over those whose sinning was not like the transgression of Adam, who was a type of the one who was to come" (Rom. 5:14).

---

1. See John 20:25 (2x); Acts 7:43, 44; 23:25; Rom. 5:14; 6:17; 1 Cor. 10:6; Phil. 3:17; 1 Thess. 1:7; 2 Thess. 3:9; 1 Tim. 4:12; Titus 2:7; Heb. 8:5; 1 Peter 5:3.
2. See *tupos* in *A Greek-English Lexicon of the New Testament and Other Christian Literature*, 3rd ed., rev. and ed. Frederick Danker (Chicago: University of Chicago Press, 2000).

- Second, Paul labels certain events in Israel's history "types" for his readers. He writes, "Now these things took place as examples [or types] for us, that we might not desire evil as they did" (1 Cor. 10:6).

- Third, the writer of Hebrews refers to the "pattern" or "type" that Moses used for the construction of the tabernacle, and this structure was a shadow of heavenly realities. He writes that the Old Testament priests "serve a copy and shadow of the heavenly things. For when Moses was about to erect the tent, he was instructed by God, saying, 'See that you make everything according to the pattern that was shown you on the mountain'" (Heb. 8:5).

- Fourth, in Luke's record of Stephen's speech, the martyr speaks of this same "pattern" that Moses had received concerning the tabernacle. Stephen says, "Our fathers had the tent of witness in the wilderness, just as he who spoke to Moses directed him to make it, according to the pattern that he had seen" (Acts 7:44).[3]

Toward Defining a Type

The Standard Definition

Paul's use of *tupos* in Romans 5:14 is about a person. Paul's use of *tupos* in 1 Corinthians 10:6 is about certain events in Israel's history. And both Luke in Acts and the writer of Hebrews connect *tupos* to the building of Israel's tabernacle. These occurrences of *tupos* give credence to the standard definition of a type: a person, event, or institution that prefigures an antitype (the person or thing foreshadowed by the type).[4] But the presence of the word *tupos* does not limit the concept of a type in the biblical text.[5]

Shadows and Copies

For an example of the presence of a type without the author using that particular word, the author of Hebrews speaks of the sacrifices of the law as a

---

3. The word "pattern" in Hebrews 8:4 and Acts 7:44 is from *tupos*.
4. The word "antitype" might sound negative at first—if *anti-* means *against*, why use a word that means "against type"? But *anti-* can mean *opposite*, and that is the sense in the word "antitype." The fulfillment (or antitype) of a type is *opposite* the type along the timeline of salvation history. Put another way, the antitype is what *corresponds to* the earlier type.
5. In secular Greek, concrete uses of *tupos* "include a hollow mould for casting images of metal, a die for casting coins, engraved marks, a carved or moulded figure; thus by extension an exact replica or image, the shape of something, the general character of something (as in a stereotypical character in a drama), a prescribed form to be imitated, or a pattern or model capable of and intended for reduplication" (Richard Ounsworth, *Joshua Typology in the New Testament* [Tübingen: Mohr Siebeck, 2012], 34).

"shadow" of the things that were to come: "For since the law has but a shadow of the good things to come instead of the true form of these realities, it can never, by the same sacrifices that are continually offered every year, make perfect those who draw near" (Heb. 10:1). He also calls the priestly offerings a "shadow" of heavenly things (Heb. 8:5). In Colossians, Paul refers to food/drink regulations and to the Israelite calendar as a "shadow" of the things to come. He writes, "Therefore let no one pass judgment on you in questions of food and drink, or with regard to a festival or a new moon or a Sabbath. These are a shadow of the things to come, but the substance belongs to Christ" (Col. 2:17).

In Hebrews 9, the author is writing about the practice of sprinkling with blood for the sake of purification (Heb. 9:21–22), and he says it was necessary for "copies" of heavenly things to be thus purified (9:23), referring to the tabernacle and its vessels as copies of heavenly realities. He then calls the handmade holy places "copies" of the true things found in the presence of God where Christ appears now for us (9:24). Peter argues that baptism corresponds to Noah's flood in the sense that Noah's flood is a "copy" of what baptism would be (1 Peter 3:21).[6]

Correspondence and Escalation

After briefly surveying the New Testament's language about types, shadows, and copies, we can conclude that the presence of a biblical type requires correspondence and escalation between type and antitype.

Correspondence refers to the point(s) of connection between type and antitype. There is no minimum number of correspondences. Let's look at some correspondences present in the passages we have already seen.

- In Hebrews 9:11–28, the writer draws attention to the fact that the priests offered sacrifices and that Jesus offered a sacrifice.

- In Matthew 12:41, Jesus says that just as Jonah experienced a descent for a period of three days, he would also experience a descent for a period of three days.

- In 1 Peter 3:21, we are reminded that those in the ark were brought safely through the water and that people are brought through water in the ordinance of baptism.

The correspondences between type and antitype do not have to match in every respect. In fact, the previous examples have key points of dissimilarity. Levitical priests offered sacrifices, while Jesus *was* the sacrifice. Jonah was

---

6. The Greek word in 1 Peter 3:21 is identical to Hebrews 9:24, so I have rendered *antitupos* as "copy" to preserve the link.

fleeing the will of God when he descended for three days into the fish without dying, while Jesus was fulfilling the will of God when he descended for three days into the grave as a dead man.

The relationship between type and antitype will also have escalation. While priests and Jesus offered sacrifices, the sacrifice of Jesus was better. While Jonah and Jesus both experienced a descent for three days, Jesus was not alive in a fish but dead in the grave. While the ark and baptism both bring people safely through water, baptism points to the cleansed conscience and not mere outward deliverance.

"True" Fulfillment

The biblical authors may indicate a typological relationship when they use the term "true." For example, in John's Gospel, Jesus calls himself the "true bread from heaven" (John 6:32) and the "true vine" (John 15:1). The images of heavenly bread and a vine are from the Old Testament (see Exod. 16; Ps. 80), and thus they provide the background necessary to understand the surpassing person and work of Christ. "It is important to note that Jesus does not devalue the importance of the Old Testament precursors for achieving God's purposes in their own time. Rather, he is claiming to bring the fullness or fulfillment that was not present in the types."[7]

The author of Hebrews also links the type/antitype relationship with the word "true." In Hebrews 8:1–2, the earthly sanctuary pointed to the "true tent" not made with hands. And in Hebrews 9:24, the human-made holy places were copies of the "true things." Hoskins is right: "The use of 'true' (*alethinos*) to describe antitypes is consistent with the use of this adjective in English and in Greek to denote that which is real or genuine. In this case, the antitype is the real entity that fulfills the incomplete shadow that preceded it."[8]

Using the term "true," interpreters can represent christological fulfillment with expressions that call Jesus the true Joshua, the true David, the true ark, the true high priest, the true temple, the true light, the true bread, the true sacrifice, or the true Israel.

A Fuller Definition

We need an understanding of biblical typology that derives from the biblical text itself. This means we need a definition that is full enough to embrace how the biblical authors apply the language of types, shadows, and copies. Here is the definition I will draw upon throughout the rest of this book: *a biblical type is a person, office, place, institution, event, or thing in salvation history that anticipates, shares correspondences with, escalates toward, and resolves in its antitype.*

---

7. Paul M. Hoskins, *That Scripture Might Be Fulfilled: Typology and the Death of Christ* (Maitland, FL: Xulon, 2009), 29.
8. Hoskins, *That Scripture Might Be Fulfilled*, 29.

We have already seen some examples of types fitting the first half of that definition: Jonah is a person, sacrifices are part of the sacrificial institution, and deliverance through the ark was an event. We will see later, though, that offices and places and things can be types as well.

The verbs in the latter half of the definition have been carefully chosen. Types are anticipatory ("anticipates"),[9] there are correspondences between type and antitype ("shares correspondences with"), the antitype is in some way greater than the type that prefigures it ("escalates toward"), and the antitype in some sense fulfills what has prefigured it ("resolves in its antitype").

Summary

A biblical type has correspondences with and escalates toward its antitype. And a type can be a person, office, place, institution, event, or thing in salvation history. Sometimes the biblical authors speak of types, shadows, or copies of future or heavenly realities, but the practice of typology may occur without such explicit terms present.

REFLECTION QUESTIONS

1. Have you heard other writers or preachers bring up typology in Scripture? If so, did their definitions differ from what you read in this chapter?

2. Can you name at least five Old Testaments persons who are types of Christ?

3. How can Adam be a type of Christ if he was disobedient, whereas Jesus was obedient?

4. Since Jesus spoke of Jonah's descent before his own death, does the validity of the type require that Jonah died sometime before being vomited from the fish?

5. Can you think of Old Testament places that may be types in salvation history?

---

9. This is a controversial point that I will seek to defend later in the book. Were biblical types always forward-looking, or were biblical types established as anticipatory once the antitype arrived and afforded the interpreter a set of retrospective lenses? Is it possible that biblical types were always intended to be anticipatory—an intention rooted in the divine author, though not necessarily in the human author?

What Are the Theological Assumptions of Typology?

Typology does not stand without support. If you look underneath the table, typology rests on theological assumptions, and these assumptions are the legs that hold it up. These assumptions are so important that typology would not exist without them. Interpreters who do not share these assumptions may consider typology a futile and undesirable enterprise. We can identify at least five assumptions of typology.

The Providence of God

First, typology rests on the providence of God. The one true God is Lord of the world he has made. In the beginning, when God created the heavens and the earth, he did not withdraw from his creation to let it run its course. The biblical authors reject deism. They proclaim God's grand-scale kingship over, and small-scale engagement with, his world. The fullness of the earth belongs to God (Ps. 24:1), and not even a sparrow will fall to the ground apart from the Father's will (Matt. 10:29). Before all things was the Son, and in him all things hold together (Col. 1:17).

Typology would not function in a deistic world. If there is no providence, there is only coincidence. The practice of typology recognizes that salvation history has unfolded according to a design. Without God directing events, nothing earlier can be designed to correspond to later events. Paul teaches, instead, that God "works all things according to the counsel of his will" (Eph. 1:11). As ruler of creation, God orders and directs the events of history. He is a God of providence. And it is this ordering of history that makes possible the correspondences between events. "In other words, the typological interpretation of Scripture emerges from Scripture's doctrine of God, the Lord who acts in history, and it finds expression in the Old Testament as well as the New."[1]

The Unity of Scripture

Second, typology requires the unity of Holy Scripture. Scripture is the inspired record of God's will and ways in salvation history, and from Genesis to Revelation the biblical authors tell the grand story of creation, fall, redemption, and consummation. Patterns abound because the God of providence established the unity of Scripture. The unity of Scripture is the result of a divine author who carried along the biblical authors by his Spirit (2 Peter 1:21). Holding the biblical canon in our hands, we hold the story of God. Sally Lloyd-Jones is right: "There are lots of stories in the Bible, but all the stories are telling one Big Story. The Story of how God loves his children and comes to rescue them. It takes the whole Bible to tell this Story."[2]

If the stories of the Bible lacked a grander design, then arguments for typology may rest on nothing more than cleverness and literary happenstance. But if the stories of Scripture exhibit an overall unity and coherence, then the interpreter is on solid ground to propose certain biblical types. "Christ as the climax of the story gives unity and significance to all that had preceded him."[3] And if the God of providence has knit together a story with Christ at the center, "then we can have no objection to a typology which seeks to discover and make explicit the real correspondences in historical events which have been brought about by the recurring rhythm of the divine activity."[4] Yet if there is no continuity over the history of redemption, typological connections are exercises in imagination only. According to Geerhardus Vos, "The bond that holds type and antitype together must be a bond of vital continuity in the progress of redemption. Where this is ignored, and in the place of this bond are put accidental resemblances, void of inherent spiritual significance, all sorts of absurdities will result, such as must bring the whole subject of typology into disrepute."[5]

The Witness of the Spirit

Third, the mission of the Holy Spirit is to bear witness to the Son. Since Scripture is inspired by the Spirit, we should expect that the resulting revelation from God would bear witness to the Son. The Spirit of Christ directed

---

1. Dennis E. Johnson, *Walking with Jesus through His Word: Discovering Christ in All the Scriptures* (Phillipsburg, NJ: P&R, 2015), 57.
2. Sally Lloyd-Jones, *The Jesus Storybook Bible* (Grand Rapids: Zondervan, 2007), 17.
3. G. W. H. Lampe, "The Reasonableness of Typology," in *Essays on Typology* (Naperville, IL: Alec R. Allenson, 1957), 27.
4. Lampe, "Reasonableness of Typology," 29.
5. Geerhardus Vos, *Biblical Theology: Old and New Testaments* (Carlisle, PA: Banner of Truth, 1975), 146.

the prophets who wrote of Christ's sufferings and glories and yet did not fully understand their own prophecies (1 Peter 1:10–11). These Old Testament authors knew "they were serving not themselves but you, in the things that have now been announced to you through those who preached the good news to you by the Holy Spirit sent from heaven, things into which angels long to look" (1:12). The identification of biblical types is a way of showing the effectiveness of the Spirit's witness in the text of Scripture. Without the inspiration of the Spirit grounding the validity of typological interpretation, interpreters are left with human ingenuity and cleverness.

Before Jesus was arrested, he promised his disciples that when he went away, the Spirit would come to help them: "Nevertheless, I tell you the truth: it is to your advantage that I go away, for if I do not go away, the Helper will not come to you. But if I go, I will send him to you" (John 16:7). Not only would the Spirit bring conviction (16:8–11), but also he would bring the disciples remembrance and understanding. Jesus said that "the Helper, the Holy Spirit, whom the Father will send in my name, he will teach you all things and bring to your remembrance all that I have said to you" (14:26). Furthermore, the Spirit "will guide you into all the truth, for he will not speak on his own authority, but whatever he hears he will speak, and he will declare to you the things that are to come. He will glorify me, for he will take what is mine and declare it to you" (16:13–14). The theological implications of this promise are profound: when the apostles preached and wrote about Christ and interpreted the Old Testament, they did so according to the inspiration and testimony of the Spirit himself. Jesus said that "when the Helper comes, whom I will send to you from the Father, the Spirit of truth, who proceeds from the Father, he will bear witness about me" (John 15:26). The Spirit is sent by the Son from the Father in order to bear witness about the Son. Biblical types are a triune accomplishment.

The Divine Trajectory in All Things

Fourth, the God of providence acts with purpose in all he does. He wields history to accomplish his aims. The genealogies of Scripture are heading somewhere. Many early events have elements that become patterned and paralleled in later events. Acts of judgment and deliverance build the expectation for more of the same. Covenants and prophecies contain promises that leave readers looking for fulfillment. The more of the Bible you read, the more you see that God has aimed the beginning of Genesis toward the end of Revelation all along. The existence of biblical types coincides with the forward-looking nature of Scripture.

At the appointed time, God will fully and finally unite all things in Christ, things in heaven and things on earth (Eph. 1:10). This goal is the end of a trajectory planned from the foundation of the world: "He is the image of the invisible God, the firstborn of all creation. For by him all things were created, in heaven and on earth, visible and invisible, whether thrones or dominions or rulers or authorities—all things were created through him and for him" (Col. 1:15–16). All human history—and thus every type in Scripture—serves the grand purpose of the glory of Christ in the world. Biblical types are like John the Baptist—they prepare the way of the Lord!

The Authoritative Claims of Jesus

Fifth, biblical typology rests upon the authoritative claims of Jesus about how the Old Testament relates to him. After his resurrection, Jesus joined two men who were walking to Emmaus. Their conversation took a turn that is full of hermeneutical intrigue. "And beginning with Moses and all the Prophets, he interpreted to them in all the Scriptures the things concerning himself" (Luke 24:27). We should not underestimate the significance of that encounter. He later spoke of the need for everything written about him in Scripture to be accomplished: "These are my words that I spoke to you while I was still with you, that everything written about me in the Law of Moses and the Prophets and the Psalms must be fulfilled" (Luke 24:44). He insisted that the Scriptures testify of him: "You search the Scriptures because you think that in them you have eternal life; and it is they that bear witness about me" (John 5:39). Jesus said that if the leaders really believed the writings of Moses, they would believe him too, "for he wrote of me" (John 5:46).

These claims of Jesus are general but also strikingly clear. He taught that the Old Testament anticipated him. He said the biblical authors wrote about him. Contrast this claim with the words of Udo Schnelle, who said, "The Old Testament is *silent* about Jesus Christ."[6] According to Richard Hays, Schnelle's words "directly contradict the explicit testimony of the New Testament writers themselves. They emphatically do not think the Old Testament is silent about Jesus Christ."[7] And would not a correct understanding of the Old Testament be that which is closest to Jesus's view of it? Jesus's view of the Old Testament is either true or false. If we acknowledge that typology is at work in the Bible, we are saying, in effect, "The claims of Jesus are true. " Recognizing typology is one way of recognizing that Moses—and the biblical authors who followed him—wrote about Jesus.

Summary

The legitimacy of typology rests on multiple theological assumptions. If Bible readers do not share these assumptions, proposed examples of typology will have no firm place to stand. If typology is something operating in

---

6.   Udo Schnelle, *Theology of the New Testament* (Grand Rapids: Baker, 2009), 52 (emphasis original).
7.   Richard B. Hays, *Echoes of Scripture in the Gospels* (Waco, TX: Baylor University Press, 2016).

Scripture, then the assumptions undergirding it should also be grounded in Scripture. And the testimony of Scripture is that the God of providence wields all things toward a Christ-exalting goal. The same Spirit who inspired the Old Testament authors also inspired the New Testament apostles to bear witness about Christ. Moreover, Jesus himself claimed that the biblical authors wrote about him. Not only did he believe this, but he taught others that it was true and interpreted the Scriptures to show them it was true.

REFLECTION QUESTIONS

1. Why would deism undermine the notion of typology in Scripture?

2. If the Bible is not a united story, how would its disunity undermine the notion of typology?

3. Why must typology be supported by a divine trajectory for all things?

4. How would something like a genealogy serve the Christ-exalting goal of God's purposes?

5. What did Jesus teach about how the Old Testament related to him?

Should We Identify Types the New Testament Does Not Identify?

I have a vivid memory of my first class in seminary when the professor said, "The biblical authors show us how to interpret the Old Testament. We should reflect on their hermeneutical moves and then imitate them." What a bombshell! I had never heard such a thing. At the time it sounded too good to be true. How can we imitate the apostles when we're not inspired? Some writers doubt that the hermeneutical methods of the apostles should be our guide. Richard Longenecker, for example, says, "Our commitment as Christians is to the reproduction of the apostolic faith and doctrine, and not necessarily to the specific apostolic exegetical practices."[1] Yet what if the hermeneutical moves of the apostles have been given to us as a guide, even though we ourselves are uninspired? My professor thought we should pay attention to how the apostles interpreted the Old Testament and then read the Old Testament the way they did. And he was right.

Learning from Jesus

Before we consider whether we should identify types in the Old Testament that were not identified in the New, we should consider how Jesus and the apostles expect us to read the Old Testament. First, what can we learn from Jesus?

Believing Moses and Believing Jesus

In John 5, some Jews were seeking to kill Jesus for blasphemy (John 5:18). In reality Jesus was committing no such thing, for he was only speaking and doing what his Father gave him to say and do (John 5:19–20, 36). These conspiring opponents claimed to know the Scriptures, but Jesus challenged

---

1. Richard Longenecker, *Biblical Exegesis in the Apostolic Period*, 2nd ed. (Grand Rapids: Eerdmans, 1999), 219.

whether they really believed what they read: "For if you believed Moses, you would believe me; for he wrote of me. But if you do not believe his writings, how will you believe my words?" (John 5:46–47).

Jesus directly accuses his conspirers of not actually believing the writings of Moses. What is his evidence for this? They were trying to kill him! They could not say they believed Moses and, in the same breath, reject Jesus. Since Moses wrote about Jesus, believing Moses would lead to believing Jesus ("if you believed Moses, you would believe me," John 5:46). So Moses, in an ironic twist, has become their accuser rather than their ally (John 5:45).

Jesus saw himself in the writings of Moses ("he wrote of me," John 5:46), and his opponents should have seen this too. Instead, they rejected the one whom God had sent and, in doing so, proved God's word did not abide in them (John 5:38). They had even searched the Old Testament Scriptures, but they did not see how these texts pointed to Christ. Jesus referred to these texts when he said they "bear witness about me" (John 5:39).

These nonapostolic readers of the Old Testament should have seen that Moses wrote about Jesus. The obstacle was this: they had the Scriptures without understanding them. They searched the Old Testament with their eyes closed.

Cleopas and the Rest of Us

When Jesus was walking to Emmaus with two men, they did not know it was him at first (Luke 24:16). One of the men was Cleopas. He was not an apostle or a writer of any New Testament documents, yet Jesus instructed Cleopas in the interpretation of the Scriptures. He interpreted the works of Moses and the Prophets, showing how the Scriptures testified about him (Luke 24:27). This transformed how Cleopas understood the Scriptures. He later said, "Did not our hearts burn within us while he talked to us on the road, while he opened to us the Scriptures?" (Luke 24:32).

Cleopas, who would not write an inspired gospel or any authoritative letters to Christian churches, was now able to read the Scriptures with open eyes. The example of Cleopas is good news for us, because we are not apostles or inspired interpreters either. And yet, like Cleopas before he encountered Jesus, to read the Old Testament without a christological lens is to not understand what is written. Jesus showed him how the Old Testament should be read.

Learning from the Apostles and Preachers

Since Jesus expected people to see him in the writings of the Old Testament, it is reasonable that his apostles would follow suit. What can we learn from the apostles?

Opening Minds for Understanding

In Jerusalem, Jesus appeared to his disciples and interpreted the Scriptures for them as well. Things were written about him in the Law, Prophets, and

Writings, and his disciples needed to understand what these Scriptures foresaw. So "he opened their minds to understand the Scriptures" (Luke 24:45). The Messiah's suffering, resurrection, and global proclamation were all grounded in the Old Testament (Luke 24:46–47).

Conversations between Jesus and his disciples continued in the weeks ahead. He taught about the kingdom of God for forty days (Acts 1:3) before his ascension. Those weeks of instruction would have included more explanations of texts, more opening of minds, more giving of insights. And the lessons of interpretation soon showed up in the apostles' preaching and praying. When Peter preached from Psalm 16 (see Acts 2:25–28) and Psalm 110 (see Acts 2:34–35), he preached Christ. When the apostles prayed and invoked Psalm 2 (see Acts 4:25–26), they understood the Anointed One to be Jesus.

Christological Interpretation beyond Jerusalem

When Philip left Jerusalem, he eventually encountered an Ethiopian eunuch. We do not know the eunuch's name, but we know what the eunuch was reading: the prophet Isaiah. Philip asked the man, "Do you understand what you are reading?" (Acts 8:30). The man said, "How can I, unless someone guides me?" (Acts 8:31). This scene is instructive, for the man needed to know how the book of Isaiah testified of Jesus. So Philip took the eunuch's text—Isaiah 53—and proclaimed the good news about Jesus (Acts 8:32–35). The eunuch was not an apostle or a writer of New Testament documents, but he still needed to read the Old Testament in light of Jesus Christ.

When the apostle Paul went to Antioch in Pisidia, he entered the synagogue on the Sabbath and proclaimed Jesus (Acts 13:14). He said the Jewish leaders had condemned Jesus because they did not truly understand the prophets (Acts 13:27). Then he proclaimed Jesus from Psalm 2, Isaiah 55, Psalm 16, and Habakkuk 1 (Acts 13:33–41). When Paul ministered in Thessalonica, he reasoned from the Old Testament Scriptures that the Messiah had to suffer and rise from the dead (Acts 17:2–3).

Hearing Hebrews about "the Shadows"

The writer of Hebrews interprets the Old Testament in light of Christ and, even more, declares the law to be "a shadow of the good things to come" (Heb. 10:1). The "holy places made with hands" were "copies of the true things" (Heb. 9:24). Yet the writer does not proceed to unfold every typological aspect of the whole law. In Hebrews 9–10, he brings up multiple practices, places, and objects, such as the shedding of blood, the work of the high priest, the offerings of bulls and goats, the purification of the tabernacle, the Most Holy Place, and the vessels of worship. These aspects of the law are part of "the shadow" that prefigures "the true form of these realities," which arrived in and through the Lord Jesus Christ (Heb. 10:1). These practices, places, and objects are examples of types in the law, but these examples are not exhaustive.

Writing about typology and Hebrews, Jonathan Edwards says,

> To say that we must not say that such things are types of these and those things unless the Scripture has expressly taught us that they are so, is as unreasonable as to say that we are not to interpret any prophecies of Scripture or apply them to these and those events, except we find them interpreted to our hand, and must interpret no more of the prophecies of David, etc. For by the Scripture it is plain that innumerable other things are types that are not interpreted in Scripture (all the ordinances of the law are all shadows of good things to come), in like manner as it is plain by Scripture that these and those passages that are not actually interpreted are yet predictions of future events.[2]

Go and Do Likewise

Jesus and the apostles taught that the Scriptures spoke of Christ. People who were not apostles, and who did not have the New Testament yet, were shown how the Law, Prophets, and Writings testified of the Lord Jesus Christ. How does this teaching relate to typology?

An Understandable but Unnecessary Boundary

Some interpreters insist that the only valid types are ones that the New Testament identifies. But we should not set up such a boundary. The notion sounds safe, because then no one would be finding types under every gushing rock. But the New Testament authors never say they have exhausted the Old Testament types. Then why assume so if they never said so? Rather, according to Sidney Greidanus, "if typological interpretation is a sound method, it should be able to discover types of Christ which the New Testament writers did not mention."[3]

When Jesus taught the apostles, and when the apostles taught others through their preaching and writing, the result was the orientation of hearers and readers toward a christological understanding of the Old Testament. In a postresurrection era, Jesus guided the apostles into the Old Testament texts with eyes wide open. They came to comprehend how the Law, Prophets, and Writings prepared the way for the Lord, including his suffering and death and third-day resurrection.

---

2. Jonathan Edwards, "Types," in *The Works of Jonathan Edwards* (New Haven, CT: Yale University Press, 1957–2008), 11:152.
3. Sidney Greidanus, *Preaching Christ from the Old Testament: A Contemporary Hermeneutical Method* (Grand Rapids: Eerdmans, 1999), 98.

But every preacher knows that a sermon cannot cover everything that could be said. Every writer knows a letter cannot cover everything that could be written. The Four Gospels, the Acts of the Apostles, the twenty-one Epistles, and the Apocalypse engage the Old Testament in various ways, and typology is one of them. Instead of assuming that the New Testament authors provided all the types that readers should see in the Old Testament, we should understand that their inspired documents contain authoritative interpretive moves worthy of reflection and, yes, *imitation*.

Still Learning from the Apostles

Jesus and the apostles showed non-apostles how to understand and interpret the Old Testament, and they gave this instruction even before the New Testament documents were written. The modern-day reader might immediately protest that we do not have Jesus and the apostles to speak to us in that way. But—I hasten to say—we *do* have the words of Christ and his apostles written down and preserved and awaiting our meditation. Whenever the New Testament writers interpret the Old Testament, they do so infallibly and authoritatively. This is good news because, even though we are not inspired interpreters, we can study their inspired interpretations. We can pay attention to the ways they read the Old Testament. We are thousands of years removed from the ancient world of the New Testament, but we can still learn from the apostles.

For the subject of typology, what is needed is careful reflection on the hermeneutical moves of the biblical authors. And by seeking to imitate the biblical authors, we will—like Cleopas and others—understand the Old Testament with greater clarity and rejoice in its riches. We need to read the Old Testament from their perspective.

If we do not seek to imitate how the biblical authors read the Old Testament, including how they identified types, what is the alternative for interpreters? To interpret the Old Testament in ways Jesus and his apostles did not? To adopt a method assuming we will arrive at conclusions more reliable and sure than if we treated the interpretive moves of the biblical authors as lenses we should put on?

Peter Leithart's resolve is straightforward: "I want to read the Old Testament and the New as a disciple of Jesus, and that means following in the footsteps of the disciples' methods of reading."[4] Let us contemplate how the biblical authors engaged the Old Testament, and then let us go and do likewise.

---

4. Peter J. Leithart, *Deep Exegesis: The Mystery of Reading Scripture* (Waco, TX: Baylor University Press, 2009), viii.

Summary

While some interpreters may be reluctant to identify Old Testaments types that the New Testament authors never specified, that boundary is not necessary when we meditate on and seek to imitate the interpretive moves of these inerrant authors. They never claimed to have mentioned all Old Testament types. So if Jesus is the most accurate interpreter of the Old Testament who ever lived, and if those who wrote in his name also interpreted and preached the Old Testament the way in which he instructed them, then our interpretation of the Old Testament will be more faithful when it is closest to theirs. If we imitate the biblical authors, we will inevitably identify types that are not in the New Testament. And we will be doing so because we are learning from the apostles how to read the sacred writings. Will not our hearts burn within us?

REFLECTION QUESTIONS

1. Why would some interpreters be concerned about identifying Old Testament types that are not recognized by the New Testament authors?

2. According to John 5, how did Jesus's listeners show they did not believe the words of Moses?

3. What are some advantages of imitating the biblical authors when you read the Old Testament?

4. How is Cleopas a hopeful example for modern-day readers?

5. How do we know that Jesus's postresurrection teaching impacted the way the apostles interpreted the Old Testament?

Do All Types Lead to Christ?

"All roads lead to Rome," the saying goes. But do all types lead to Christ? The simple answer to the question is yes, biblical types point to Christ. He is the antitype that the earlier types prefigure and anticipate. But then an interpreter might ask, *What about the old Jerusalem pointing to the new Jerusalem? What about the deliverance of Noah and his family pointing to Christian baptism in water? What about the earthly judgment of one nation pointing to the final judgment of all nations?* These questions—and others—confirm that our simple answer is not quite so simple after all.

A Christological Prism

When you focus light at a prism, the beam goes into and through the prism, revealing beautiful colors. The same is true when you focus types at Christ: they go *into* and *through* him, revealing beautiful things.

Biblical types receive their significance when they are seen in light of Christ's person, work, and achievements. Let's return to our two questions in the opening paragraph of this chapter and answer them. While the old Jerusalem points to the new Jerusalem, Christ is the one who has inaugurated the new creation, and thus the consummation of all things—a new heaven and new earth—is inseparably connected to Christ and his accomplishment. While Noah's deliverance through the water points to the act of Christian baptism, baptism is a picture of the believer's union with Christ's death and resurrection. While the earthly judgment of one nation points to the judgment of all nations, Christ is the righteous judge who will gather the nations before him at his return and then confirm the eternal states of the righteous and the wicked.

Jesus endows types with their significance, and they are rightly understood in association with him.

A Christological Narrative

The christological significance—in some form or fashion—of types is not surprising at all, once we remember that the story of the Bible is a christological narrative. Or, as others have framed it, the Old and New Testaments have a promise-and-fulfillment relationship. In the Old Testament the Messiah is promised and patterned in multiple ways, and in the New Testament his arrival is heralded for the world to hear. As the story unfolds, the types contribute to the expectation and are themselves a form of expectation.

Consider some more examples of how the christological narrative endows types with a christological significance. Believers are truly Canaan-bound (Heb. 11:13–16), but it is Jesus who leads them into Sabbath rest in that promised land. The church is the temple of God (1 Cor. 6:19), but that identity is true because we are united to Christ, who was the Word tabernacling among sinners and whose body was torn down and then rebuilt on the third day (John 1:14; 2:19–22). Believers are heirs of God's promises to Abraham but only because we are coheirs with Christ, who is the seed of Abraham (Gal. 3:16, 29; 4:1–7).

A Covenantal Stream

When God acts toward his people in the Scriptures, he does so in covenant. Types are christological because the Old Testament covenants must be understood in light of the new covenant that Jesus made on the cross. Christological types appear in covenantal contexts.[1] A covenantal stream flows from creation to new creation. As Barrett puts it, "Through his covenant(s) God promises to redeem Adam's race, but will do so through Eve's own offspring, sending a Messiah, a Christ, who will be God's definitive covenant word to his people, providing the redemption he first promised to Adam and Abraham. In the meantime, God embeds his drama with countless types that serve to foreshadow Christ, the antitype, who is to come."[2]

Adam, a type of Christ, was in covenant with the Lord, as were Noah, Abraham, Moses, and David. The Hebrew calendar and the sacrificial system—which contain types of Christ—were part of God's covenant with Israel. The exodus, the entrance into the Promised Land, the exile, and the return from exile are all pulsing with covenantal overtones. The hope for a new David who would rule forever was based on God's covenantal promises to Israel's first king from Judah's tribe (2 Sam. 7:12–13). And of course Christ himself, born under the law to redeem those under the law, bought and sealed the long-awaited new covenant. If the antitype should be understood

---

1. See David Schrock, "From Beelines to Plotlines: Typology That Follows the Covenantal Typography of Scripture," *Southern Baptist Journal of Theology* 21, no. 1 (Spring 2017): 35–56.
2. Matthew Barrett, *Canon, Covenant and Christology: Rethinking Jesus and the Scriptures of Israel*, New Studies in Biblical Theology, vol. 51 (Downers Grove, IL: IVP Academic, 2020), 3–4.

in some way with the new covenant, then it makes sense that the Bible's types are flowing in a covenantal stream. David Schrock is right: "We do not need to fear typology nor create new spiritual meaning. Rather, following the terrain of the text, we need to keep reading the Bible until we like beekeepers find the sweet scent of gospel honey in the pages of God's Word."[3]

Since the covenantal stream takes us to Christ and the new covenant, interpreters should follow the stream to its endpoint no matter at what point earlier in the stream they begin. Paul believed in the christological reading of the Old Testament and its covenants. He wrote about unbelieving Jews: "For to this day, when they read the old covenant, that same veil remains un-lifted, because only through Christ is it taken away. Yes, to this day whenever Moses is read a veil lies over their hearts. But when one turns to the Lord, the veil is removed" (2 Cor. 3:14–16). Believers behold the covenantal stream of Scripture with the veil removed. The Lord has lifted it, and now we can truly *see* when we read the Old Testament.

Parallels between Pre-Christ Characters

Before Jesus the Antitype is born into the world, there are correspondences among previous people in the Bible, and we need to think through how to characterize these characters. It is notable, for instance, that Adam and Noah have significant parallels. Both men are blessed and given the command to be fruitful and multiply (Gen. 1:28; 9:1). Both men work the ground (3:17–19; 9:20). Both men sin with fruit (3:6; 9:20–21). Both men have an experience where nakedness and shame collide (3:7–10; 9:22–24). With these correspondences, the biblical author is reminding us of the story of Adam as we read the story of Noah. How should we conceive of the Adam-Noah relationship?

An interpreter might say, "Noah is a type of Adam." And that use of "type" is meant to capture a real literary relationship between the characters. There is an Adamic shadow in the story of Noah. But when someone uses "type" in this way, they're probably not implying that Adam is the antitype. Rather, the story of Adam contains narrative features that surface in the story of Noah, and these parallels or patterns have a likeness that seems worthy of the word "type."

To be more precise with our language, however, we could say that "Noah is a new Adam." Or we could say that "Noah is an ectype of Adam." An *ectype* is an imitation of something prior. In the case of Adam and Noah, Adam was first in the biblical storyline and then the story of Noah contains features that remind us of Adam. Noah, then, is the ectype, and both Adam and Noah are types that point to Jesus the antitype. If an interpreter still prefers the term "type" to describe parallels between pre-Christ characters in the Bible, it will be important for the term not to lose its greater significance, which is its christological *telos*, or goal.

---

3. Schrock, "From Beelines to Plotlines," 48–49.

Horizontal and Vertical Directions

Typology moves in more than one direction.[4] When interpreters think and speak about typology, normally they mean typology in a linear movement, from a type at one point in history to the antitype later in history. This is known as horizontal typology, for it moves along earthly planes of redemptive history. If the sacrificial system is an Old Testament type of Christ, then Jesus's death on the cross is the horizontal fulfillment of that type. The sacrificial system was established at an earlier point in history, and then time passed along the earthly plane until Jesus said "It is finished" later in history. Or, as Richard Ounsworth puts it, "The People of God move 'forward' into the eschatological Promised Land . . . and this is pictured via the 'horizontal' typological relationship of the historical entry of the Israelites into Canaan to the real 'rest' of God made available in Christ."[5]

Typology can move not only forward but *upward* as well. Vertical typology recognizes that earthly types may have heavenly counterparts, like the earthly tabernacle being a type of the heavenly presence of God. According to Hebrews 9:11, at his ascension, Jesus entered through "the greater and more perfect tent" that was not made with hands. This interpretation shows that the earthly tabernacle was patterned after something else, something enduring and beyond this world. Vertical typology is about correspondences existing "between the reality of heaven and the human realm."[6] According to Hebrews 9:24, "Christ has entered, not into holy places made with hands, which are copies of the true things, but into heaven itself, now to appear in the presence of God on our behalf." Vertical typology is concerned with the true things of heaven, not with copies made with hands on earth.

Summary

Whether biblical types move in a vertical or horizontal direction, and no matter the covenantal context in which they occur, they should be understood in light of Christ's person, work, and achievements, even if those achievements are currently promises awaiting consummation. The greatest significance of a biblical type is its christological significance. After all, biblical types occur within a story whose center and goal is the Lord Jesus Christ. All types were created by him and through him and for him, and in him all types hold together.

---

4. See the discussion about vertical and horizontal typology in Bill DeJong, "On Earth As It Is in Heaven," in *The Glory of Kings: A Festschrift in Honor of James B. Jordan*, eds. Peter J. Leithart and John Barach (Eugene, OR: Wipf & Stock, 2011), 135.

5. Richard Ounsworth, *Joshua Typology in the New Testament* (Tübingen: Mohr Siebeck, 2012), 5.

6. Ounsworth, *Joshua Typology in the New Testament*, 53.

REFLECTION QUESTIONS

1. Can you think of three people who are types of Christ and identify their respective covenantal context?

2. Can you think of any types that receive their greatest significance in an antitype unrelated to Jesus Christ?

3. How does Christ endow typological significance on the final judgment and the new creation?

4. Give some examples of vertical and horizontal typology.

5. How does the illustration of a prism help to relate biblical types to Christ?

Are Types Only Recognizable in Hindsight?

When interpreters study typology, the issue arises as to whether types are seen through the windshield or in the rearview mirror. If types are recognizable only in hindsight and thus after the antitype has arrived, then typology is retrospective. If types are recognizable even before the antitype has come, then typology is prospective. Well, as it turns out, you can see through the windshield *and* in your rearview mirror. Some types are retrospective; others are prospective.

Retrospective Types

In a carefully crafted story, a seemingly meaningless detail may later prove not to have been meaningless at all but crucial, even decisive, to the grand plot. From the reader's perspective, however, the significance was not understood until you read further into the story. The same kind of literary insight happens to Bible readers as they traverse the canon.

Once Christ had come, there are certain people whom the reader of Scripture might consider to be types. Characters like Job, Boaz, or Samuel may be recognized as christological types retrospectively, but it is not necessarily clear within their stories that they signify an antitype beyond their days. Sometimes a New Testament author identifies a christological type that was not exactly apparent in the Old Testament era, types like Jonah or the rock that gave water or the bronze serpent that Moses lifted up.

The reason for retrospective types is that the biblical authors wrote better than they knew. The divine author has woven together the people, offices, places, things, institutions, and events that point to Christ, and some of these types were not clear until after Christ came and died and rose. However, a retrospective type is simply retrospective from *our* perspective! The divine author's intent is always accomplished in his Word, no matter the stage in progressive revelation.

Prospective Types

A prospective type is advanced within the biblical text itself and is thus recognizable prior to the advent of the antitype.[1] Advancing a type may occur through a character's speech, a narrator's description, or a series of correspondences that recall something or someone earlier in the biblical story. Through certain words and events, the biblical author may use narrative recapitulation to evoke an earlier part of Scripture.

Notions of sacrifice or a dwelling place or the exodus are used by the biblical authors themselves to form patterns and stimulate expectations (see, for example, Gen. 3:21; 4:4; 22:2; Exod. 12:6; Lev. 1–7; 16:1–10; Isa. 53:1–12; Dan. 9:24–27; Matt. 26:26–28). And people like Adam or Moses or David have features that are woven into other narratives and characters, suggesting that they have a typological significance before the antitype arrives.

Though the biblical authors advance certain types as God's story unfolds, not necessarily every historical listener would have recognized them. Some Israelites may have been ignorant of significant biblical types. This possibility doesn't negate the fact that these types have been inscripturated. The written nature of this revelation is what matters. How could we know with accuracy what listeners would have thought or what the characters within the stories themselves understood about what Scripture says? Our focus must be the words of the biblical text, not the reconstruction of the situation that preceded it or the understanding of the characters behind it or the speculation about stages of composition. The point is that biblical authors have written, and what they have written has been inspired by the Spirit. The Spirit inspired prospective types that, whether or not they were fully appreciated at the time, were truly *there* in the text. If the biblical authors saw these types and advanced them in their writings, the readers were meant to see them too.

Divine Design in the Types

To this point in the chapter, we have been thinking about biblical types from the reader's perspective. Sometimes a type is recognized as such before the antitype comes, while other times a type is best discerned in hindsight. In both cases there should be textual evidence—correspondences between type and antitype, escalation from type to antitype, and christological significance—before a type is considered valid.

Keep in mind, however, that the Bible is not merely a set of documents composed by human authors. A divine author is telling the story, and he has superintended the details from Genesis 1 to Revelation 22. There is a major implication of this reality on biblical types: a valid type (whether seen retrospectively or prospectively) had been installed by the divine author along the

---

1. See the discussion in G. K. Beale, *Handbook on the New Testament Use of the Old Testament: Exegesis and Interpretation* (Grand Rapids: Baker Academic, 2012), 13–25.

progressive revelation of Scripture, and so, in a true sense, all biblical types are prospective from the divine perspective. God has ordered all the persons, offices, places, institutions, events, or things in salvation history. And since the sending of Christ was the plan of God from the foundation of the world, we would rightly expect the Old Testament storyline to pulsate with christological significance as the plan of God unfolds and escalates toward the Redeemer's advent.

The Old Testament is full of Christ, and this is God's design. And since God loves the Son whom he sends to redeem us, it is God's delight to fill the Old Testament with the Son he loves.

Typology and Prophecy

Since God has authored all the types in Scripture, and since these types look toward the antitype to come, we can speak of types possessing a prophetic quality. Indeed, the New Testament authors write of Christ "fulfilling" Old Testament texts that do not seem to be direct messianic prophecies.

Consider Matthew 2:15, where Jesus has been spared the wrath of wicked King Herod, and the gospel writer says, "This was to fulfill what the Lord had spoken by the prophet, 'Out of Egypt I called my son,'" quoting Hosea 11:1. Interpreters might be tempted to say that Matthew wrongly used the Old Testament. After all, when Hosea was writing, his words were about *Israel*, God's firstborn son (see Exod. 4:22). Hosea was recalling that God brought Israel—God's son—out of Egypt in the exodus. Yet, as Garrett points out, "We need look no further than Hosea 11 to understand that Hosea, too, believed that God followed patterns in working with his people. Here the slavery in Egypt is the pattern for a second period of enslavement in an alien land (v. 5), and the exodus from Egypt is the type for a new exodus (vv. 10–11)."[2] Matthew is not misusing the Old Testament when he speaks of Jesus fulfilling Hosea 11:1. Matthew is recognizing that Jesus embodies the stories of Israel. And as Matthew writes about the story of Jesus's escape from Herod, he rightly sees that Jesus—God's Son—has gone "out of Egypt," as it were. A new exodus is afoot. Matthew is showing that the greatest significance of Hosea 11 is not the old exodus but the new exodus.[3]

Jesus fulfills more than just direct predictions about the Messiah. Back in Matthew 2, for example, Herod learned that the Christ was to be born in Bethlehem (see Matt. 2:6; Mic. 5:2), and this birth was a direct prophecy that Jesus had fulfilled (see Matt. 2:1). But when Matthew writes of Jesus fulfilling Hosea 11:1 (in Matt. 2:15), or when he says Jesus fulfilled "what was spoken by the prophets" when he was called a Nazarene (Matt. 2:23), something other

---

2. D. A. Garrett, *Hosea, Joel*, New American Commentary 19a (Nashville: Broadman & Holman, 1997), 222.
3. See the discussion in Beale, *New Testament Use of the Old Testament*, 63–64.

than a direct prophecy is being fulfilled. It is best to speak of some kind of *pattern* being fulfilled. There were evident correspondences between Jesus and earlier biblical passages, and these correspondences denoted a pattern that Jesus took up and embodied, so the language of "fulfillment" is appropriate.

We should think of biblical types as *indirect prophecies*. By "indirect," we are distinguishing biblical types from a direct—or explicit—statement about God's appointed deliverer. The language of fulfillment is important, even necessary, when we talk about types because the inspired and authoritative biblical authors use the language of fulfillment. If we think about fulfillment the way the biblical authors do, we will see that biblical types have a prophetic quality.

When a biblical author interprets a previous passage typologically, that author is not dismantling or contradicting the meaning of the earlier text. Instead, Scripture interprets Scripture and Scripture develops Scripture. Aubrey Sequeira and Samuel Emadi point out that "Scripture often develops the meaning of a type beyond the original intent of the author while in no way . . . contravening a text's original meaning."[4] The divine intent surpasses the intent of the human author, but it does not reject the intent of the human author. Types are ultimately designed by God to forecast christological realities, and in this sense all christological types are prospective.[5] "Later biblical authors may unfurl the significance of an OT person, event, or institution but they do not retroactively *confer* typological status."[6]

Summary

A type is prospective when the biblical text is advancing it along the story line of Scripture before the antitype has arrived. But sometimes a type is clear only retrospectively, after the antitype has come. These two categories—prospective and retrospective—are both from the interpreter's vantage point. But there is a higher vantage point than ours. From the divine perspective, all types are prospective because God has inspired the story that takes us to Christ, and thus these types are prefigurements designed to be fulfilled in Christ. The biblical authors speak about the fulfillment not just of direct messianic prophecies but of patterns in Scripture. Since the relationship between type and antitype entails correspondence and escalation, the pattern takes on a prophetic quality that anticipates fulfillment. While the language of "fulfillment" may naturally evoke a preceding promise that is being fulfilled, prophecies are God's promises that he, in due time, will keep. So Christ fulfills both direct and indirect prophecy. The Bible's patterns become promises, and all God's promises find their Yes in him.

---

4.   Aubrey Sequeira and Samuel C. Emadi, "Biblical-Theological Exegesis and the Nature of Typology," *Southern Baptist Journal of Theology* 21, no. 1 (Spring 2017): 19.
5.   Sequeria and Emadi, "Nature of Typology," 19–20.
6.   Sequeria and Emadi, "Nature of Typology," 19 (emphasis original).

REFLECTION QUESTIONS

1. Besides the retrospective types suggested in this chapter, can you think of other types that are recognizable in hindsight?

2. Why might interpreters object to seeing a prophetic quality in biblical types?

3. How is the unity of divinely authored Scripture an important argument for the prospective nature of types?

4. What evidence is there that the New Testament authors understood types to function prophetically?

5. If biblical types were only recognizable in hindsight, what would be some of the implications and theological costs of that position?

Are All Types Historical?

The New Testament authors treat the Old Testament people and events as historical, and we should imitate the perspective of these authors. After writing to the Corinthians about what their forefathers had experienced—crossing the Red Sea, divine guidance by a pillar of cloud, manna from heaven, a rock that gushed water when struck, the judgment of Israelites in the wilderness (1 Cor. 10:1–5)—Paul said, "Now these things took place as examples for us" (1 Cor. 10:6). Did you catch that verb? These things *took place*.

Nonfictional Types

When Jesus spoke about Noah and the flood (see Matt. 24:37–39), he was not relying on a fictional figure and event in order to prophesy the coming judgment. When Jesus spoke about the unbelief among his contemporaries despite the mighty works he had done, he declared that "if the mighty works done in you had been done in Sodom, it would have remained until this day" (Matt. 11:23). As Jesus rebuked his contemporaries for their unbelief, he did so by alluding to the real destruction of a real city. When some religious leaders asked Jesus for a sign, he said, "No sign will be given . . . except the sign of the prophet Jonah. For just as Jonah was three days and three nights in the belly of the great fish, so will the Son of Man be three days and three nights in the heart of the earth" (Matt. 12:39–40). Jesus treated Jonah as a historical character and interpreted the events in the book of Jonah as historical events.

We have defined a biblical type as *a person, office, place, institution, event, or thing in salvation history that anticipates, shares correspondences with, escalates toward, and resolves in its antitype.* In that definition, the phrase "salvation history" matters because things that did not actually happen, or people who did not truly exist, cannot share historical correspondences with or be fulfilled by an antitype.

The Inseparable Historical Component

Biblical typology has history built into it. As David Baker puts it, "The fundamental conviction which underlies typology is that God is consistently active in the history of this world—especially in the history of his chosen people—and that as a consequence the events in this history tend to follow a consistent pattern."[1] As the one sovereign over history, "God has directed history so that foreshadowings occur."[2]

To set aside the historical nature of the element being investigated is to deviate into something other than typology. In vertical typology, something earthly is a copy or pattern of something heavenly, and in horizontal typology, something earthly will correspond to and escalate toward something on an earthly plane. The realness, or historicity, of the type is vital, no matter if the movement is upward or forward.

If historicity is nonnegotiable for a type, then the typological lens of the biblical authors reinforces the historicity of major Old Testament features. We can believe that an ark really survived a flood, Sodom and Gomorrah were really destroyed in a divine judgment, Isaac really was the promised son who faced death and lived, the exodus out of Egypt really happened, the tabernacle was really built, sacrifices were really offered, Moses really led the Israelites through the wilderness, David really reigned as king, Jonah really lived for three days and nights in a fish, the Israelites really returned from exile, and so on.

Because typology has an inseparable historical component, the identification of Adam as a type also argues for the historicity of Adam. In Romans 5, Paul treats Adam as a historical figure who committed disobedience in history and whose actions had historical consequences. The historical existence and actions of Adam are what makes him an appropriate type of Christ, whose historical person and work brings life and justification to sinners. If there was no historical Adam who sinned in history the way the Bible teaches, then the typological power of Romans 5 is deflated. Paul's gospel argument in Romans 5:12–21 depends on typology, which depends on history.

The Importance of History for Israel

When Israel entered the Promised Land, they were surrounded by neighboring peoples who had adopted mythical accounts of creation and human origins. In fact, throughout the ancient Near East, there were stories of gods birthing and creating and battling and dying. Against the tales about these gods, the biblical authors declare the true story of the world. History was

---

1. David L. Baker, *Two Testaments, One Bible: A Study of Some Modern Solutions to the Theological Problem of the Relationship between the Old and New Testaments*, rev. ed. (Downers Grove, IL: InterVarsity, 1991), 195.
2. J. D. Currid, "Recognition and Use of Typology in Preaching," *Reformed Theological Review* 53 (1994): 128.

important for Israel because the living God, the God who was and is and is to come, had made himself known in history. There were historical deeds to recount, redemptive events to remember. As Joshua Philpot puts it, "the command to recount the past acts of God for future generations is foundational to Israel's belief system and worship."[3]

The feasts of Israel were historical acts that remembered historical acts. The songs of Israel embedded the redemptive activity of God in their lyrics. From generation to generation, the Israelites were to proclaim what the Lord had done. Philpot explains the implications of this emphasis upon history: "If history in the biblical mindset is instruction in the ways of God, and if the truth of the narratives must be preserved, then it is implausible that types might be based on abstractions."[4] Being a people whose Scripture undermines myth with truth, the Israelites would not have valued typological interpretation that was essentially mythological interpretation.

Looking for Exceptions

A reader might conclude that types within historical narratives are historical, but what about poetic sections of Scripture? Could exceptions be found where, say, the figure Leviathan is mentioned in the book of Job? Leviathan evokes the ancient Near Eastern chaotic beast that no mere human can tame. In Job 41, Leviathan may point to an enemy like Satan or may even be Satan himself in the guise of metaphor. Yet if Leviathan, or any other poetic character, actually has a historical referent, then this example is not an exception after all. Philpot argues, "The point is not whether typology employs metaphors to recall persons/events, but whether the type is a historical person or occurrence."[5]

Exceptions to historical types would cause a great disruption in biblical genealogies, for biblical characters appear, again and again, in genealogies that trace ancestors and descendants. Adam is in genealogies (see Gen. 5; 1 Chron. 1; Luke 3). Noah is in genealogies (Gen. 5; Luke 3). David is in genealogies (Ruth 4; Matt. 1). The preservation of these lines depends on people like Achim and Eliud (Matt. 1:14), about whom we know nothing—and yet their names are given because historical lineage truly matters. The natural sense of these passages is that the names are historical figures. And if any of these figures are types of Christ, they are *historical* types because there is no other kind. "If just one link in a strong chain is broken or weak, the entire chain fails. Thus it is with typology. From Adam to Noah to Abraham to David to Jesus, the historical correspondence within the chain must be solid and

---

3.　Joshua M. Philpot, "See the True and Better Adam: Typology and Human Origins," *Bulletin of Ecclesial Theology* 5, no. 2 (October 2018): 88.

4.　Philpot, "Typology and Human Origins," 88.

5.　Philpot, "Typology and Human Origins," 89n51.

without any weak parts (i.e., abstractions). If one of the types in the strand is not historical, then the whole typological pattern collapses."[6]

More Than Literary Connections

Biblical types are not simply clever literary connections. Rather, "OT events can function as types because they are both historically factual and recorded as part of written history."[7] The literary connections matter because they are based on true realities in God's plan. Richard Ounsworth rightly insists on an *ontological typology*, which means that the typological relationship reflects a *real* relationship. He explains that "while similarities in the wording of Scripture may serve to highlight correspondences between different aspects of the story of Israel's relationship with her God, our audience would understand that these correspondences are not created, as it were artificially, by a literary device, but only brought to light by verbal similarities."[8]

The historical realities—not just the literary presentations—of Old Testament types are shaped by God's nature and providential love, which is why "we find the same patterns repeated again and again in that history: the ontological relationship arises from the fact that these related events are both stamped with the same character of God's nature; and this relationship is uncovered, not created, by typological exegesis."[9] The literary relationship between the type and antitype is based in the providential working of the living God in history. Typological connections are not merely the result of the human author's creativity but, instead, are due to the divine author's sovereign control over all things.

Summary

When the biblical authors interpret earlier texts in a typological manner, they do so in a way that implies the historicity of the type. In fact, these authors do not treat any type as nonhistorical, so neither should we. After all, the antitype does not have true correspondences with an earlier type if that type did not truly exist. Typological connections are not based in the literary creativity of the human authors. God's providential hand has truly been working within history, and so a type/antitype relationship has a transcendent origin and a historical manifestation. "Put simply, if types are not historical, then Christ is not the culmination of a providentially ordained history or the fulfillment of any actual, historical promise."[10] Typology and historicity are inseparable, and what God has joined together, let no one separate.

---

6. Philpot, "Typology and Human Origins," 89.
7. Richard Ounsworth, *Joshua Typology in the New Testament* (Tübingen: Mohr Siebeck, 2012), 52.
8. Ounsworth, *Joshua Typology in the New Testament*, 4.
9. Ounsworth, *Joshua Typology in the New Testament*, 6.
10. Aubrey Sequeria and Samuel C. Emadi, "Biblical-Theological Exegesis and the Nature of Typology," *Southern Baptist Journal of Theology* 21, no. 1 (Spring 2017): 19.

REFLECTION QUESTIONS

1. Do you agree or disagree with the following claim? "While the Bible may contain types of Christ, those types—such as certain people or events—are not necessarily historical."

2. If the Old Testament types that Jesus referenced were not actually historical, how would their fictional status undermine the words and promises of Jesus?

3. Other than the examples mentioned in this chapter, can you think of passages in the Four Gospels where Jesus uses typology and thus affirms the historicity of someone or something in the Old Testament?

4. In Romans 5:12–21, how does Paul form a typological argument from historical people and events?

5. Though some Bible readers are skeptical of a historical Adam or a historical Jonah, why should the New Testament's use of those characters provoke these readers to rethink their skepticism?

Is Typology the Result of Exegesis or Something Else?

Is typology a form of biblical application? Is it an interpretive method that starts outside the text, yet is brought to bear upon the text? Is it the result of exegesis? There is no consensus among biblical scholars on the question of this chapter. David Baker says, "Typology is not a method of exegesis or interpretation, but the study of historical and theological correspondences between difference parts of God's activity among his people in order to find what is typical there."[1] Some conclusions I have already reached, as well as some arguments I have already made, will inform how I address the question differently.

Typology is an interpretive method rooted in exegesis. Now why would I say such a crazy thing?

Defining Exegesis

Simply put: exegesis is the effort to see and interpret what the biblical text means. Klyne Snodgrass says that "exegesis seeks to analyze the significance of the particular words used and the relations into which they are set to discern the intent of the communication."[2] To exegete a biblical passage is to engage, inevitably, in interpretation. Sound exegesis is the nonnegotiable foundation for sound interpretation. Typology is an interpretive method, but it is not baseless. Typology is an attempt to interpret *what is there* in the text, not what is not there in the text.

---

1. David L. Baker, *Two Testaments, One Bible: A Study of Some Modern Solutions to the Theological Problem of the Relationship between the Old and New Testaments*, rev. ed. (Downers Grove, IL: InterVarsity, 1991), 197.
2. Klyne Snodgrass, "Exegesis," in *Dictionary for Theological Interpretation of the Bible*, ed. Kevin J. Vanhoozer (Grand Rapids: Baker Academic, 2005), 203.

Interpreters who value grammatical-historical exegesis should appreciate and embrace typology, for typology depends on the grammar and history of the text in view. Grammatical-historical exegesis is committed to the very words of Scripture. This method emphasizes that the meaning of the text is what the author intended to communicate—the ultimate author being God himself.

Words, phrases, clauses, and sentences matter because they communicate meaning. If an interpreter suggests a typological connection between Job and Jesus or between the Promised Land and the new creation, simply asserting a connection will do no good. There must be arguments! Arguments based on what? There must be arguments based in the biblical text itself. The whole notion of historical correspondences assumes that I—the interpreter—can demonstrate how something in this text over here corresponds to something in that text over there. A focus on grammar is inescapable, for sometimes a single word or a set of words, or even a common concept, can unite a type with its antitype.[3] And in the previous chapter, we affirmed how important historicity is to typology—there is no such thing as a nonhistorical biblical type.

The recognition of types is the result of attention given to the grammar and history of words, concepts, patterns, and ultimately the whole storyline of Scripture itself.

The Context of the Canon

According to Francis Foulkes, "Typology reads into Scripture a meaning which is not there in that it reads in the light of the fulfillment of the history. This is not exegesis, drawing out from a passage what the human author understood and intended as he wrote."[4] This is too narrow an understanding of exegesis. Sometimes when later biblical authors use earlier texts, they are showing meaning present in those earlier texts. Added to the reality of the human author is the divine author who has superintended the entirety of the biblical witness. Beale is right: "If typology is classified as partially prophetic, then *it can be viewed as an exegetical method* since the New Testament correspondence would be drawing out retrospectively the fuller prophetic meaning of the Old Testament type which was originally included by the divine author."[5]

---

3. Consider how the word "lamb" in John 1:29 evokes the Passover of Exodus 12:1–28, or how the gambling for Christ's garments in Mark 15:24 recalls the language of David in Psalm 22:18, or how the sorrow and suffering of the righteous Jesus connects to Old Testament righteous sufferers like Job.

4. Francis Foulkes, *The Acts of God: A Study of the Basis of Typology in the Old Testament* (London: Tyndale, 1958), 39.

5. G. K. Beale, "Did Jesus and His Followers Preach the Right Doctrine from the Wrong Texts? An Examination of the Presuppositions of Jesus' and the Apostles' Exegetical Method," *Themelios* 14 (1988–1989): 93 (emphasis added).

When interpreters recognize a type, they are reading a biblical text in light of redemptive history and progressive revelation. A carpenter is still engaging in his craft no matter if he is repairing a kitchen table or building a house. The scope and scale, however, is vastly different. With exegesis, an interpreter may be focusing on a specific passage or a series of passages across the canon. Typology is exegesis across the canon of Scripture. Truly, the largest context in which to understand any passage is the context of the canon. If I am exegeting and interpreting the story of Noah, I should do so within Genesis 6–9, within the book of Genesis, within the Old Testament storyline, and ultimately within the whole biblical canon. "The canonical extension of the context of a passage being interpreted does not by itself transform the interpretative procedure into a noninterpretative one. Put another way, the expansion of the database being interpreted does not mean that we are no longer interpreting but only that we are doing so with a larger block of material."[6] Canonical interpretation does not diminish, but enriches, a biblical passage. Canonical interpretation does not obscure biblical texts but shines greater light upon them.

Not everyone holds the same presuppositions about Scripture, and this fact can determine how typology is "classified."[7] Beale explains:

> For example, if we concede that God is also the author of OT Scripture, then we are concerned not only with discerning the intention of the human author but also with the ultimate and wider divine intent of what was written in the OT, which could well transcend and organically grow out of the immediate written speech of the writer but not contradict it. The attempt to draw out the forward-looking typological aspect of the human and/or the divine intention of an OT text is certainly part of the interpretative task. And above all, if we assume the legitimacy of an inspired canon, then we should seek to interpret any part of that canon within its overall canonical context (given that one divine mind stands behind it all and expresses its thoughts in logical fashion).[8]

The Example of Adam

In Romans 5, the apostle Paul calls Adam "a type of the one who was to come" (Rom. 5:14). As Paul considers the far-reaching and saving effects of Jesus's work, he contrasts it with the far-reaching yet disastrous results of Adam's

---

6. G. K. Beale, *Handbook on the New Testament Use of the Old Testament: Exegesis and Interpretation* (Grand Rapids: Baker Academic, 2012), 25.
7. Beale, *New Testament Use of the Old Testament*, 24.
8. Beale, *New Testament Use of the Old Testament*, 24.

sin. Since there is a surpassing greatness to Christ's work when it is compared with Adam, Paul sees an escalation of both quality and degree: "where sin increased, grace abounded all the more" (5:20). Paul is exegeting the story and example of Adam across the canon, and he's taking it to its christological *telos*. While Adam's work brought sin and death and condemnation, God's free gift of Christ Jesus, through the cross, brought life and grace and justification.

When we read the story of Adam, there is no reference in Genesis 2 or 3 to him being a type of God's deliverer. Yet there is an obvious role he plays as the head of people in creation. He is the head of the human race, for God gave him the command not to eat of a certain tree (Gen. 2:16–17), and his sin affected everyone after him. He had been told to serve and guard the garden of Eden (2:15), yet temptation exercised dominion over him. Adam's actions were extremely consequential, which makes his comparison with Christ both appropriate and powerful. If the first Adam's disobedience brought such disaster, how much more would the last Adam's obedience bring deliverance!

Across the Old Testament, there is an Adamic mold that subsequent characters resemble. As G. K. Beale writes, "A later OT author may style some historical character being narrated about according to the pattern of an earlier OT character in order to indicate that the earlier historical person is a typological pointer to the later person in focus."[9] Noah is a new Adam with the commission to be fruitful and multiply and serve as the new head of the human race.[10] Abraham is a new Adam who enters God's promised sacred space and will be a source of blessing for the world (Gen. 12:1–3). Solomon is a new Adam who dwells in the Promised Land and acts with wisdom and dominion (1 Kings 3–4). Paul calls Jesus the "last Adam" (1 Cor. 15:45). Jesus is the agent of blessing for the cursed world, and his perfect atoning work on the cross achieves reconciliation between sinners and God. Sinners who are estranged in Adam can be forgiven in Christ. Jesus is the head of a new people—the people of God in the new creation work of the Spirit.

Paul's words about Adam in Romans 5 make sense in a canonical context. Paul understands that the significance and depth of Adam's story is by no means exhausted in the context of Genesis or even the Old Testament. Paul isn't misusing the Genesis story in order to say positive things about the work Jesus accomplished. Instead, Paul believes that the single story of God's redeeming plan, which culminates in Christ, began in Genesis. Thus, Paul reads the story of Adam christologically. Reading the story of Adam this way is not imparting a new meaning into the text. The meaning of a biblical passage is not fully evident until the widest scope has enveloped it. Paul's words in Romans 5 have correctly exegeted the typological significance of Adam in Genesis 2–3.

---

9. Beale, *New Testament Use of the Old Testament*, 16.
10. Richard Ounsworth, *Joshua Typology in the New Testament* (Tübingen: Mohr Siebeck, 2012), 42; Beale, *New Testament Use of the Old Testament*, 16.

Summary

Typology is canonical exegesis. It sees correspondences and escalation between type and antitype, a relationship spanning books and even Testaments. Since an interpreter must offer textual reasons for any typological relationship, the grammatical-historical method of interpretation matters for typology. And since types need textual arguments, we can rightly understand typology as an exegetical enterprise. A typological reading is an effort to reveal what was always in the text because of the unity of the Testaments and the divine authorship of Scripture. When biblical authors read earlier Scripture in a typological way, they were not ignoring the original context of a passage. And neither should we ignore the context of a passage. An exegete must be interested in what the text says and the context in which it is said. "Context is king," the saying goes. Yes, and amen. And if context is king, the canon is the king of kings.

REFLECTION QUESTIONS

1. Is there a difference between biblical exegesis and biblical interpretation?

2. What context(s) should be considered when interpreting a biblical passage?

3. What is meant by "canonical exegesis"?

4. What is grammatical-historical exegesis?

5. How does grammatical-historical exegesis relate to typology?

SECTION B

Typology in Church History

How Was Typology Practiced in the Early Church?

How did the use of typology fare after the first century of the early church? That question is not easy to answer, because two thousand years of interpretive history are behind us. Yet, "typological interpretation of the Bible is present in every century of Christian history."[1] In Questions 10–15, we will survey church history and make some major observations about how typology has been used. We begin with the era of the church fathers, spanning approximately AD 100–450.

The Education of the Saints

In the early centuries of the church, believers preached the gospel and taught the faith once for all entrusted to the saints. Sermons were crafted, treatises were penned, and commentaries were written. For patristic commentators, "the purpose of biblical exegesis, implicit and explicit, was to form the practice and belief of Christian people, individually and collectively."[2]

The use of typology served this catechetical purpose. Though not exactly distinguishing typology from allegory, the church fathers did see and teach Christ from the Old Testament. Their writings demonstrate a conviction that Scripture is a unity, and that what was promised in the Old Testament has been fulfilled in the New.[3] Peter Leithart is right: "The church

---

1. John J. O'Keefe and R. R. Reno, *Sanctified Vision: An Introduction to Early Christian Interpretation of the Bible* (Baltimore: Johns Hopkins University Press, 2005), 70.
2. Frances M. Young, *Biblical Exegesis and the Formation of Christian Culture* (Grand Rapids: Baker Academic, 1997), 299.
3. See Brian E. Daley, "Is Patristic Exegesis Still Usable?," in *The Art of Reading Scripture*, eds. Ellen F. Davis and Richard B. Hays (Grand Rapids: Eerdmans, 2003), 74–80.

fathers regularly read ancient literature typologically, seeing in it anticipations of the Christ."[4]

By reading the Old Testament as anticipating Christ, the fathers were trying to imitate the apostles. "In interpreting the Old Testament christologically, the fathers considered themselves to be faithful followers of the apostles, who were teaching what the risen Lord had taught them."[5] Irenaeus (AD 130–202) said, "A person who reads the Scriptures in the manner we have indicated" is following the practice of the disciples with whom "the Lord used this kind of discourse . . . after his resurrection from the dead."[6]

The Rule of Faith

A key development in the thinking and exegetical work of Irenaeus was his summary of the "rule of faith," the oral tradition that abridged the preaching of the apostles. According to Irenaeus:

> This then is the order of the rule of our faith, and the foundation of the building, and the stability of our conversation: God, the Father, not made, not material, invisible; one God, the creator of all things: this is the first point of our faith. The second point is: The Word of God, Son of God, Christ Jesus our Lord, who was manifested to the prophets according to the form of their prophesying and according to the method of the dispensation of the Father: through whom all things were made; who also at the end of the times, to complete and gather up all things, was made man among men, visible and tangible, in order to abolish death and show forth life and produce a community of union between God and man. And the third point is: The Holy Spirit, through whom the prophets prophesied, and the fathers learned the things of God, and the righteous were led forth into the way of righteousness; and who in the end of the times was poured out in a new way upon mankind in all the earth, renewing man unto God.[7]

---

4. Peter Leithart, *Deep Exegesis: The Mystery of Reading Scripture* (Waco, TX: Baylor University Press, 2009), 180.
5. Craig A. Carter, *Interpreting Scripture with the Great Tradition: Recovering the Genius of Premodern Exegesis* (Grand Rapids: Baker Academic, 2018), 141.
6. Irenaeus, *Against Heresies* 4.26.1, in Karlfried Froehlich, *Biblical Interpretation in the Early Church*, Sources of Early Christian Thought (Philadelphia: Fortress, 1984), 45.
7. Irenaeus, *Demonstration of Apostolic Preaching* 6, in Steven D. Cone and Robert F. Rea, *A Global Church History: The Great Tradition through Cultures, Continents and Centuries* (London: T&T Clark, 2019).

This summary was an important interpretive lens through which to read the Old Testament. The rule of faith affects the way the Old Testament is to be read. And in the timeline of events early in church history, it is helpful to situate the rule of faith before the total number of New Testament books was recognized.

According to Christopher Seitz, "The rule of faith is the scripturally grounded articulation, based upon a proper perception of the hypothesis of Scripture, that Jesus Christ is one with the god who sent him and who is active in the Scriptures inherited, the Holy Spirit being the means of testifying to his active, if hidden, life in the 'Old Testament' and our apprehension of that."[8]

Christological reading of the Old Testament was in keeping with the rule of faith, for such reading identified the shadows of Christ in the text and confirmed the prophetic witness to him. "For Irenaeus, the Christ proclaimed in the rule of faith is the key to the Scripture."[9]

The Defense of the Faith

The early church fathers had to engage criticism from multiple fronts, dealing with hostile Jews and heretics and dissenters. Using biblical and theological arguments, church leaders desired to equip the saints to stand firm and to answer the accusations of opponents.

When the fathers insisted that Jesus was the Messiah whom the Old Testament prophesied, typology was useful for their apologetic arguments. The writers could show parallels and correspondences between the Old Testament and the person and ministry of Jesus. Such connections would surely demonstrate that Jesus uniquely fulfilled Old Testament shadows and patterns and so was God's deliverer. Apologists such as Justin Martyr, Tertullian, and Irenaeus used the typological approach against Judaism and gnosticism.[10] Typology also played a role in the conflict with Manicheanism, which adopted gnostic errors about the Old Testament.[11] Through typology, the apologists were able to show the value of the Old Testament (contra gnosticism) and the fulfillment of the Old Testament in the New (contra Judaism).[12]

---

8. Christopher R. Seitz, *The Character of Christian Scripture: The Significance of a Two-Testament Bible*, Studies in Theological Interpretation (Grand Rapids: Baker Academic, 2011), 198.
9. Keith D. Stanglin, *The Letter and Spirit of Biblical Interpretation: From the Early Church to Modern Practice* (Grand Rapids: Baker Academic, 2018), 36.
10. Friedbert Ninow, *Indicators of Typology within the Old Testament: The Exodus Motif* (Frankfurt: Peter Lang, 2001), 24.
11. Jean Danielou, *From Shadows to Reality: Studies in the Biblical Typology of the Fathers*, trans. Dom Wulstan Hibberd (London: Burns & Oates, 1960), 2.
12. Richard M. Davidson, *Typology in Scripture: A Study of Hermeneutical TUPOS Structures* (Berrien Springs, MI: Andrews University Press, 1981), 20.

The Alexandrian and Antiochene Schools

According to an interpretive method that became known as the Alexandrian School, the sense of Scripture was not limited to the words on the surface of the text. Deeper meanings existed that should be pursued and uncovered. In response to the Alexandrian School, another interpretive method, known as the Antiochene School, insisted on interpretive restraint. These interpreters criticized the Alexandrian School for fanciful interpretations and for minimizing—or ignoring—the historical and grammatical features of the biblical text.

There is a danger in oversimplifying these two schools. A caricature has long existed that the Alexandrians were all about allegorical interpretation while the Antiochenes were all about literal interpretation. Rather than pitting the two schools against each other as opposites, it is more accurate to speak of a *spectrum* between them.[13]

Both the Alexandrian and Antiochene schools recognized spiritual and literal meanings in the biblical text. As Carter explains, "The main concern of the Alexandrians was that the literal sense apart from the spiritual killed the meaning; while the main concern of the Antiochenes was that 'the biblical historical sequence could be lost in timeless symbolism.'"[14] Or as Karlfried Froehlich summarizes it, the difference between Alexandria and Antioch was the methodological emphases and priorities of the two schools, for the latter emphasized rational analysis of biblical language more than analysis of spiritual reality, and the former subordinated history to a higher meaning intended by the divine author.[15] Indeed, "in acknowledging the divine author of Scripture both sides sought deeper meaning and hidden treasures of revelation in the sacred text."[16] For example, while Theodore of Mopsuestia (AD 350–428) was frustrated with the allegorists, he believed that the most exalted sense of Scripture was the sense revealed by typology.[17]

John Chrysostom (AD 349–407), who represented the Antiochene School, also upheld the importance of typology. He said a type can be compared to the drawing of a king that someone has sketched in outline form, later to be filled in with colors.[18] The colors fill up—or fulfill—the outline, and the antitype fulfills the type. The early church fathers, and both the Alexandrian and Antiochene schools, saw sketches and outlines of Christ and his work throughout the Old Testament. The New Testament "coloring" gave these interpreters eyes to see, and see they did.

---

13. Young, *Biblical Exegesis*, 120.
14. Carter, *Interpreting Scripture with the Great Tradition*, 99. See Stanglin, *Letter and Spirit of Biblical Interpretation*, 48–68.
15. Karlfried Froehlich, *Biblical Interpretation in the Early Church*, Sources of Early Christian Thought (Philadelphia: Fortress, 1984), 20–21.
16. Froehlich, *Biblical Interpretation in the Early Church*, 22.
17. Ninow, *Typology within the Old Testament*, 25.
18. John Chrysostom, *Homilies on Philippians* 10.4.

Examples of Types among the Church Fathers

Basil (AD 329–379) wrote, "The nature of the divine is very frequently represented by the rough and shadowy outlines of the types; but because divine things are prefigured by small and human things, it is obvious that we must not therefore conclude the divine nature to be small. The type is an exhibition of things expected, and gives an imitative anticipation of the future."[19] For the church fathers as a whole, "typological interpretation is best understood as an ever-expanding network of patterns and associations that refer back to the apostolic witness about Jesus Christ."[20]

The early fathers saw types in many Old Testament stories. While the fathers did not finely distinguish typology from allegory, we are able to study their writings and make such distinctions in hindsight. When the writers offer historical correspondences and then interpret something or someone in the Old Testament with a christological escalation, we can detect typological exegesis at work. Later in this book we will observe allegorical interpretations in their writings, but for the purposes of this chapter, the following examples are different types that the fathers discussed.

Adam and Jesus

The typological relationship between Adam and Jesus is brought out explicitly by the apostle Paul in Romans 5, and the early church fathers discussed these connections as well as the fact that both Adam and Jesus faced temptation.[21]

The Flood and the Ark

No theme occurs more frequently in the writings of the church fathers than the symbolism of Noah's ark as a type of the church, which delivers sinners from divine judgment.[22] The devastation of the flood foreshadowed the wrath of God at the final judgment, and the provision of the ark pointed to God's rescue of his people from his wrath.[23] Sometimes deliverance from the flood would be related to baptism.[24]

The Sacrifice of Isaac

Tertullian wrote about ways the mystery of the cross was set forth in Old Testament types. When Isaac, at his father's instruction, journeyed to the place

---

19. Basil, *Treatise on the Holy Spirit* 14.31, in Robin M. Jensen, *Baptismal Imagery in Early Christianity: Ritual, Visual, and Theological Dimensions* (Grand Rapids: Baker Academic, 2012), 16.
20. O'Keefe and Reno, *Sanctified Vision*, 76.
21. See Justin Martyr, *Dialogue* 103; Irenaeus, *Against Heresies* 3.18.7; Origen, *Romans* 5.1.7; Cyril of Alexandria *John* 1.9; 2.1.
22. Danielou, *From Shadows to Reality*, 69.
23. Justin Martyr, *Dialogue* 138.
24. Ambrose, *Sermons on the Sacraments* 2.1.

of sacrifice with wood upon his back, this episode was a type of Christ whom the Father sent to journey to the place of crucifixion.[25] Melito of Sardis said that if you want to see the mystery of Christ, behold Isaac who was tied up.[26]

The Story of Joseph

Tertullian saw Joseph in Genesis as a type of Christ.[27] When Gregory of Nyssa interpreted the Joseph story, he linked together the release from prison and the final resurrection on the last day.[28] Melito saw the trading of Joseph as prefiguring what would happen to Jesus.[29]

The Passover

In Exodus 12, the Lord fulfills his promise to lead the captive Israelites out of Egypt through his servant Moses, and their departure is after the Passover. Early Christian writers treated the Passover the way the New Testament does—as a type pointing to Christ's suffering and death. In an early Christian sermon, Melito of Sardis spoke of the Passover events in Exodus 12 as a "type" that anticipated the "reality" of Christ's atoning work.[30]

The Hands of Moses Outstretched

The raised hands of Moses during the battle against Amalek in Exodus 17 provided fascinating imagery for the early church fathers. Moses's hands held out the wooden staff of God, and this scene foreshadowed the cross and the victory of Jesus.[31] Tertullian questioned why Moses would not have simply been prostrate in prayer or beating his breast with pleas for Israel's deliverance; he reflected on the fact that Moses had his arms outstretched for the duration of Israel's battle against Amalek.[32] Tertullian concluded that it was necessary for Moses to stretch his arms like this, since Moses prefigured the Lord Jesus who would conquer the devil on the cross with outstretched arms.[33]

The Rock, the Sea, and the Cloud

Some church fathers saw sacramental significance in Old Testament types. Theodoret noted a typological relationship between the Red Sea and the

---

25. Tertullian, *Against Marcion* 3.18.
26. Melito of Sardis, *On Pascha*, trans. and ed. by A. Stewart-Sykes (Crestwood, NY: St Vladimir's Seminary Press, 2001), 52.
27. Tertullian, *Against Marcion* 3.18.
28. Gregory of Nyssa, *In Sanctum Pascha*.
29. Melito, *On Pascha*, 53.
30. Melito, *On Pascha*, 37–38.
31. See Cyprian, *Testimonia* 2.21; Theodoret, *Questions on the Octateuch*, Exod 34; Justin Martyr, *Dialogue* 90, 97.
32. Tertullian, *Against Marcion* 3.18.
33. Tertullian, *Against Marcion* 3.18.

baptismal font, the cloud and the Holy Spirit, and Moses and Christ.[34] Ambrose compared the rock (from which the water flowed in Moses's day) with the Eucharist.[35] According to Cyprian, the water gushing from the rock found fulfillment when Christ was pierced by the Roman spear, and he tied that image to the waters of baptism as well.[36] When Basil wrote about the gushing rock, he said the rock is Christ and the water from it is a type of Christ's power.[37]

The Law

The law in the early church was filled with mysteries that figuratively revealed the plan of the gospel and the kingdom of God.[38] According to Hilary of Poitiers, the Bible contains "true authentic prefigurations" of what Christ would come to do in birthing, sanctifying, calling, choosing, and redeeming the church.[39] Indeed, "Everything which Christ would fulfill had then been prefigured since the beginning of the world."[40] According to Melito of Sardis, the decrees of the gospel were proclaimed ahead of time by the law, the law serving thus as a type.[41]

The Bronze Serpent

The bronze serpent was lifted up in the wilderness in Numbers 21:4–9. Some early fathers wrote about this scene as a type of Christ's cross, in keeping with Jesus's interpretation in John 3:14–15.[42]

Joshua and Jesus

In the literature of the early church fathers, Joshua is nearly universally interpreted as a type of Christ, especially since the Septuagint renders his name *Iesous*, the name used for Jesus in the New Testament.[43] The earliest text where Joshua typology appears is the *Epistle of Barnabas* (12:8–10). Attention is given to the name of Joshua and how it relates to the Greek name for Jesus in the New Testament. "It is quite certain that the similarity of the names is a main reason why the Fathers see in Joshua a type of Jesus."[44] For example, Justin appealed to Joshua's name and links him typologically to Christ.[45] Augustine spoke of

---

34. Theodoret, *Questions on the Octateuch*, Exod 27.
35. Ambrose, *Sermons on the Sacraments* 5.1.
36. Cyprian, *Epistles* 63.8.2.
37. Basil, *Treatise on the Holy Spirit* 14.31.
38. Danielou, *From Shadows to Reality*, 11.
39. Hilary of Poitiers, *Tractatus Mysteriorum* 1.1.
40. Hilary of Poitiers, *Tractatus Mysteriorum* 1.1.
41. Melito, *On Pascha*, 47.
42. See Justin Martyr, *Dialogue* 91; Tertullian, *Against Marcion* 3.18.
43. O'Keefe and Reno, *Sanctified Vision*, 74.
44. Danielou, *From Shadows to Reality*, 231.
45. Justin Martyr, *Dialogue* 113.

Joshua as a type, for just as Joshua led the Israelites into the earthly Canaan, Christ would lead his church to occupy the future heavenly Canaan.[46]

The Scarlet Cord of Rahab

The author of 1 Clement—a letter attributed to Clement of Rome who died in approximately AD 101—wrote that the scarlet cord of Rahab showed beforehand that redemption shall come through the blood of Jesus for all who believe in him (see 1 Clem. 12:7). Justin also considered the scarlet cord to point toward the blood of Christ through which sinners from the nations would be saved.[47]

Summary

For centuries, the early church fathers saw Christ in the Old Testament, and one way they saw him was through Old Testament types. Their convictions about the unity of Scripture and God's christological purposes in Israel's history stirred and enhanced their vision as readers to see their Savior in the shadows. Certain Old Testament people and events pointed not only to Christ but to the church and its sacraments. Typological readings were useful for educating the saints and for defending the Christian faith. The church fathers believed they were reading the Old Testament in the manner Christ had taught his apostles to read it. As Irenaeus put it, "Anyone who reads the Scriptures attentively will find in them the word concerning Christ and the prefiguration of the new calling," for Christ is the treasure hidden in the field—that is, Christ is hidden in the Scriptures.[48]

REFLECTION QUESTIONS

1. How was typological exegesis useful for the education of Christians in the early church?

2. Why was typological exegesis important to defenders of the Christian faith?

3. What were some common Old Testament people or events that the early church fathers treated as types?

4. What was the difference between the Alexandrian and Antiochene schools?

5. According to Irenaeus, how crucial was typology for understanding the Old Testament?

---

46. See Sidney Greidanus, *Preaching Christ from the Old Testament: A Contemporary Hermeneutical Model* (Grand Rapids: Eerdmans, 1999), 100.
47. Justin Martyr, *Dialogue* 111.
48. Irenaeus, *Against Heresies* 4.26.1.

How Was Typology Practiced in the Middle Ages?

Typological interpretation did not disappear after the first few centuries of the Christian church. Theologians in the Middle Ages—a span of time stretching across a thousand years (AD 450–1450)—continued to see multiple senses in the biblical text. Henri de Lubac summarizes the big picture: "The Christian tradition understands that Scripture has two meanings. The most general name for these two meanings is the literal meaning and the spiritual ('pneumatic') meaning."[1] Paramount, then, was the recognition that the Old Testament has a christological meaning embedded there by the divine author. And one way interpreters in the Middle Ages saw Christ within the Old Testament was through typology.

The Influence of Augustine and John Cassian

There is no pivotal moment when the Middle Ages arrived, but there may have been a pivotal person. David Baker identifies the work of Augustine (who lived from AD 354–430) as "the transition from the early Church to the Middle Ages: it is the culmination of several centuries of Christian thought and forms the foundation of theology in the West for the following centuries."[2]

A focus upon Augustine is especially appropriate for a discussion about typology in church history. After all, to Augustine, Christ was *the* key for understanding the Old Testament. Augustine wrote, "Everything in those Scriptures speaks of Christ, but only to him that has ears. He opened their

---

1. Henri de Lubac, *Medieval Exegesis: The Four Senses of Scripture*, vol. 1, trans. Mark Sebanc (Grand Rapids: Eerdmans, 1998), 225.
2. David L. Baker, *Two Testaments, One Bible: A Study of Some Modern Solutions to the Theological Problem of the Relationship between the Old and New Testaments*, rev. ed. (Downers Grove, IL: InterVarsity, 1976), 47.

minds to understand the Scriptures; and so let us pray that he will open our own."[3] Augustine was clear that while the Scriptures speak of Christ, such understanding is not completely self-evident to readers. We need our ears and minds opened. We need divine help.

Prayerful dependence and divine help were important because of the conviction that there was more than one sense to Scripture. In the era of the early church, Origen had taught that Scripture has three senses (the body, the soul, and the spirit), and Ambrose also taught a threefold sense (the literal-historical, the moral, and the mystical). Augustine added a fourth sense, which searched for an eschatological meaning. This fourfold set of senses was important for John Cassian (AD 360–435), a contemporary of Augustine. John Cassian established the standard form of the fourfold sense. In his work *Conferences*, he wrote of the literal, allegorical, tropological, and anagogical senses.[4] This fourfold sense is also known as The Quadriga—the "four-horse chariot."

The Quadriga

Use of the Quadriga flourished in the Middle Ages. The literal sense was foundational for the spiritual sense, which was divided into the allegorical, tropological, and anagogical senses.

1. The literal sense focuses on the facts.

2. The allegorical sense focuses on how the facts prefigure something else.

3. The tropological sense focuses on moral explanation and exhortation.

4. The anagogical sense focuses on hope.[5]

How does typology intersect with the Quadriga? If the Old Testament literal sense points beyond itself to Christ, then christological significance is found in the spiritual sense. And if the spiritual sense can be divided threefold—allegorical, tropological, and anagogical—then in which category does typology fall? The term "allegorical," in the way it is used in the Quadriga, is a large enough umbrella to incorporate typology. This may seem like a counterintuitive point, because this book does not argue that typology equals allegory, yet early interpreters did not make hard and fast distinctions between allegory and typology.

---

3. Augustine, *Homilies on 1 John* 2.1, in Sidney Greidanus, *Preaching Christ from the Old Testament: A Contemporary Hermeneutical Model* (Grand Rapids: Eerdmans, 1999), 100.
4. John Cassian, *Conferences* 14.8. These four terms will be explained in the following section on the Quadriga.
5. See de Lubac, *Medieval Exegesis*, 1:1.

So, in the Middle Ages, christological types in the Old Testament fit best under the spiritual sense, and specifically the allegorical sense, for the second part of the Quadriga was the label given to the deeper and christological understanding of a biblical text. To engage the allegorical sense of a text was to participate in "a systematic and openly Christocentric theological digestion of Old and New Testament together."[6] As Keith Stanglin puts it, "Allegory encompasses types that link the Old and New Testaments together."[7]

Question 8 argued that biblical types are historical. Their historicity means that the engagement of the allegorical sense does not ignore or negate the literal sense. Rather, using the Quadriga, typology incorporates *both the literal and allegorical senses*. Historical facts are affirmed which then prefigure something else. For example, the story of David's defeat of Goliath in 1 Samuel 17 is a historical story that also has a deeper meaning in the fullness of the biblical canon, foreshadowing David's greater son who conquered the serpent.[8]

Understanding how the Quadriga functioned is crucial to rightly discerning the use of typology in the Middle Ages. As Karlfried Froehlich summarizes:

> The attention to be given to the literal sense preserved the grammatical and historical emphases of the Antiochene school; the allegorical sense expressed the typological understanding of the Old Testament and its rich early Christian tradition; the tropological sense allowed for the interests of Jewish and Christian moralists from the rabbis and Philo to Tertullian and Chrysostom; the anagogical sense kept alive the central concern of Alexandrian exegesis for a spiritual reading of Scriptures.[9]

The Unity of Scripture

Interpretation during the Middle Ages, particularly the Quadriga, depended on the unity of Scripture. If the Old and New Testaments are not a unity, the Quadriga collapses. This presupposition about unity undermines much of modern scholarship, which treats Scripture as a compilation of fragments, yet this presupposition is very much in line with the period of the early church that affirmed the coherence of the Bible's big story.

---

6. Karlfried Froehlich, *Sensing the Scriptures: Aminadab's Chariot and the Predicament of Biblical Interpretation* (Grand Rapids: Eerdmans, 2014), 57.
7. Keith D. Stanglin, *The Letter and Spirit of Biblical Interpretation: From the Early Church to Modern Practice* (Grand Rapids: Baker Academic, 2018), 97.
8. See James Hamilton, "The Skull Crushing Seed of the Woman: Inner-Biblical Interpretation of Genesis 3:15," *Southern Baptist Journal of Theology* 10, no. 2 (Summer 2006): 30–54.
9. Karlfried Froehlich, *Biblical Interpretation in the Early Church*, Sources of Early Christian Thought (Philadelphia: Fortress, 1984), 28–29.

There were writers who spoke boldly about the relationship of the Testaments. For example, Stephen Langton (1150–1228) said that just as Isaiah's seraphim "proclaim the praises of God to one another," the Old and New Testaments—"each one of which contains the other"[10]—testify to the same truths. The New is in the Old, and the Old is in the New. The unity of Scripture was indispensable for medieval hermeneutics. In fact, when we consider the medieval emphasis on the divine inspiration of Scripture, the importance of a virtuous interpreter, and the role of the church's rule of faith, "medieval exegesis is simply a continuation of patristic exegesis."[11]

The Foundation of the Literal Sense

One of the marks of interpretation in the Middle Ages was a widespread commitment to the spiritual sense. Yet, we should not allow the literal sense to be neglected or negated. Rather, if we think of the Quadriga as a house, the literal sense is the foundation. While Jerome had spoken of the literal sense as the foundation for right interpretation, Gregory the Great (540–604) expanded the metaphor: the foundation is laid (*littera*), next the walls are put up (*allegoria*), and then the house is painted (*tropologia*, the other word for moral interpretation).[12] A fourth sense—anagogy (*anagogia*)—is the roof. Alcuin (735–804) said, "The foundation in history must be laid first, so that the roof of allegory can be built more suitably on the first-established structure."[13]

Throughout the Middle Ages, some interpreters perceived a neglect of the literal sense. A trajectory had formed where interpretations majored heavily on the spiritual sense of a text, and this emphasis often led to conclusions unwarranted by the text. There was widespread, even seemingly unbridled, allegorical interpretation (see part 3 of this book).

The neglect of the literal sense was not universal, though. For example, Rupert of Deutz (1075–1129) said that "the literal sense must be taken seriously in every instance."[14] And Hugh of St. Victor (1096–1141) opposed warrantless allegorizing and favored the literal meaning of the text. Hugh taught that responsible interpreters study the literal or historical sense of a text. In his work on hermeneutics, *Didascalicon: On the Study of Reading*, Hugh—like Jerome and Gregory before him—compared Scripture to the structure of a great building. The historical sense was its foundation and allegory its superstructure:

10. De Lubac, *Medieval Exegesis*, 1:256.
11. Stanglin, *Letter and Spirit of Biblical Interpretation*, 78.
12. *The Letters of Gregory the Great* 5.53a, trans. John R. C. Martyn, Medieval Sources in Translation 40 (Toronto: Pontifical Institute of Medieval Studies, 2004), 382.
13. Cited in Henning G. Reventlow, *History of Biblical Interpretation*, vol. 2, *From Late Antiquity to the End of the Middle Ages*, trans. James O. Duke, Resources for Biblical Study 61 (Atlanta: Society of Biblical Literature, 2009), 123.
14. Cited in Reventlow, *History of Biblical Interpretation*, 2:155.

But just as you see that every building lacking a foundation cannot stand firm, so also is it in learning. The foundation and principle of sacred learning, however, is history, from which, like honey from the honeycomb, the truth of allegory is extracted. As you are about to build, therefore, lay first the foundation of history; next, by pursuing the typical meaning; next, build up a structure in your mind to be a fortress of faith. Last of all, however, through the loveliness of morality, paint the structure over us with the most beautiful colours.[15]

Thomas Aquinas and Nicholas of Lyra

The literal sense was important for recognizing biblical types, because types are rooted in historical realities. Typology could only flourish where the literal sense was affirmed and respected. Bonaventure (1221–1274) said no one can be a competent interpreter of Scripture who is not familiar with "the letters of the Bible."[16] Yet Bonaventure still focused on the "illuminative" aspect of Scripture, identifying types apart from allegory.[17]

When the literal sense was respected and emphasized as the foundation of proper interpretation, types could be discerned. For example, in a twelfth-century Cistercian homily, the historical Joseph was viewed as a type of Christ: "What I have placed before you, brethren, is like an egg or a nut; break the shell and you will find the food. Beneath the image of Joseph you will find the Paschal Lamb, Jesus, the one for whom you yearn."[18] The writer talks about Joseph's distinction among his brothers, Joseph's blameless actions, his prudent judgments, his rejection and humiliation, and his elevation and vindication and reward—all things that correspond to and escalate toward the Lord Jesus.

Of medieval theologians who pushed back against the abuses of the spiritual sense and who strongly emphasized the literal sense, perhaps no writers are more noteworthy than Thomas Aquinas (1225–1274) and Nicholas of Lyra (1270–1349).[19] Stanglin represents the evaluation of others when he calls Thomas Aquinas "the most influential theologian after Augustine" in the Western church.[20] While Aquinas did not distinguish between typology and allegory, he maintained that the spiritual sense is grounded in the literal

---

15. Jeremy Taylor, ed. and trans., *The Didascalicon of Hugh of St Victor* (New York: Columbia University Press, 1961), 138.
16. Cited in Reventlow, *History of Biblical Interpretation*, 2:210.
17. Friedbert Ninow, *Indicators of Typology within the Old Testament: The Exodus Motif* (Frankfurt: Peter Lang, 2001), 26.
18. Guerric of Igny, *Liturgical Sermons [by] Guerric of Igny*, vol. 2, trans. Monks of Mount Saint Bernard Abbey, Cistercian Fathers 32 (Spencer, MA: Cistercian, 1971), 81.
19. Stanglin, *Letter and Spirit of Biblical Interpretation*, 110.
20. Stanglin, *Letter and Spirit of Biblical Interpretation*, 103.

sense. The Scripture "sets up no confusion, since all meanings are based on one, namely the literal sense."[21] While Aquinas stressed the literal sense in his exegetical practice, his concept of the literal sense enveloped conclusions previously attributed to the spiritual sense.[22] When Aquinas wrote about Isaiah 12, which promises Israel's return from Babylonian captivity, he believed that such consolation foreshadowed the ultimate release from captivity that is found in Christ.[23] And when he treats Isaiah 40–66, he often joins together a literal and typological sense, such as with the figure of Cyrus, whom he interprets as both a historical figure and a type of Christ.[24] Yet any spiritual sense that the interpreter pursues should not be the basis for doctrine. For Aquinas, "nothing necessary for faith is contained under the spiritual sense that is not openly conveyed through the literal sense elsewhere."[25]

Nicholas of Lyra agreed with Thomas Aquinas that, though there may be a number of mystical or spiritual meanings in a text, they all presuppose the literal sense as the foundation (*fundamentum*).[26] In fact, with Aquinas and Nicholas, we see the spiritual sense being drawn back into the literal sense to comprise what could be called the "double-literal sense" or "extended literal sense."[27] This is an important development in the Middle Ages because the christological significance of a passage could be thought of as the plain sense, if the literal sense is extended to overlap with what would have previously been relegated wholly to the spiritual sense. Nicholas also perpetuated the building image for the multiple senses of Scripture. The literal sense was the foundation of the interpretive building, and "a mystical interpretation that deviates from the literal sense is to be judged inappropriate and inadequate."[28]

Summary

Following the centuries of the early church, the thousand-year period of the Middle Ages continued to see the practice of typological interpretation. The Quadriga was an interpretive grid that included a christological dimension. The united Testaments preserved the prefigurements of Christ and the fulfillment of those types. Typology rests on the acknowledgement of the

---

21. Thomas Aquinas, *Summa Theologiae* 1.1.10, trans. Blackfriars (New York: McGraw-Hill, 1964–1981). For the same argument, see Sidney Greidanus, *Preaching Christ from the Old Testament: A Contemporary Hermeneutical Model* (Grand Rapids: Eerdmans, 1999), 106–7.
22. Craig A. Carter, *Interpreting Scripture with the Great Tradition: Recovering the Genius of Premodern Exegesis* (Grand Rapids: Baker Academic, 2018), 99.
23. Brevard S. Childs, *The Struggle to Understand Isaiah as Christian Scripture* (Grand Rapids: Eerdmans, 2004), 156–57.
24. Childs, *Isaiah as Christian Scripture*, 158. See Thomas Aquinas, *In Isaiam Prophetam Expositio, Opera Omnia*, vols. 18–19 (Paris: Louis Vives, 1876).
25. Thomas Aquinas, *Summa Theologiae* 1.1.10, trans. the Black-friars, 1:38–39.
26. Stanglin, *Letter and Spirit of Biblical Interpretation*, 106.
27. Carter, *Interpreting Scripture with the Great Tradition*, 101.
28. Cited in Reventlow, *History of Biblical Interpretation*, 2:250.

literal sense of a biblical text, and this literal sense was foundational for interpreters in the Middle Ages. When abuses of the spiritual sense occurred that departed or diminished the literal sense, voices rose to defend the literal sense while at the same time not denying the deeper significance to the biblical text. This renewed emphasis on the literal sense was a trajectory picked up during the next era of church history.

REFLECTION QUESTIONS

1. What are the four parts of the Quadriga?

2. How did the image of a building illustrate the stages of interpretation?

3. Why was emphasis on the literal sense an important feature to maintain for typological interpretation?

4. What roles did Thomas Aquinas and Nicolas of Lyra play when the literal sense was not being appropriately recognized and stressed?

5. What are some ways that interpretation in the Middle Ages overlapped with interpretation in the early church era?

How Was Typology Practiced in the Early Modern Era?

The early modern era (1450–1650) included the period of the Protestant Reformation, so this was a span of time feverishly devoted to studying and interpreting the biblical text. Theologians continued to employ typology when reading the Old Testament, which was a strategy continuing from the Middle Ages and the centuries of the early church. Interpretive practices in the period of the Reformation were picking up a trajectory from the previous years.

Emphasis on the Literal Sense

A renewed emphasis on the literal sense—which had marked the work of figures like Thomas Aquinas and Nicholas of Lyra in the Middle Ages—continued during the early modern era. During the Reformation years, "the literal sense became more prominent, even if more complex as it absorbed more and more of the content of the spiritual meanings."[1] There was a discernible hesitancy among Reformers to deviate from the literal sense and so delve into realms of speculation and fanciful interpretations. Their hesitancy was justified by a long Christian tradition that attended to the literal sense of Scripture as foundational for sound exegesis.[2]

Nevertheless, emphasis on the literal sense did not mean a denial of other senses. Two of the most famous figures from this era—Martin Luther (1483–1546) and John Calvin (1509–1564)—believed the biblical text contained multiple senses.

---

1. Timothy George, *Reading Scripture with the Reformers* (Downers Grove, IL: IVP Academic, 2011), 27.
2. Iain Provan, *The Reformation and the Right Reading of Scripture* (Waco, TX: Baylor University Press, 2017), 202.

Martin Luther

Born in 1483, Martin Luther was trained in the Quadriga, which was to be expected, for the Quadriga had been used for a thousand years by that point. Luther's study of Scripture led him to be critical of the allegorization of biblical texts. He pinpointed men like Jerome, Origen, and Augustine as examples of allegorizers. Yet Luther's criticisms did not prevent him from pursuing a spiritual sense in the biblical text.

Luther emphasized the literal sense of the text but remained open to a spiritual sense as well. The reason he saw the biblical text as having this two-fold sense was because of his assumption about its unity. He believed that all of the Old Testament applied to Christ, and thus he made many typological identifications.[3] Luther identified types of Christ in Old Testament people like Melchizedek, Aaron, David, and Solomon, in events like the crossings through the Red Sea and the Jordan River, and in things like the manna, the water from Horeb's rock, and the bronze serpent.[4]

As Luther himself put it, "The Old Testament pointed toward Christ. The New, however, now gives us what was previously promised and signified through figures in the Old Testament."[5] Luther's typology was thoroughly christocentric and firmly rooted in history, though in his effort to see the christological dimension of the Old Testament, his interpretations occasionally veered into allegory.[6]

John Calvin

John Calvin recognized types in his reading and interpretation of the Old Testament. For Calvin, typology was not a slight interpretive interest—it was dominant, imposing, central. To be clear: "Without typology . . . Calvin would not be Calvin; for typology occupies a central and significant role in his theology."[7] He was convinced that the Old Testament revealed Christ everywhere in its sacred pages, though not in full glory, of course, but in types and shadows that Christ fulfilled.[8] For Calvin, typology was the key to opening up the Old Testament.[9]

---

3. Friedbert Ninow, *Indicators of Typology within the Old Testament: The Exodus Motif* (Frankfurt: Peter Lang, 2001), 27.
4. Thomas M. Davis, "The Traditions of Puritan Typology," in *Typology and Early American Literature*, ed. Sacvan Bercovitch (Amherst: University of Massachusetts Press, 1972), 37.
5. Quoted in Paul Althaus, *The Theology of Martin Luther*, trans. Robert C. Schultz (Philadelphia: Fortress, 1966), 95.
6. Richard M. Davidson, *Typology in Scripture: A Study of Hermeneutical TUPOS Structures* (Berrien Springs, MI: Andrews University Press, 1981), 30.
7. Davis, "Traditions of Puritan Typology," 38.
8. Davis, "Traditions of Puritan Typology," 39.
9. See the explanations in John Calvin, *Institutes of the Christian Religion*, ed. John T. McNeill, trans. Ford Lewis Battles, 2 vols., Library of Christian Classics (Philadelphia: Westminster, 1960), 2.11.

In his many commentaries, Calvin claimed that Joseph, Aaron, Samson, David, Zedekiah, Cyrus, and Zerubbabel were all types of Christ.[10] Calvin wrote, "The Gospel points with the finger to what the Law shadowed under types."[11] He considered types to be a key distinction between the Old and New Testaments, for types exhibited "only the image of truth, while the reality was absent, the shadow instead of the substance," while the antitype exhibited "both the full truth and the entire body."[12]

Emphasis on the literal sense continued in the writings and preaching of Calvin. But while previous interpreters typically considered christological types to be located in the spiritual sense of a biblical text, Calvin located types in the literal sense itself.[13] In other words, guided by his commitment to historical interpretation of a biblical text, Calvin believed the literal meaning of a text *included* the types that foreshadow Christ.[14] By extending the literal sense to include biblical types of Christ, Calvin's typological interpretation arrived at what he considered to be the "plain sense" of the text.[15] Carter summarizes it this way: "All meaning is found in the plain sense, which can be understood as a combination of the literal and spiritual senses, which are unified by Jesus Christ as the great theme and center of the Old and New Testaments understood as one book."[16]

William Perkins

After Luther and Calvin, William Perkins (1558–1602), a popular English Reformed preacher and theologian, had substantive international influence, especially on those later called the Puritans.[17] He engaged the Old Testament with typological instincts. For example, when Perkins read Exodus 12, he interpreted it in a twofold way: first, the Passover was intended to celebrate Israel's deliverance from Egypt, and second, the Passover was a type of our "spiritual deliverance from everlasting death, by the sacrifice of Christ Jesus the immaculate Lambe of God."[18]

---

10. Peter J. Leithart, "The Quadriga or Something Like It: A Biblical and Pastoral Defense," in *Ancient Faith for the Church's Future*, eds. Mark Husbands and Jeffrey P. Greenman (Downers Grove, IL: IVP Academic, 2008), 111.
11. John Calvin, *Institutes*, 2.9.3.
12. Calvin, *Institutes* 2.10.4.
13. Craig A. Carter, *Interpreting Scripture with the Great Tradition: Recovering the Genius of Premodern Exegesis* (Grand Rapids: Baker Academic, 2018), 169.
14. Ninow, *Typology within the Old Testament*, 27.
15. Carter, *Interpreting Scripture with the Great Tradition*, 165.
16. Carter, *Interpreting Scripture with the Great Tradition*, 176.
17. Keith D. Stanglin, *The Letter and Spirit of Biblical Interpretation: From the Early Church to Modern Practice* (Grand Rapids: Baker Academic, 2018), 142.
18. William Perkins, *The Works of That Famous and Worthy Minister of Christ in the Universitie of Cambridge M. William Perkins*, 3 vols. (London, 1631), 3:151. See Erwin R. Gane, "The

According to Perkins, the Quadriga of the Middle Ages did not accurately reflect the number of senses in the biblical text. A text had a single sense—the literal sense, which included any literary features or figurative elements. He said, "To make many senses of scripture, is to overturn all sense, and to make nothing certain. As for the three spiritual senses (so called) they are not senses, but applications or uses of scripture."[19] Perkins was concerned that multiple senses implied the instability of meaning. According to his interpretive approach, any biblical type was located in the literal sense of a biblical text.

Perkins's emphasis on the literal sense, however, still incorporated conclusions that earlier exegetes might have attributed to the spiritual sense. According to Stanglin, "Like Luther, who decried allegorical interpretation yet simultaneously practiced it, Perkins also acknowledged a fuller meaning of Scripture in ways consistent with patristic and medieval exegesis."[20] And Perkins unhesitatingly affirmed a christological reading of the Old Testament. In fact, he directed students of the Bible to read Romans and the Gospel of John before moving to Old Testament books, so that they would have an increased capacity to see typological and christological meaning.[21]

The Cocceian School

Johannes Cocceius (1603–1669) lived after the time of Luther, Calvin, and Perkins, near the end of the early modern era. He distinguished between types that Scripture explicitly identified and ones that he said were implied though unidentified by Scripture. Cocceius did not establish any interpretive controls for typology, so "the door was opened" to an increasing number of possible types.[22]

Cocceius's approach to Scripture provoked criticism from others in the years to come. Two centuries after Cocceius, Patrick Fairbairn (1805–1874) said the former interpreter had "left ample scope for the indulgence of a luxuriant fancy."[23] If typological exegesis could be practiced without sufficient controls for the interpreter, would not the practice eventually and inevitably devolve into subjectivity? Despite any criticism that came after Cocceius, his

---

Exegetical Methods of Some Sixteenth-Century Puritan Preachers: Hooper, Cartwrights, and Perkins. Part II," *Andrews University Seminary Studies* 19, no. 2 (1981): 99–114.

19. William Perkins, *A Commentarie, or, Exposition upon the Five First Chapters of the Epistle to the Galatians* (London: John Legatt, 1617), 304–5.

20. Stanglin, *Letter and Spirit of Biblical Interpretation*, 143.

21. Stanglin, *Letter and Spirit of Biblical Interpretation*, 143. See William Perkins, *The Arte of Prophecying, or, a Treatise concerning the Sacred and Onely True Manner and Methode of Preaching*, in Perkins, *Works*, 2:736, col. 2.

22. Ninow, *Typology within the Old Testament*, 28.

23. Patrick Fairbairn, *The Typology of Scripture: Viewed in connection with the Whole Series of the Divine Dispensations*, 2 vols., 6th ed. (Edinburgh: T&T Clark, 1876), 1:29.

hermeneutic flourished, especially in Britain and in the writings of the New England Puritans.[24]

Francis Turretin

While Johannes Cocceius was alive, a man named Francis Turretin (1623–1687) was born. With centuries of interpretation based on the Quadriga preceding him, it is important to see how Turretin engaged the fourfold lens of interpretation: he rejected it. He embraced "only one and genuine sense," the literal sense, which could be simple and historical or composite and typological.[25]

Like some interpreters before him, however, Turretin does not sideline a spiritual sense to the text—he simply subsumes it in the literal sense itself. He writes, "A composite or mixed meaning is found in oracles containing typology, part of which [oracle] is type and part antitype. This does not constitute two meanings, but two parts of one and the same meaning intended by the Holy Spirit, who covered the mystery with literal meaning."[26] When it comes to the allegorical, tropological, or anagogical senses of the Quadriga, Turretin says they "are not different meanings, but applications of the single literal meaning; allegory and anagogy apply to instruction, and tropology applies to discipline."[27]

While Turretin majors on the literal sense of the text, he believes this literal sense can still encompass what previous theologians had called the spiritual sense or the allegorical, tropological, and anagogical senses of the Quadriga. For Turretin, "the literal sense embraces a fuller sense that allows for typological and christological readings of the Old Testament," and he considers "the three spiritual senses as legitimate in terms of uses or applications."[28]

Summary

Interpreters of the early modern era, specifically the Reformers, paid great attention to the literal sense, even subsuming under it the kinds of christological conclusions that previously belonged to the spiritual sense. Typology continued to be used by interpreters like Luther, Calvin, Perkins, Cocceius, Turretin, and others. These theologians were wary of abuses of the spiritual sense, and they criticized theologians of the early church and Middle Ages who seemed to major in senses that neglected or ignored the literal sense. The Quadriga, which had been used during the previous thousand years, was not

---

24. Ninow, *Typology within the Old Testament*, 28.
25. Stanglin, *Letter and Spirit of Biblical Interpretation*, 145; Francis Turretin, *Institutes of Elenctic Theology*, trans. George Musgrave Giger, ed. James T. Dennison Jr. (Phillipsburg, NJ: P&R, 1992), 2.19.1–4 (1:149–50).
26. Turretin, *Institutes of Elenctic Theology*, 2.19.2 (1:149–50).
27. Turretin, *Institutes of Elenctic Theology*, 2.19.6 (1:150–51).
28. Stanglin, *Letter and Spirit of Biblical Interpretation*, 146.

affirmed or advocated by these theologians. Nevertheless, their emphasis on the literal sense incorporated christological readings of the Old Testament.

REFLECTION QUESTIONS

1. What assumptions about interpreting the biblical text does the early modern period have in common with the eras of the early church and the Middle Ages?

2. How did Martin Luther engage the notion of types in the Old Testament?

3. What are some implications of John Calvin extending the literal sense to include Old Testament types?

4. Why was Johannes Cocceius significant in the historical discussion of typology?

5. How did Francis Turretin understand the value of the Quadriga?

How Was Typology Practiced in the Enlightenment?

In the years following the Reformation, typology was strongly featured in the work of the Puritans. But the years of the Enlightenment (1650–1800) also had negative effects on typology, for the elevation of human reason influenced how people viewed and read the Bible. Therefore, while some interpreters continued to treat the Bible as a supernatural book with united testaments that exalted Christ, other interpreters treated the Bible with suspicion, questioned long-held presuppositions, and contributed to the diminished view of typology.

The Rise of the Puritans

The Puritans lived and preached and wrote during the sixteenth and seventeenth centuries. The Reformers acknowledged the presence of biblical types, and the Puritans followed suit. "The Reformers were, in fact, among the most earnest practitioners of typology, and the Puritan practice is clearly based on Reformational precedent."[1] But the Puritans' practice of typological exegesis goes deeper than the Reformation years; it is rooted "deep in the traditions of the Church Fathers."[2] A couple examples of Puritan typological exegesis will suffice: Thomas Goodwin and Samuel Mather.

Thomas Goodwin (1600–1680) wrote a book called *The Heart of Christ*, and in it he made multiple typological observations. He said the marriage of Adam to his wife was a type and shadow of Christ's marriage to his church.[3]

---

1. Thomas M. Davis, "The Traditions of Puritan Typology," in *Typology and Early American Literature*, ed. Sacvan Bercovitch (Amherst: University of Massachusetts Press, 1972), 12.
2. Davis, "Traditions of Puritan Typology," 12..
3. Thomas Goodwin, *The Heart of Christ* (1651; repr., Carlisle, PA: Banner of Truth Trust, 2011), 83.

He considered the Holy of Holies a type of the highest seat in heaven, where Christ sits.[4] He called Christ the truth and substance of the ceremonial types.[5] He viewed Moses as a type of Christ.[6] And he said that the high priests "were types of our great high priest."[7]

Puritan interpretation strongly emphasized the historicity of the biblical accounts. "The Puritan sense of the literal historicity of Scripture was nowhere more vigorously manifested than in Mather's defense of typological correspondences, which were based on literal events in the Old Testament and were in no way allegorical fictions or fanciful analogies."[8] From March 1666 to February 1668, Samuel Mather (1626–1671) preached a systematic treatment of typology. After his death, his younger brother Nathanael published these sermons in London in 1673 under the title *The Figures or Types of the Old Testament, by which Christ and the Heavenly Things of the Gospel Were Preached and Shadowed to the People of God of Old, Explained and Improv'd in Sundry Sermons, by Samuel Mather.*[9] Mason Lowance Jr. notes, "The influence and popularity of this work is indicated by the three distributions of the first edition, and by the demand for a second edition in 1705."[10]

According to Samuel Mather, "A type is some outward or sensible thing ordained of God under the Old Testament, to represent and hold forth something of Christ in the New."[11] He identified many biblical characters as types of Christ, such as Adam, Noah, Melchizedek, Abraham, Isaac, Jacob, Joseph, Moses, and Joshua.[12] He identified "typical things" such as Noah's ark, Jacob's ladder, the burning bush, and the manna.[13] And he identified "typical actions" such as the exodus out of Egypt, the crossing through the Red Sea, the journey in the wilderness, the crossing of the Jordan River, and the exile to Babylon.[14] He said the temple "typified the Body of Christ,"[15] and he said the garments of Aaron "typified and shadowed out the beauty of Christ, our true High Priest, in all those glorious graces of the Spirit of holiness in him."[16]

---

4. Goodwin, *Heart of Christ*, 105.

5. Goodwin, *Heart of Christ*, 84.

6. Goodwin, *Heart of Christ*, 63, 88.

7. Goodwin, *Heart of Christ*, 49, 94, 99, 103.

8. Mason I. Lowance Jr., introduction to Samuel Mather, *Figures or Types of the Old Testament, Opened and Explained*, 2nd ed., v–xxiii (1705; repr., New York: Johnson Reprint, 1969), xiv.

9. Ursula Brumm, *American Thought and Religious Typology* (New Brunswick, NJ: Rutgers University Press, 1970), 40.

10. Lowance, introduction to Mather, *Figures or Types*, xvi.

11. Mather, *Figures or Types*, 52.

12. Lowance, introduction to Mather, *Figures or Types*, xviii.

13. Lowance, introduction to Mather, *Figures or Types*, xviii–xix.

14. Lowance, introduction to Mather, *Figures or Types*, xix.

15. Samuel Mather, *A Testimony from the Scripture against Idolatry and Superstition* (Boston, 1725), 61.

16. Mather, *Testimony from the Scripture*, 31.

The Bible and Human Reason

During the years of the Enlightenment, the rise of Baruch Spinoza (1632–1677) was a significant and ominous development. Craig Carter calls him a "heretical Jew . . . who blazed the trail for the development of rationalistic biblical criticism, and his motives were political in nature."[17] Spinoza's ambitions were not small: he wanted to free society from the superstition of religion, for he regarded all religions as breeding grounds for cruelty, fear, hatred, and violence.[18] If religion was associated with superstitions, then the Bible itself came to be viewed with suspicion and, ultimately, with an antisupernatural bent.

It is the eighteenth century above all that is associated with the title "Age of Enlightenment," with such key figures as Voltaire (Francois-Marie Arouet, 1694–1778), David Hume (1711–1776), Jean-Jacques Rousseau (1712–1778), Adam Smith (1723–1790), and Immanuel Kant (1724–1804).[19] By and large, the thinkers of the Enlightenment wanted to break the power of the church in society, and one key move to accomplish this goal was to assert that morality could be based on reason alone, with no need for special revelation.[20]

The elevation of human reason was not merely the rejection of a supernatural worldview; it was the establishment of a natural worldview. If human reason could be trusted to the extent that special revelation was not needed, then the Bible did not necessarily have the authority that interpreters once believed it did. And if natural explanations could be pursued and scientific theories posited for where we came from and why we're here, then the supernatural elements of the Bible seemed, quite frankly, antiquated and primitive. The Bible was an ancient literary document that could now be studied as any other piece of literature.[21]

Under the continued inflation of human reason and antisupernaturalism, the presuppositions about the Bible began to crack. No longer did interpreters need virtue to understand the sacred text. No longer did the tradition of church theologians provide a faithful guide for Bible readers. No longer did the message of the Bible depend upon a unity spanning both testaments. "Now, Scripture was considered to be a collection of various strands of traditions and origins that had no connection whatsoever with each other."[22]

The effect upon typology was disastrous. Without the unity and inspiration of Scripture, typology is impossible. Textual correspondences are

---

17. Craig A. Carter, *Interpreting Scripture with the Great Tradition: Recovering the Genius of Premodern Exegesis* (Grand Rapids: Baker Academic, 2018), 114.
18. Carter, *Interpreting Scripture with the Great Tradition*, 114.
19. Iain Provan, *The Reformation and the Right Reading of Scripture* (Waco, TX: Baylor University Press, 2017), 391.
20. Carter, *Interpreting Scripture with the Great Tradition*, 16.
21. Friedbert Ninow, *Indicators of Typology within the Old Testament: The Exodus Motif* (Frankfurt: Peter Lang, 2001), 33.
22. Ninow, *Typology within the Old Testament*, 33–34.

reduced to historical coincidence instead of divine providence. And if the biblical text was not authoritative and inspired, it was not necessarily trustworthy on historical matters either. If we reject divine authorship of the biblical text, then the Bible is merely a human book, and humans are known to err. Since typology depends on true historical events, the skepticism of antisupernaturalism meant that events in the Bible might not have happened. "Typology was no longer viewed as a legitimate approach to Scripture. . . . Thus the typological method of interpretation became an odd relic with little or no significance."[23]

The Different Eyes of Edwards and Marsh

Jonathan Edwards (1703–1758) was born during the Age of the Enlightenment, while skepticism about the Bible was challenging and eroding the theological presuppositions long held by interpreters. When Edwards interpreted the Old Testament, he believed types pervaded the biblical accounts. Types were not limited to what the New Testament identified.[24] Rather, the Old Testament "was, as it were, a typical world."[25] It is "rational to suppose that Scripture abounds with types."[26] For instance, he affirmed Melchizedek as a type of Christ, and he saw the Pool of Siloam as a type of Christ's grace and mercy.[27] Still, Edwards did not want the identification and interpretation of types to "give way to a wild fancy."[28]

Herbert Marsh (1757–1839) affirmed types in the Old Testament, but he did not have as open a typological grid as Edwards did. Marsh wanted a more restrictive approach to types in the Old Testament. He argued that a type is valid only when it is identified by Jesus or his apostles in the New Testament.[29] He was probably the ablest defender of a much more constrictive view of biblical types.[30] He expressed his doubts about asserting unidentified types: "But if we assert that a person or thing was designed to prefigure another person or things, where no such prefiguration has been declared by divine authority, we make an assertion for which we neither have, nor can have, the slightest foundation."[31]

---

23. Ninow, *Typology within the Old Testament*, 34.
24. Jonathan Edwards, "Types," in *The Works of Jonathan Edwards* (New Haven, CT: Yale University Press, 1957–2008), 11:146–47.
25. Edwards, "Types," 11:146.
26. Edwards, "Types," 11:151.
27. Edwards, "Types," 11:146–48.
28. Edwards, "Types," 11:148.
29. Herbert Marsh, *Lectures on the Criticism and Interpretation of the Bible* (Cambridge, UK: C&J Rivington, 1828), 373.
30. Richard M. Davidson, *Typology in Scripture: A Study of Hermeneutical TUPOS Structures* (Berrien Springs, MI: Andrews University Press, 1981), 36.
31. Marsh, *Criticism and Interpretation of the Bible*, 373.

Biblical Studies and the Term "Typology"

Johann David Michaelis (1717–1791) believed that the Old Testament "was to be read as the literary remains of an important ancient civilization"[32] and to be studied for the sake of its aesthetic power, its political insights, and as a resource for moral philosophy and the study of language.[33] Viewed in this way, the Bible no longer provided "an overarching, unified narrative, typologically integrated and centered on Christ and interpreting all of human existence."[34] Michaelis helped lay the foundation for the discipline of biblical studies that flourished in Europe after his time. Iain Provan explains, "The birth of this discipline with its newly conceived Bible, we now understand, was a direct consequence of the death of Scripture as conceived by Christians for seventeen hundred years beforehand—and indeed, it was part of a concerted ongoing effort to make sure that Scripture stayed in its grave and did not climb back out again."[35]

While the word "type" was used in years prior to the Enlightenment, the term "typology" did not appear until the mid-1750s.[36] The person who coined "typology" was J. S. Semler (1721–1791).[37] There is an irony with Semler and typology, for this man who coined the term was no advocate for the practice! Instead, he was "one of the leading forces in discrediting the validity of typological interpretation."[38] Semler said, "He who assumes no types . . . is deprived of nothing whatever; and even he who is most fond of typology cannot, for all that, place it among the fundamentals of Christianity."[39]

Summary

The Age of the Enlightenment brought major changes to the practice of typological interpretation. The elevation of human reason led to the diminishment of the church's theological assumptions about the Bible. With many interpreters no longer approaching Scripture as an inspired and united story whose redemptive message is Jesus the Christ, typology was viewed as an outdated reading strategy. The old theological assumptions of the Great Tradition had no validity in modernity. These major interpretive developments did not mean every Bible reader and preacher shunned typology. There were Puritans

---

32. Provan, *Reformation and the Right Reading of Scripture*, 398.
33. Michael C. Legaspi, *The Death of Scripture and the Rise of Biblical Studies* (New York: Oxford University Press, 2010), 31.
34. Provan, *Reformation and the Right Reading of Scripture*, 399.
35. Provan, *Reformation and the Right Reading of Scripture*, 399–400.
36. Ninow, *Typology within the Old Testament*, 23.
37. Ninow, *Typology within the Old Testament*, 29n56.
38. Davidson, *Typology in Scripture*, 37–38
39. This quote, along with the first appearance of the term "Typologie," comes from Semler's notes in A. H. Sykes, *Paraphrasis des Briefes an die Hebräer*, trans. Johann S. Semler (Halle, n.p., 1779), 86n96.

in the seventeenth century and theologians like Jonathan Edwards in the eighteenth century who were committed to Scripture as God's inspired Word and who interpreted the Old Testament typologically, rooted in the Great Tradition and not blown into skepticism and naturalism by the prevailing winds of enlightenment.

REFLECTION QUESTIONS

1. How did the Puritans view typological interpretation?

2. How did the elevation of human reason affect the practice of typology?

3. In what ways did Jonathan Edwards read the Bible differently from prevailing naturalistic presuppositions?

4. How did Herbert Marsh recognize types in the Old Testament?

5. When did the term "typology" first appear?

How Was Typology Practiced in the Late Modern Era?

During the period of the Enlightenment, the use of typology experienced major shifts as the elevation of human reason eroded the presuppositions that interpreters held throughout the eras of the early church, Middle Ages, and early modern era. This trend in the academy was not reversed in the late modern era (1800–1900). Basically, the assumptions behind the historical-critical method in the Enlightenment were being driven to their logical conclusions in the nineteenth century.[1] The rising confidence in science continued during these decades and solidified the disintegration of the Bible's unity and story. How could there be room for typology in an environment cramped with such enlightened minds?

Typology and the New Criticism

With the Bible's unity being a notion akin to a primitive way of life deserving pity and then a hard pass, the deconstruction of biblical texts became the venture to pursue. Instead of devoting scholarly energies to the canonical presentation of Genesis through Revelation, what mattered was the stages of a text's composition, what lay *behind* the text. Additionally, various forms of criticism arose that did not assume divine authorship or christological dimensions of biblical texts.

Richard Davidson accurately presents the lay of the land with regard to typology in the late modern era:

> Those passages in the NT which had previously been regarded as indicating a typological correspondence were explained by critical scholars as a first-century cultural accommodation

---

1. Keith D. Stanglin, *The Letter and Spirit of Biblical Interpretation: From the Early Church to Modern Practice* (Grand Rapids: Baker Academic, 2018), 174.

which no longer had validity in the modern worldview. From the rise of the Age of Enlightenment through the nineteenth century, traditional views of biblical typology were largely disregarded within critical scholarship.[2]

As the application of the historical-critical method detracted from the overall message of the Bible for the people of God, that message became harder to hear. According to Carter, "historical criticism, like liberal theology in general, has done much to weaken the conviction of the church that the Bible is a unified book, uniquely inspired and authoritative, with a crucially important message for all of humanity that one can understand by reading it and listening to sermons that explain it."[3]

In his book that explores the interpretation of Isaiah in church history, Childs notes some interpreters in particular whose works were marked by historical criticism: Wilhelm Gesenius (1786–1842) and Ferdinand Hitzig (1807–1875). The scholarship of Gesenius had a "heavy dose of Enlightenment rationalism," and Hitzig was "extremely hostile to traditional Christian interpretation, which he regarded as an enemy to genuine exegesis."[4]

Julius Wellhausen (1844–1918) was a German scholar who offered the Documentary Hypothesis, a theory about the composition of the Pentateuch. Wellhausen rejected the authorship of Moses and proposed various sources behind the Pentateuch: the Yahwist, Elohist, Deuteronomic, and Priestly sources. This theory in higher-critical studies encouraged further speculation through scholarly imagination. "It was now the exegete's job, qua historian, to peel away not only the interpretive traditions of later Christian theology but also the layers resident in the Bible itself, to jettison anything that seems historically unlikely."[5] And, of course, since typological exegesis depends inextricably on the historicity of the Bible's characters and events, an implication of deconstructed texts is the demolition of typology.

Looking for Jesus
The tentacles of skepticism and historical-critical methodology stretched across both testaments. Getting "behind the text" to what really happened meant taking apart the Four Gospels. With a bias toward the supernatural now disallowed, interpreters had to realize that Jesus did not say all that the Gospels report him saying, nor did he do all the things the Gospels report

---

2. Richard M. Davidson, *Typology in Scripture: A Study of Hermeneutical TUPOS Structures* (Berrien Springs, MI: Andrews University Press, 1981), 38.
3. Craig A. Carter, *Interpreting Scripture with the Great Tradition: Recovering the Genius of Premodern Exegesis* (Grand Rapids: Baker Academic, 2018), 23.
4. Brevard S. Childs, *The Struggle to Understand Isaiah as Christian Scripture* (Grand Rapids: Eerdmans, 2004), 265–66.
5. Stanglin, *Letter and Spirit of Biblical Interpretation*, 174.

him doing. The real Jesus, the historical Jesus, was to be found somewhere in the Gospels, and it was time to mount up quests to find him.

People like David Strauss (1808–1874) rejected theism, the doctrine that God created the world, the possibility of miracles, the divinity of Christ, and Christianity in general.[6] The rejection of these theological convictions in approaching the Bible made typology an impossibility. The effect of literary criticism contributed to the "breaking down of the old conception of the unity of Scripture and the consequent discrediting of the typological and prophetical exegesis familiar to so many generations of Christians."[7] In 1835, Strauss published a book called *Life of Jesus*, questioning the historicity of the Four Gospels. He explained with "myth" language why certain seemingly supernatural things were associated with the ministry of Jesus, and he also put forward ways to distinguish historical facts in the Gospels from legendary elements.

Treatment of the Four Gospels with historical-critical filters brought about a dichotomy between the "Jesus of history" and the "Christ of faith." The former figure could be affirmed, and the latter figure could not. Many scholars became captivated by the quest for the historical Jesus, taking up Strauss's trajectories in subsequent studies.[8] Speculation continued about what really happened in the ministry of Jesus. Since typological interpretation is rooted in the providence of God and divine authorship of a united biblical story, such interpretation wavers and collapses in the quest for the real Jesus.

Some Who Stood Firm

If the popular academic position was to be skeptical of Scripture and reject the theological assumptions of the Great Tradition, then not everyone did what was popular. E. W. Hengstenberg (1802–1869) set forth a conservative response to "the critical biblical scholarship of the end of the eighteenth century and especially the beginning of the nineteenth," and his positions were clear in his book *Christology of the Old Testament*, in which he devoted a chapter to the christological sections of Isaiah.[9] Hengstenberg's influence spread to Great Britain and to the United States.

In the mid-1850s, some scholars "sought to place the typological method upon a sound footing. They attempted to avoid either extreme of the Cocceian or Marshian positions by the identification and application of basic principles of typological hermeneutics gleaned from the biblical use of types."[10] For example, Patrick Fairbairn (1805–1874), who overlapped almost exactly with

---

6. Carter, *Interpreting Scripture with the Great Tradition*, 117.
7. G. W. H. Lampe, "The Reasonableness of Typology," in *Essays on Typology*, Studies in Biblical Theology 22 (Naperville, IL: A. R. Allenson, 1957), 17.
8. Stanglin, *Letter and Spirit of Biblical Interpretation*, 177.
9. Childs, *Isaiah as Christian Scripture*, 266. See E. W. Hengstenberg, *Christology of the Old Testament*, 4 vols. (Edinburgh: T&T Clark, 1854).
10. Davidson, *Typology in Scripture*, 38.

David Strauss, published a work that became the classic nineteenth-century treatment on typology. In 1857 his *Typology of Scripture* was released, and it went through multiple revisions and reprintings. He criticized not only the loose typological approach of Cocceius but also the constrictive typological approach of Marsh, "as if there were no way for Scripture to furnish a sufficient direction on the subject, except by specifying every particular case."[11]

These nineteenth-century scholars who affirmed the reality of typology in Scripture did so because they affirmed the divine authorship, inspiration, and unity of the Old and New Testaments. These interpreters certainly stood out from their higher-critical contemporaries in the late modern era, but they were in blessed historical continuity with the cloud of witnesses from the early church onward.

Summary

Much scholarship in the nineteenth-century solidified the skeptical trajectories stemming from the Enlightenment. While not every interpreter rejected the theological convictions held heretofore by faithful readers of the Bible, the practice of the historical-critical method undermined the reality and helpfulness of typology for understanding the biblical text. The spiritual sense had no place in such a method. Traditional affirmations of the spiritual sense were part of ancient biases that needed to be immediately set aside for the sake of what lay behind the passages. "Skepticism became the default attitude toward the biblical text."[12] This situation explains why "within historical-critical scholarship the contemporary relevance and validity of biblical typology has largely been repudiated."[13]

REFLECTION QUESTIONS

1. How did the Enlightenment affect views on typology in the late modern era?

2. How does historical-criticism and deconstruction impact typological interpretation?

3. How did the German scholars Gesenius and Hitzig view the Enlightenment?

4. What does the dichotomy between "Jesus of Christ" and "Christ of faith" mean?

5. Why was Patrick Fairbairn significant to the subject of typology?

---

11. Patrick Fairbairn, *The Typology of Scripture: Viewed in Connection with the Whole Series of the Divine Dispensations*, 2 vols., 6th ed. (Edinburgh: T&T Clark, 1876), 1:43.
12. Stanglin, *Letter and Spirit of Biblical Interpretation*, 183.
13. Davidson, *Typology in Scripture*, 45.

How Was Typology Practiced in the Postmodern Era?

In our final chapter on the historical survey of typology, we arrive at the postmodern era (1900–present day). Due to the prevalence in the academy of antisupernatural presuppositions and the historical-critical method, typology had been largely ignored as a legitimate exegetical method. In the 1900s, this academic posture was taken up by more scholars, but a renewal of interest in typology occurred as well.

Some Higher-Critical Voices

Rudolf Bultmann (1884–1976) rejected the authority and value of the Old Testament, and with that rejection, typology is voided automatically. He was the heir of skepticism passed along by theologians like J. S. Semler and Julius Wellhausen. "Being especially influenced by the literary-critical school of Wellhausen, he declared that the Old Testament is of no more value to the Christian than a pagan document."[1]

Friedrich Baumgärtel (1888–1981) spoke clearly about the notion of incorporating typological interpretation into the current historical-critical milieu: "To desire to build theological bridges . . . by renewing typological and christological ways of understanding . . . means basically to exclude modern historical-critical thinking from the process of understanding."[2]

---

1. Friedbert Ninow, *Indicators of Typology within the Old Testament: The Exodus Motif* (Frankfurt: Peter Lang, 2001), 34. See R. Bultmann, "The Significance of the Old Testament for the Christian Faith," in *The Old Testament and the Christian Faith: A Theological Discussion*, ed. B. W. Anderson (New York: Herder & Herder, 1969), 31–32.
2. F. Baumgärtel, "The Hermeneutical Problem of the Old Testament," trans. M. Newman, in *Essays on Old Testament Hermeneutics*, eds. C. Westermann and. J. L. Mays (Richmond, VA: John Knox, 1963), 157.

Typology and the 1940s

Though surrounded by higher-critical forces seeking to extinguish its influence, typological interpretation did not die. A German scholar named Gerhard von Rad (1901–1971) thought typology was a legitimate way of relating the Old and New Testaments. He offered eight characteristics of typological interpretation.[3] But von Rad did not describe typology as possessing a prospective sense; rather, he saw it as purely retrospective, allowing interpreters to see prefigurations of the Christ event in hindsight. In identifying types, interpreters see that "the same God who revealed himself in Christ has also left his footprints in the history of the Old Testament covenant people."[4] Ninow explains that "von Rad's approach made biblical theology acceptable within historical-critical scholarship. He demonstrated how one could appropriate the phenomenon of biblical typology without giving up the foundational presuppositions that govern the critical approach."[5]

Leonhard Goppelt (1911–1973) released the first comprehensive survey of New Testament typology from a modern historical perspective. He concluded that "typology is the method of interpreting Scripture that is predominant in the New Testament and characteristic of it."[6] Goppelt published the book (his dissertation) *TYPOS: The Typological Interpretation of the Old Testament in the New* in 1939. This book has become a classic work on typology, which subsequent scholars must engage when they write in the areas of biblical studies and typology.

The following decade, in the 1940s, multiple studies were undertaken dealing with biblical theology. In Britain, William J. T. P. Phythian-Adams and Arthur G. Hebert attempted to explain the ways God worked in the Old and New Testament eras. Austin M. Farrer sought to establish a philosophical basis for the typological method and explored a possible typological schema in Revelation. In the United States, Charles T. Fritsch delivered a series of lectures on biblical typology at Dallas Theological Seminary. And Samuel Amsler wrote a dissertation examining the use of typology in the Pauline corpus. Speaking of these works in the decade of the 1940s, Davidson says, "These studies represent various attempts to embrace both biblical typology and the results of historical criticism. Aside from these works and a few cursory treatments on the subject, by the end of the 1940s, typology was still largely ignored within critical biblical scholarship."[7]

---

3. Gerhard von Rad, "Typological Interpretation of the Old Testament," in *Essays on Old Testament Hermeneutics*, ed. Claus Westermann (Richmond, VA: John Knox, 1963), 36–39.
4. Von Rad, "Typological Interpretation of the Old Testament," 36.
5. Ninow, *Typology within the Old Testament*, 39.
6. Leonhard Goppelt, *TYPOS: The Typological Interpretation of the Old Testament in the New* (Grand Rapids: Eerdmans, 1982), 198.
7. Richard M. Davidson, *Typology in Scripture: A Study of Hermeneutical TUPOS Structures* (Berrien Springs, MI: Andrews University Press, 1981), 56–59.

Typology Revived

In the decades since 1940, renewed interest in biblical typology "bloomed."[8] Authors advocating a hermeneutically controlled typology (like that of Fairbairn) included Geerhardus Vos, Louis Berkhof, and J. Barton Payne.[9] Vos (1862–1949) wrote a theology of the Old and New Testaments that was published in 1948 as *Biblical Theology*. He emphasized the importance of identifying what a type symbolized before an interpreter proceeds to identifying the antitype:

> A type can never be a type independently of its being first a symbol. The gateway to the house of typology is at the farther end of the house of symbolism. This is the fundamental rule to be observed in ascertaining what elements in the Old Testament are typical, and wherein the things corresponding to them as antitypes consist. Only after having discovered what a thing symbolizes, can we legitimately proceed to put the question what it typifies, for the latter can never be aught else than the former lifted to a higher plane. The bond that holds type and antitype together must be a bond of vital continuity in the progress of redemption. Where this is ignored, and in the place of this bond are put accidental resemblances, void of inherent spiritual significance, all sorts of absurdities will result, such as must bring the whole subject of typology into disrepute.[10]

An important preacher and writer on the subject of Christ in the Old Testament was Edmund Clowney (1917–2005). Clowney was an evangelical scholar who wrote, taught, and preached with a commitment to typology. For Clowney, the redemptive history of the Old Testament carried along a rich paradigm of figures with the focus on God's dwelling among humankind, and all these figures lead to the New Testament revelation in which God in Christ dwelled among humans.[11] In his book *The Unfolding Mystery*, he says the Old Testament is filled with signs that point to Christ. He illustrates the gospel with the story of Abraham's near-sacrifice of Isaac. "God did what Abraham did not have to do: He made His Son an offering for sin. . . . Without the typology of Abraham's sacrifice, we could not understand the depth of meaning in the New Testament teaching about God's love in giving His Beloved."[12] In

---

8. Ninow, *Typology within the Old Testament*, 16–17.
9. Davidson, *Typology in Scripture*, 48.
10. Geerhardus Vos, *Biblical Theology* (Carlisle, PA: Banner of Truth, 1948), 145–46.
11. Ninow, *Typology within the Old Testament*, 68–69.
12. Edmund P. Clowney, *The Unfolding Mystery: Discovering Christ in the Old Testament* (Phillipsburg, NJ: P&R, 1988), 59.

Preaching Christ in All of Scripture, Clowney says a biblical type must find its realization, its antitype, in what is "climactic, eschatological, Christocentric."[13] And Clowney doesn't limit types to the ones that the New Testament identifies, for "that is a little like saying that you can find solutions to math problems only by looking in the back of the book, since you haven't a clue as to how to work the problems."[14]

In his book *Jesus and the Old Testament*, R. T. France (1938–2012) distinguished between typology and exegesis,[15] though he believed the latter was required for the former. France recognized correspondences and escalation between type and antitype. As the New Testament writers interpreted the Old, they believed that God worked "in a consistent manner, and that in the coming of Christ his Old Testament acts are repeated and consummated. This is New Testament typology."[16]

A more comprehensive approach to typology that was written in the 1900s was the dissertation of David Baker, published in 1975, called *Two Testaments, One Bible: A Study of Some Modern Solutions to the Theological Problem of the Relationship between the Old and New Testaments*. He concluded that the use of *tupos* in the Septuagint and New Testament has the general meaning of "example or "pattern," and he stated two principles underlying typology: first, types are historical, and second, real correspondences exist between type and antitype.[17] But "typology is not an exegesis or interpretation of a text, but the study of relationships between events, persons and institutions recorded in biblical texts."[18] Baker denied that typology had any designed prefigurement with a christological *telos*.

E. Earle Ellis (1926–2010) studied and wrote about the ways the New Testament authors used the Old Testament. Like Goppelt before him, Ellis believed that typology was the primary way the New Testament authors used earlier Scripture. Typology was "thoroughly christological in its focus."[19] Ellis refers to "typological exegesis" and says it is "grounded firmly in the historical significance of the 'types.'"[20] It is insufficient, Ellis contends, to characterize typology with correspondences while jettisoning divine intent. "For the NT writers a type has not merely the property of 'typicalness' or

13. Edmund P. Clowney, *Preaching Christ in All of Scripture* (Wheaton, IL: Crossway, 2003), 31.
14. Clowney, *Preaching Christ in All of Scripture*, 31.
15. R. T. France, *Jesus and the Old Testament* (London: Tyndale, 1971; Vancouver: Regent College Publishing, 1998), 41.
16. France, *Jesus and the Old Testament*, 43.
17. David L. Baker, *Two Testaments, One Bible: A Study of Some Modern Solutions to the Theological Problem of the Relationship between the Old and New Testaments*, rev. ed. (Downers Grove, IL: InterVaristy, 1991), 41, 195.
18. Baker, *Two Testaments, One Bible*, 190.
19. E. Earle Ellis, *Prophecy and Hermeneutic in Early Christianity* (Grand Rapids: Baker, 1993), 166.
20. E. Earle Ellis, *Paul's Use of the Old Testament* (Grand Rapids: Baker, 1981), 127.

similarity; they view Israel's history as *Heilsgeschichte* [salvation history], and the significance of an OT type lies in its particular *locus* in the Divine plan of redemption."[21]

In 1981, Richard Davidson (born 1946) published his dissertation *Typology in Scripture: A Study of Hermeneutical TUPOS Structures*. In this comprehensive book, Davidson surveys the previous literature on typology, explores the use of *tupos* in biblical and nonbiblical literature, and builds an inductive argument for the use of typology in the two testaments. Davidson concludes that biblical types are salvation-historical realities that God designed to correspond to, and prospectively predict, their escalated antitypes.[22]

A major force in the realm of biblical theology is G. K. Beale (born 1949). In his *Handbook on the New Testament Use of the Old Testament*, Beale says that the essential characteristics of a type are analogical correspondence, historicity, pointing-forwardness, escalation, and retrospection.[23] Crucial to Beale's position on typology is his emphasis on the prospective nature of Old Testament types. There is a divine intent that Old Testament types look forward, so types have a prophetic sense, though in an indirect way.[24]

Kevin Vanhoozer (born 1957) affirms and practices typological interpretation. He says that typological discourse doesn't add a second, spiritual sense to the biblical text but, rather, *extends* the literal sense.[25] He explains:

> Typological exegesis therefore discovers the plain sense of the author, yet it also discovers that the human authors tell more than they can know, for they are not always cognizant of the ultimate referent of their discourse. It is only when we read the plain sense of the human author in canonical context that we discern the divinely intended "plain canonical sense," together with its "plain canonical referent": Jesus Christ.[26]

A prolific writer on biblical theology and typology is James M. Hamilton Jr. (born 1974), to whom this book is dedicated. In *What Is Biblical Theology?* he says, "Types are not arbitrary correspondences invented by the biblical authors but genuine accounts of what really took place. The biblical authors are

21. Ellis, *Paul's Use of the Old Testament*, 127.
22. Davidson, *Typology in Scripture*, 421.
23. G. K. Beale, *Handbook on the New Testament Use of the Old Testament: Exegesis and Interpretation* (Grand Rapids, Baker Academic, 2012), 14.
24. Beale, *New Testament Use of the Old Testament*, 17.
25. Kevin J. Vanhoozer, "Ascending the Mountain, Singing the Rock: Biblical Interpretation Earthed, Typed, and Transfigured," in *Heaven on Earth? Theological Interpretation in Ecumenical Dialogue*, eds. Hans Boersma and Matthew Levering (Hoboken, NJ: Wiley-Blackwell, 2013), 218.
26. Vanhoozer, "Ascending the Mountain," 218.

drawing attention to people, events, and institutions where the divine author has caused actual resemblance."[27]

Summary

The twentieth and twenty-first centuries witnessed a renewal of interest in typology. But this renewal was not exactly a full-blown return to the theological assumptions present from the early church through the early modern era. For example, some scholars have sought to advocate typology while remaining within the historical-critical method themselves, but this position cannot sustain the prospective nature of biblical types. Antisupernatural trajectories within the historical-critical method must be denied in order to affirm the unity and divine design of the biblical canon. In the last half of the twentieth century, there were theologians publishing conclusions about typology that were more in line with premodern convictions, and that blessed trend has continued into the first part of the twenty-first century as well. S. Lewis Johnson is right: "We must not succumb to the biting ridicule of those who denigrate typology. We may then be guilty of ignoring what God has stressed. One of the happier results of twentieth-century scholarship has been the rediscovery of the importance of typology for the understanding of the Bible."[28]

REFLECTION QUESTIONS

1. How did Rudolf Bultmann view the value of the Old Testament for the Christian?

2. How did Gerhard von Rad understand typology?

3. Why was the decade of the 1940s important for the subject of typology?

4. What role did Edmund Clowney play in the revival of typology?

5. How did Leonhard Goppelt and E. Earle Ellis view typology?

---

27. James M. Hamilton Jr., *What Is Biblical Theology? A Guide to the Bible's Story, Symbolism, and Patterns* (Wheaton, IL: Crossway, 2014), 78. See also James M. Hamilton Jr., *God's Glory in Salvation through Judgment: A Biblical Theology* (Wheaton, IL: Crossway, 2010).
28. S. L. Johnson, "A Response to Patrick Fairbairn and Biblical Hermeneutics as Related to the Quotations of the Old Testament in the New," in *Hermeneutics, Inerrancy, and the Bible*, eds. E. D. Radmacher and R. D. Preus (Grand Rapids: Zondervan, 1984), 794–95.

Identifying Types

How Do We Identify Types?

In keeping with what Jesus taught, what the apostles wrote, and what the history of interpretation affirms, the Old Testament is about Jesus Christ. If the Old Testament before Christ was like a dimly lit room full of shadows and figures, we can now read those books with all the lights on because of his resurrection. Christ is the key to the lock, the substance of the mystery, the crescendo of the story. How shall we identify Old Testament types?

New Testament Identification

The first—and surest—way to recognize an Old Testament type is if a New Testament author does so in his writing(s). While the New Testament authors do not identify every possible Old Testament type, their writings are a helpful starting point. When they specify a type, we have their inspired interpretation of the Old Testament, and their words are authoritative and trustworthy. They do not misunderstand or distort the Old Testament, they do not dismiss original contexts, and they do not make untraceable hermeneutical moves.

If the New Testament writers recognize Jonah (Matt. 12:40–41), Solomon (Matt. 12:42), and Adam (Rom. 5:14) as types of Christ, then we have multiple persons whom God designed to point forward to his Son. If the New Testament writers recognize the manna (John 6:51), the rock (1 Cor. 10:4), and the lamb (John 1:29) as types of Christ, then we have multiple things that God designed to point forward to his Son. If the New Testament writers recognize priests (Heb. 7:26), kings (Matt. 1:1), and prophets (Acts 3:22) as types of Christ, then we have multiple offices that God designed to point forward to his Son. Based on these instances and others, interpreters can discern how the New Testament authors read the Old Testament typologically. In Question 3 we established the following definition of a type: *a biblical type is a person, office, place, institution, event, or thing in salvation history that anticipates, shares correspondences with, escalates toward, and resolves in its antitype.*

Parallels to Identified Types

Sound typological exegesis should not and must not be arbitrary. One way readers can see unidentified Old Testament types is by discerning parallels with identified types.[1] A few examples will illustrate this notion. If the Bible recognizes Adam as a type of Christ (Rom. 5:14), and if we notice that Noah has correspondences to Adam (Gen. 9:1), then we can see Noah as a type of Christ. "Nowhere in the NT, however, does it say that Noah is a type of Christ. Nevertheless, if Noah is a partial antitype of the first Adam but does not fulfill all to which the typological first Adam points, then Noah also can plausibly be considered a part of the Adamic type of Christ in the OT."[2] A similar argument can be made about Joshua. "Since the original reader/observer would have been justified in interpreting Joshua as a second Moses figure (cf. Deut. 31; Josh. 1; 3:7), and since Jesus may also be viewed as a second Moses, it is possible to correlate the significance of Joshua's acts of salvation and conquest of the promised land to the work of Christ."[3] If the Bible recognizes David as a type of Christ, and then we see that Boaz has correspondences to David, we can see Boaz as a type of Christ.[4]

Even though we might note parallels between an identified type and an unidentified type, the need for correspondences and escalation to Christ is nonnegotiable. If an interpreter can make a case for correspondences and escalation between someone/something in the Old Testament and Christ, then we are dealing with a plausible christological type. In other words, there needs to be a redemptive or covenantal significance to the type. If such significance exists, along with correspondences and escalation to Christ, then the interpreter has discerned a type.

Symptoms and Diagnosis

Think of the preceding typological components—correspondences, escalation, and a redemptive or covenantal significance—as symptoms of a type, just like there are symptoms of a sickness. To borrow a negative analogy for the sake of a positive point, the presence of certain symptoms increases the likelihood of a certain diagnosis. As interpreters, when we diagnose a type, we do so because of the presence of certain symptoms. And for those who study diseases and symptoms, a diagnosis is hardly guesswork or a shot in the dark.

To carry the sickness metaphor a bit further, let's imagine two patients: one who has been diagnosed with certainty and one who hasn't. Patient A can

---

1. See G. K. Beale, *Handbook on the New Testament Use of the Old Testament: Exegesis and Interpretation* (Grand Rapids: Baker Academic, 2012), 21.
2. Beale, *New Testament Use of the Old Testament*, 21.
3. G. P. Hugenberger, "Introductory Notes on Typology," in *Right Doctrine from the Wrong Texts?*, ed. G. K. Beale (Grand Rapids: Baker, 1994), 341.
4. See Mitchell L. Chase, "A True and Greater Boaz: Typology and Jesus in the Book of Ruth," *Southern Baptist Journal of Theology* 21, no. 1 (Spring 2017): 85–96.

become something of a model, or a template, for others. So if Patient B starts showing the same symptoms that Patient A had, we would not be surprised by an identical diagnosis. Typological exegesis is an act of diagnosing types through a deliberate (not arbitrary) and careful (not reckless) evaluation of correspondences, escalation, and redemptive or covenantal significance.

Prayerful and Patient Whole-Bible Reading

The New Testament authors had a deep familiarity with the Old Testament, and this shows up in how their writings use it through quotations, allusions, and echoes. We need to grow in our familiarity with Holy Scripture, and this will increase our sensitivity to Old Testament correspondences and parallels. Typological exegesis requires whole-Bible reading. "All of Scripture *already* is written with a plotline that flows from Eden through Israel's hills and valleys until it terminates and overflows in the person and work of Jesus Christ," and this acknowledgment helps us to "hear what the Spirit originally intended as we pay careful attention to the contours of the biblical plotline."[5]

If we overcompartmentalize the books of the Bible, then that frayed and fractured unity will obscure (at least partially) the patterns and inner-biblical connections across the testaments. Since the two testaments are united in their theological history and message, interpreters should be compelled to read and reread passages, even large swaths of text, in order to see the fullness of the Bible's beauty more clearly. Faithful interpretation of the Old Testament, and specifically typological exegesis, requires time and focus, so our minds need to be patient. Delight in the slow work of pondering passages. There is no secret formula that guarantees a certain outcome if you plug in the right factors. Baptize your Bible reading in prayer. Cry out for God's help, and I don't mean sparsely or mechanically. Immerse your interpretation of Scripture in prayer. God is faithful to help our minds think and our eyes see!

Seeing with the Saints

Faithful interpretation is aided by dialogue and engagement with a faithful confessing community. If we read the Bible and talk with others about what we see, we will be in a better position for our faithful interpretations to be affirmed as well as our skewed readings to be corrected. Interpreting the Bible should not be merely a solo endeavor. While we are not inspired by the Spirit like the biblical authors, we are indwelt by the Spirit and knit together in a body of Christ that needs our engagement, thoughtfulness, and care. And part of our careful, thoughtful engagement should involve thinking out loud about the Bible. We need to see Scripture with present-day saints.

---

5. David Schrock, "From Beelines to Plotlines: Typology That Follows the Covenantal Typography of Scripture," *Southern Baptist Journal of Theology* 21, no. 1 (Spring 2017): 48–49.

Along with engaging our fellow believers, we also need to dialogue with the saints of old. As we seek to read the Bible—and, in particular, the Old Testament—faithfully and christologically, we should do so with a growing awareness of how the Bible was read before us. Our interpretations will benefit from a historical perspective, and there is a two-thousand-year history of interpretation behind us. By growing in familiarity with ancient interpreters, we can be kept from errors such as thinking that christological readings of the Old Testament are spiritually dangerous, historically rare, and contextually dishonest. Ever since the early church, the Great Tradition has embraced the Bible as God's inspired Word that testifies of Christ, first preparing his way and then declaring his arrival. And this Great Tradition has seen typology as a valid way of relating the Testaments to each other.

Summary

If we will labor over Scripture with prayer and patience, and if our posture toward Scripture is characterized by faithful convictions about its divine authorship and unity, we will sense the importance of reading the Old Testament with christological lenses.[6] As we study the hermeneutical moves of the New Testament authors, we can more faithfully interpret the Old Testament as we imitate them. We will see how identified types can help us recognize unidentified types. And knowing we are not inspired interpreters, we need to be convinced of how crucial current and past voices are, for these voices can spur us on to faithful interpretation. We do not need to fear typological exegesis, because we are surrounded by this cloud of witnesses who can help guard and guide our readings of the sacred text.

REFLECTION QUESTIONS

1. What is the surest way of noting a biblical type?

2. What is the value of seeing parallels between unidentified and identified types?

3. How does reading and rereading the Bible relate to typological interpretation?

4. What personal relationships do you have that include, among other things, dialogue and engagement on interpreting the Bible?

5. How can you improve your own Bible reading with voices from church history?

---

6. See Matt Smethurst, *Before You Open Your Bible: Nine Heart Postures for Approaching God's Word* (Leyland, England: 10Publishing, 2018).

What Types Are in Genesis?

In the beginning, God created types. The first book of the Bible, Genesis, is the launching pad for the christological trajectory of Scripture. While the following sections are not an attempt to exhaust the types in Genesis, they will represent the kinds of shadows that anticipate the light of the Savior's person and work.

Genesis 1–3

The Heavens and the Earth

The Bible opens with creation and ends with new creation. This book-ended display of God's power frames the biblical story. In Genesis 1, God formed and filled the heavens and the earth. From nothing he made everything and declared it good. The word "beginning" (Gen. 1:1) eventually leads us to the end, when all things are made new. The heavens and the earth in Genesis 1 are a type of the new heavens and new earth. In John's final vision, he saw "a new heaven and a new earth, for the first heaven and the first earth had passed away" (Rev. 21:1). While the first creation was temporary, the new creation will be everlasting. While the first creation was tainted by sin, life in the new creation will have no tears, death, mourning, or pain (21:4). Isaiah conveyed God's promise: "For behold, I create new heavens and a new earth, and the former things shall not be remembered or come into mind" (Isa. 65:17). There is a clear escalation from the first to new creation, since the new heavens and earth are not merely a return to the way things were before the fall. The new heavens and new earth will don, as it were, a garment of immortality.

New creation is a christological hope (Rom. 8:18–21), confirming that the first creation is a christological type. Johnson explains: "Isaiah's interpretation of the original creation as a pattern—a type—of God's final work of salvation, the creation of a new heavens and a new, curse-free earth, would subsequently be elaborated by the Holy Spirit in the New Testament."[1] The work of redemption was accomplished at the cross, and this work of redemption will make its blessings flow far as the curse is found. The resurrection of believers will signal the renewal of the whole creation (Rom. 8:21–23). The resurrection of the saints will occur at the return of Christ, when the last enemy—death—is defeated (1 Cor. 15:23, 26). The Son of Man will gather the nations through bodily resurrection, and he will summon the saints to inherit the everlasting kingdom that was prepared "from the foundation of the world" (Matt. 25:34). When we read about the foundation of the world being laid in Genesis 1, the endgame of new creation was all part of the christological plan.

The Garden of Eden

God created sacred space in his good world, and Adam and Eve were to exercise dominion and be fruitful and multiply (Gen. 1:28; 2:8). This sacred space, the garden of Eden, was a type of the coming new Jerusalem. In the garden was the tree of life and a river (Gen. 2:9–10), and the new Jerusalem is characterized by a river and the tree of life (Rev. 22:1–2). The glory of Eden's paradise was real but only temporary. Through Adam and Eve's sin, the couple defiled God's sacred space and was exiled (Gen. 3:24). The garden of Eden would one day be surpassed by a sacred space that is cosmic in scope (Rev. 21–22). The story of God's people goes from a garden to a city, where the aim of the garden is fulfilled.[2]

The garden of Eden was a mini-temple, a microcosmic dwelling place.[3] Adam and Eve were to guard and keep the sacred space, subduing anything that might defile it (Gen. 1:26–28; 2:15). Their instructions from God confirmed the vulnerability of the garden. Yet in the final state of God's new world, nothing will bring corruption. There will be nothing accursed (Rev. 22:3), and nothing unclean will ever enter it (Rev. 21:27). All that dwell there will be characterized by everlasting life and glory. The new Jerusalem will be a new and better Eden.

Adam and Eve

The first union (Adam and Eve) points forward to the last union (Christ and his church). Adam was the head of humankind, and his actions affected all those in him. Christ was the head of the new humanity, and his actions affect all

---

1. See Dennis E. Johnson, *Walking with Jesus through His Word: Discovering Christ in All the Scriptures* (Phillipsburg, NJ: P&R, 2015), 67–68.
2. See Johnson, *Walking with Jesus*, 202–6.
3. See G. K. Beale, *The Temple and the Church's Mission*, New Studies in Biblical Theology, ed. D. A. Carson (Downers Grove, IL: InterVarsity, 2004); J. Daniel Hays, *The Temple and the Tabernacle: A Study of God's Dwelling Places from Genesis to Revelation* (Grand Rapids: Baker, 2016).

those in him. Paul calls Adam "a type of the one who was to come" (Rom. 5:14).[4] Jesus is "the last Adam" (1 Cor. 15:45). Whereas condemnation and death came through the first, justification and eternal life came through the last. Adam was tempted and failed, but Christ was tempted and prevailed. Adam was supposed to exercise dominion as an image-bearer, yet he compromised his responsibility and dishonored the Lord. As the image of the invisible God (Col. 1:15), Jesus exercised dominion over sickness and demons and death, and he is reigning at the right hand of God and exercising dominion over his enemies (1 Cor. 15:25–26; Heb. 1:3). Jesus is the true and better Adam.[5]

Eve is a type of the church, which is in Christ.[6] Eve is the first bride, and the church is the last bride. Paul "betrothed" the Corinthians "to one husband, to present you as a pure virgin to Christ" (2 Cor. 11:2). But the church, like Eve, faced the deceptive wiles of "the serpent" (2 Cor. 11:3). Though Adam did not faithfully protect Eve when he was there with her at the eating of the forbidden fruit (Gen. 3:6), Christ will faithfully protect and preserve the church, and nothing can separate the church from God's love in Christ (Rom. 8:31–39).

Marriage

Adam woke from a deep sleep, and there was Eve, whom he called "bone of my bones and flesh of my flesh" (Gen. 2:23). Their one-flesh union was the first marriage, and this marriage was a covenant formed in the presence of God between a man and a woman. The covenant of marriage was an institution foreshadowing Christ and the church. When Paul wrote about husbands and wives and referred to this one-flesh relationship, he said, "This mystery is profound, and I am saying that it refers to Christ and the church" (Eph. 5:32).[7]

The Old Testament nation of Israel was in covenant with God, and the prophets sometimes depicted this relationship in marital terms (see Exod. 24; Ezek. 16; Hos. 1). If Israel kept God's covenant, they were being a faithful wife; if they broke God's law, they were committing spiritual adultery. Such depictions show that marriage, even in the Old Testament, had a significance beyond itself. In fact, one way to capture the story of Scripture is that of a gracious God pursuing and redeeming a bride. Marriage bookends the Bible.

---

4. See David Schrock, "From Beelines to Plotlines: Typology That Follows the Covenantal Typography of Scripture," *Southern Baptist Journal of Theology* 21, no. 1 (Spring 2017): 38–39.

5. Joshua M. Philpot, "See the True and Better Adam: Typology and Human Origins," *Bulletin of Ecclesial Theology* 5, no. 2 (2018): 77–90.

6. See Edmund P. Clowney, *The Unfolding Mystery: Discovering Christ in the Old Testament* (Phillipsburg, NJ: P&R, 1988), 24.

7. See Nicholas P. Lunn, "'Raised on the Third Day according to the Scriptures': Resurrection Typology in the Genesis Creation Narrative," *Journal of the Evangelical Theological Society* 57, no. 3 (September 2014): 526.

God's people anticipate "the marriage supper of the Lamb" (Rev. 19:9), and the new creation is described as "coming down out of heaven from God, prepared as a bride adorned for her husband" (Rev. 21:2).

The Tree of Life

In the midst of the garden God planted, he placed a tree of life (Gen. 2:9). Of the other trees that God provided in the garden (Gen. 2:16), only this one had the designation "of life," and the reason for this designation is the effect upon the one who eats from it. We learn later that to eat of this tree is to live forever (Gen. 3:22). When the serpent tempts Eve to eat, he does not provoke her curiosity with the tree of life. Instead, she eats from the forbidden tree (Gen. 2:17; 3:2–6). And then the couple is cut off from the tree of everlasting life.

John's Gospel tells us that God loved the world in this way: he gave his only Son so that whoever believes in Jesus would not perish but have everlasting life (John 3:16). This hope and promise connect us to the life from which sin has separated us. Barred from the tree of life because of our unrighteousness, we once again have access to this life because of Christ's righteousness. When he died on the cross in our place and bore the wrath of God, the tree of judgment for him became the tree of life for us. The tree of life in the garden of Eden is a type of Christ's work on Calvary's hill.

Garments of Skins

God is a God who covers the sin of his people. When Adam and Eve rebelled against the Lord, they sewed fig leaves together for loincloths and then hid among the trees of the garden (Gen. 3:7–8). But God covered their shame with garments he provided. Adam and Eve's self-covering was inadequate. The Lord "made for Adam and for his wife garments of skins and clothed them" (Gen. 3:21). These skins would have been the skins of animals, and acquiring these skins meant the death of these animals.

Since something was sacrificed that covered Adam and Eve, these garments of skins were a type of the cross where Jesus died to cover his bride. In Christ, we are clothed with righteousness not our own (Phil. 3:9). The scene in Genesis 3 showed God's initiation: he is the one who made the clothing as well as the one who clothed them. Adam and Eve had rebelled against God, yet mercy came through judgment. When Israel later had a sacrificial system that pointed to Christ, they would also know stories like Genesis 3:21, where God acted to cover the shame of his people.

Exile from the Garden

Adam and Eve, now covered by garments of skin that the Lord provided, left the garden of Eden in exile (Gen. 3:24). While tragic, this exile was necessary, lest Adam "reach out his hand and take also of the tree of life and eat, and live forever" (Gen. 3:22). Redemption was needed. The exile they experienced would ensure their death, for they were cut off from the sanctuary of the garden. They left the place of blessing and stepped upon the ground under the curse of God.

The exile from Eden foreshadowed the judgment that Christ bore on our behalf. We too deserve exile and the curse, returning to the dust from which we came. We deserve to be banished from the fellowship of God's presence. The garden exile bore witness to the horror of the human condition. In Adam, all sinned (Rom. 5:12), and all were exiled in him too. Yet in Christ our exile would be reversed, and through his work upon the cross we would once more have access to the tree of life, that we might live forever in the presence of God as his redeemed people.

Genesis 4–11

Abel

Adam and Eve had Cain and Abel, and according to the writer of Hebrews, Abel walked by faith (Heb. 11:4; cf. Gen. 4:1–2). The birth of sons was significant for Eve, for God had said that a future son would be born who would overcome the serpent (Gen. 3:15). Would Abel be the promised seed of the woman?

We don't know how old Abel was when Cain killed him, but Abel's death was the first death of an image-bearer. And as an innocent man facing persecution from the hostile serpent's seed, Abel was a type of the ultimate righteous sufferer.[8] Abel and Jesus were both descendants of Eve, and Jesus faced the persecution of contemporaries as well. Jesus walked by faith and did so without sin. The blood of Abel was still the blood of a sinner, but the blood of Jesus was the blood of the Savior. Abel's blood cried out from the ground for justice (Gen. 4:10), but Jesus's blood spoke a better word (Heb. 12:24). Jesus mediated a new covenant, and his blood cried out for mercy as he drank the cup of justice for us. Hanging on the cross, Jesus prayed, "Father, forgive them, for they know not what they do" (Luke 23:34). Jesus was the seed of the woman long ago promised to Eve. He is the true and better Abel.

Seth

After Cain killed Abel, Adam and Eve had another son whom they named Seth. Eve said, "God has appointed for me another offspring instead of Abel, for Cain killed him" (Gen. 4:25). Seth was the new Abel, the new seed of the woman. During his days, "people began to call upon the name of the Lord" (Gen. 4:26), which may indicate the reality of Seth's faith and his influence.

---

8. Those who oppose God and his people are the seed of the serpent because such opposition corresponds to the hostile heart of the Evil One (Gen. 3:15; John 8:39–44).

Seth was a type of Christ because he was the new son of Eve. He, like Abel, anticipated the true seed of the woman who would not only call on the name of the Lord but would actually be the Lord himself, the Word made flesh.[9] Seth was also Adam's son and is called a "son in his own likeness, after his image" (Gen. 5:3). Schrock notes, "As the rest of Scripture confirms, Adam is the fountainhead for all personal types. Because his image and likeness is passed down from Adam to Seth (Gen 5:3), the train of redemptive history picks up steam as one generation of image-bearers bears another."[10] While Cain's murder of Abel seemed to throw the promised line into jeopardy, Seth's birth was the resurrection of that hope. And while the cross seemed to be the defeat of Jesus, hope was raised up with him from the dead.

Enoch

There was a man in Genesis who did not die. Enoch walked with God for more than three centuries until God took him (Gen. 5:22–24). While he lived on earth, he lived by faith (Heb. 11:5) and warned of God's coming judgment upon the ungodly (Jude 14–15). The taking of Enoch apart from death was an unprecedented act, for those generations before and after him continued to die. Death's jaws did not consume Enoch. He seemed to have defeated death!

Enoch was a type of Christ. The Lord Jesus walked by faith and lived obediently, without any transgression. He too proclaimed the coming of judgment upon the ungodly, and his time on earth ended in an unprecedented way as well. Though Jesus died on the cross, he was raised from the dead on the third day in a glorified body. Enoch may have been taken before death, but he did not enjoy a glorified physical body. Jesus was the firstfruits of all who would be raised in him (1 Cor. 15:20). Jesus also ascended to be with God, but his ascension was to reign at the right hand of God until he put all enemies under his feet (1 Cor. 15:25). Jesus, not Enoch, was the true victor over death.

Noah

After the flood had killed everything not in the ark, the world needed a new Adam, and that new Adam was Noah. Noah's father, Lamech, had been hopeful about his son's destiny, for the name "Noah" sounds like the Hebrew word for "rest." Lamech hoped his son would bring "rest" from the toilsome labor and cursed ground (Gen. 5:29). Lamech was looking for the seed of the woman (Gen. 3:15). While Noah would not be the Savior, he would be a type. Through Noah, God delivered a remnant for the sake of his name.

Noah was righteous among his wicked generation (Gen. 6:9). He walked with God, like Enoch. By faith and out of reverence for God, Noah built an ark and became an heir of the righteousness that comes by faith (Heb. 11:7).

---

9. See Clowney, *Unfolding Mystery*, 42.
10. Schrock, "From Beelines to Plotlines," 38.

His obedience secured deliverance for those in his family. After the flood waters receded, Noah would lead the new humanity. He was a new Adam who was told to be fruitful and multiply (Gen. 1:28; 9:7). Adding another layer of significance, the story of Noah is flavored with covenant language (Gen. 6:18; 9:9–17). Noah is a type of Christ, whose mission and work was connected to the new covenant and would inaugurate new creation. Noah was a new Adam who pointed to the last Adam.[11] The life of Christ was marked by faith and reverence. And the obedience of Christ secured deliverance for all who come to him to join his family.

The Ark and Flood

The ark survived the tumultuous flood upon the earth, and this was a type of merciful deliverance from God's righteous judgment. Jesus said that the return of the Son of Man would be sudden and unexpected, like those who were caught unaware by the deluge in the days of Noah (Matt. 24:38–39). Christ Jesus is our ark, a refuge for sinners and the only stay from God's wrath. The deluge around Noah pointed to "the day of judgment and destruction of the ungodly" (2 Peter 3:7). Earthly judgments anticipate the final judgment.

Peter links baptism to the events in Noah's story (1 Peter 3:20–22). Just as the ark preserved those who were inside safely through the water, union with Christ preserves sinners safely through the day of judgment. This union is pictured by baptism, for Christ died and was buried and was raised, and in union with him we identify with his death, burial, and resurrection (Rom. 6:3–5). Our baptism is an image of going under the waters of judgment with Christ and then emerging vindicated.

Genesis 12–25

Abraham

God called Abraham to leave his kin and country and travel to a new land (Gen. 12:1). By faith, Abraham obeyed and made his journey to the land of promise (Heb. 11:8–9). God promised him many descendants and an inheritance, and God couched these promises in a covenant (Gen. 12:2–3; 15:5, 8). Through Abraham's family, God would bless all families of the earth (Gen. 12:3). Since through Adam came the curse, Abraham was a new Adam through whom will come blessing.[12] This global aim of blessing is crucial

---

11. See Richard Ounsworth, *Joshua Typology in the New Testament* (Tübingen: Mohr Siebeck, 2012), 42; Peter J. Link Jr. and Matthew Y. Emerson, "Searching for the Second Adam: Typological Connections between Adam, Joseph, Mordecai, and Daniel," *Southern Baptist Journal of Theology* 21, no. 1 (Spring 2017): 129.
12. Schrock, "From Beelines to Plotlines," 40.

when we remember the global problem of the curse of sin. God set apart Abraham for the sake of the world.

Jesus is a true and greater Abraham.[13] He left the glory he shared with his Father and humbled himself in true humanity. Through his work on the cross, a new covenant was established. He himself was the fulfillment of God's pledge to Abraham that blessing would come to all families of the earth.

The Promised Land

The introduction of the "Promised Land" recalls the loss of sacred space in Eden (Gen. 3:24). While Adam and Eve were exiled from Eden, Abraham and his family would inherit a land of promise (Gen. 12:7). The family would be fruitful and multiply and exercise dominion. The problem for Abraham was his death before inheriting the land. He dwelled there only as a stranger and pilgrim. He died possessing the promise of the land and not the land itself.

According to the author of Hebrews, Abraham died in faith, "not having received the things promised" (Heb. 11:13). Yet the promise was not revoked. Abraham would inherit what God had promised, for he was seeking a better homeland (Heb. 11:14). Abraham desired "a better country, that is, a heavenly one," and God prepared for Abraham's family "a city" (Heb. 11:16). Ounsworth says, "Jesus has succeeded where Moses failed, in granting the People of God access to the heavenly rest of which the earthly Land was but a type or shadow."[14] The Promised Land foreshadowed the new Jerusalem, the city whose builder and maker is God (Heb. 11:10). Abraham's faith was not in vain, for his death did not nullify his inheritance. Abraham will be raised from the dead at the return of Christ, and his inheritance will be all that the Promised Land pointed to. Paul said that Abraham and his offspring "would be heir of the world" (Rom. 4:13). The Promised Land, like Eden before it, looked toward the new creation to be received in Christ Jesus.[15]

Melchizedek

After Abraham rescued his kidnapped nephew and defeated forces in battle (Gen. 14:1–17), he encountered an intriguing man. A priest-king named Melchizedek brought bread and wine and blessed Abraham (Gen. 14:18–20). Abraham tithed a tenth of everything he had to Melchizedek (Gen. 14:20), and that sacrificial act was the last mention of Melchizedek until Psalm 110. Written by David, Psalm 110 tells of God's words to the Messiah, that the anointed king will sit at God's right hand until his enemies are made a footstool (Ps. 110:1). The Messiah will rule with a mighty scepter and is thus

---

13. Benjamin Keach, *Preaching from the Types and Metaphors of the Bible* (1855; repr., Grand Rapids: Kregel, 1972), 973–74.
14. Ounsworth, *Joshua Typology in the New Testament*, 66–67.
15. See the *Epistle of Barnabas* 6.

a king (Ps. 110:2). But the Messiah is also "a priest forever after the order of Melchizedek" (Ps. 110:4). Since Israel's priests came from the tribe of Levi, and since Israel's kings came from the tribe of Judah, it is not clear how the Messiah could be both priest and king. Melchizedek is a helpful type who is himself a king and priest.

Jesus was from the tribe of Judah and not Levi. So while his royal pedigree is established (Matt. 1:1–17), the legitimacy of his permanent priesthood is not so obvious. How is Jesus both king and priest? He is king and priest like Melchizedek. Melchizedek, then, was a type of Christ.[16] The author of Hebrews—who is the only New Testament writer to mention the ancient priest-king—devotes significant space to explaining how Jesus's priesthood relates to Melchizedek (see Heb. 7). Jesus's superior priesthood is typified by Melchizedek, who was superior to Abraham (Heb. 7:7) and whose priesthood was superior to the priesthood of Abraham's descendants (Heb. 7:9–10). Like Melchizedek, Jesus was the superior priest and king.

Circumcision

Circumcision was the sign of God's covenant with Abraham (Gen. 17:11). On the eighth day, Hebrew males were to be circumcised and so demonstrate their consecration to God. In fact, the refusal to circumcise a male infant would result in being cut off from the people of Israel and violating God's covenant (Gen. 17:14). This sign would be kept century after century, generation after generation.

Not only does the sign of circumcision point back to God's covenant with Abraham (Gen. 15:18), but it points forward to the new covenant that Christ would establish on the cross. The outward sign in Genesis anticipated the inward work that God would do through his Son. The circumcision made with hands foreshadowed the circumcision made without hands (Col. 2:11). Christ was cut off for our sake. He was rejected so that we might be gathered in. And now "neither circumcision counts for anything, nor uncircumcision, but a new creation" (Gal. 6:15). Because of the new covenant, Jews in Christ and Gentiles in Christ have been circumcised in the heart, by the Spirit and not by the letter (Rom. 2:28–29).[17]

Sodom and Gomorrah

The cities of Sodom and Gomorrah are famous for the fiery judgment that fell upon them (Gen. 19:24, 28). And the judgment on these wicked cities is a type of the final judgment upon all the wicked. In Abraham's

---

16. See Ralph Allan Smith, "The Royal Priesthood in Exodus 19.6," in *The Glory of Kings: A Festschrift in Honor of James B. Jordan*, eds. Peter J. Leithart and John Barach (Eugene, OR: Pickwick, 2011), 105–10; Keach, *Types and Metaphors of the Bible*, 973.

17. Keach, *Types and Metaphors of the Bible*, 993.

dialogue with the Lord (Gen. 18:22–33), the righteous would not be swept away with the wicked. Abraham learned that the Judge of all the earth would do what is just (Gen. 19:25).

Those who perished in Sodom and Gomorrah would be raised up in the last day for judgment (Matt. 11:24). The historical judgment in Genesis 19 was a type of the eschatological judgment that Christ would administer at his return. According to Peter, the condemnation of Sodom and Gomorrah was "an example of what is going to happen to the ungodly" (2 Peter 2:6). The righteous, however, need not fear the final judgment. Just as God could distinguish between the righteous and the unrighteous in Sodom and Gomorrah, God will spare his people from the outpouring of his wrath.

Isaac

Isaac is the promised son of Abraham, born because of the power of God (Gen. 11:30; 18:10; 21:1–7). Barren Sarah was barren no more, and the age of the couple was no obstacle for God. The son of promise faced hostility from his brother Ishmael, who was the son of the slave woman Hagar (Gen. 16:15; 21:9–10). Nevertheless, Isaac would be the heir of the promises and the successive bearer of the covenant. Through Isaac, the descendants of Abraham would come (Gen. 21:12). God tested Abraham's trust when he asked the patriarch to sacrifice Isaac on a mountain, and then the mountain became a place of substitution when a ram was offered in Isaac's place (Gen 22:1–3, 11–13).[18]

Both Isaac and Jesus are the sons of Abraham (Gen. 22:2; Matt. 1:1). By the power of God, the virgin Mary conceived (Luke 1:35), reminding us of God's power in the Old Testament that accomplished miraculous conceptions. As Isaac was Abraham's beloved promised son (Gen. 22:2), Jesus was his Father's beloved promised Son (Mark 1:11; John 3:16). As the ultimate seed of Abraham, Jesus is the one to whom God's promises to Abraham truly belong (Gal. 3:16).[19] Isaac was opposed by Ishmael, and Jesus came to his own people only to be rejected by them (John 1:11). Though Isaac was spared on the mountain of sacrifice, Jesus would not be spared. Isaac was delivered from death, yet Jesus was delivered through death—by resurrection. Jesus is the true and greater Isaac.[20]

Genesis 25–50

Jacob

God's promises and covenant were given to Abraham but also *through* him—to Isaac and then to Jacob. In Genesis 25, the story of Jacob begins.

---

18. See Tertullian, *Against the Jews* 10; *Epistle of Barnabas* 7.
19. See Keach, *Types and Metaphors of the Bible*, 974.
20. See Clowney, *Unfolding Mystery*, 54–59.

He was a trickster, deceiving and plotting to acquire what was not rightfully his (Gen. 25:29–34). Jacob's cunning ways caused severe tension with his brother, Esau. Years later, while traveling to meet up with his estranged brother, Esau, Jacob wrestled with an unidentified man until daybreak (Gen. 32:24). Afterward, the figure pronounced Jacob's new name to be "Israel," which means, "striving with God" (Gen. 32:28). Jacob realized his striving had been with a divine figure. "I have seen God face to face," he said, "and yet my life has been delivered" (Gen. 32:30).[21]

Jesus was a greater Jacob.[22] He was no trickster like that patriarch. Jesus humbled himself and laid down his life for us (Phil. 2:8). He acted to acquire for us what we did not deserve but so desperately needed: redemption and new creation.[23] Like Jacob, Jesus encountered sibling tension. Jesus's own brothers did not believe in him before his resurrection (John 7:5; Acts 1:14), and sometimes they sought to intervene when they believed he was out of his mind (Mark 3:20–21, 32). Jesus was greater than Jacob, for while Jacob saw the presence of the Lord manifested in Genesis 32, Jesus alone has dwelt eternally and unimpeded with the Father. Jacob, like a new Adam, was told to "be fruitful and multiply" (Gen. 35:11). Yet only Christ, the last Adam and greater Jacob, would produce innumerable offspring from every nation, tribe, people, and tongue (Rev. 7:9).

Joseph

Joseph dreamed he would rule over his brothers (Gen. 37:7–10). But according to God's plan, this reign would be achieved through rejection and suffering. Joseph's brothers plotted against him, and his descent into a pit was followed by being sold for silver (Gen. 37:12–28). While in Egypt, Joseph faced false accusations and imprisonment (Gen. 39:13–20). But in the Lord's good providence, Joseph interpreted a dream for the pharaoh and became prime minister over Egypt, second only to the pharaoh himself (Gen. 41:43–46). Famine drove Joseph's family to Egypt, and unbeknownst to them, they came to their rejected brother and needed his provision (Gen. 42:7–8). Joseph eventually revealed himself to them and reconciled with them (Gen. 45:1–15). What the brothers had meant for evil, God had designed for good (Gen. 50:20).

Jesus is a true and greater Joseph.[24] Jesus would reign as King of kings, but this rule would be accomplished through rejection and suffering (Mark 8:31). Fellow Israelites plotted against him, one of his disciples denied him, and another disciple betrayed him for silver (Matt. 26). The betrayal led to arrest,

---

21. See Keach, *Types and Metaphors of the Bible*, 974–75.
22. See Clowney, *Unfolding Mystery*, 76–77.
23. Leonhard Goppelt, *TYPOS: The Typological Interpretation of the Old Testament in the New* (Grand Rapids: Eerdmans, 1982), 186–87.
24. See Tertullian, *Against the Jews* 10; Peter J. Leithart, *A House for My Name: A Survey of the Old Testament* (Moscow, ID: Canon, 2000), 65.

the arrest led to false accusations, and a verdict of death meant crucifixion.[25] So outside the city of Jerusalem, Jewish and Roman forces opposed Jesus and delighted in his defeat. But what they meant for evil, God meant for good. Jesus's descent into the pit of death was followed by resurrection and vindication. He revealed himself to his disciples, he restored Peter, and he commissioned them to spread the good news (Matt. 28; John 20–21). Jesus achieved the greatest work of reconciliation: he brought together not merely estranged siblings but sinners and a righteous God. And God gave Jesus the name that is above every name, that at his name every knee will bow (Phil. 2:9–11).

Judah

Judah was one of Jacob's twelve sons (Gen. 29:35). After he and his brothers cast Joseph into a pit, Judah suggested they sell him to the Ishmaelites instead of killing him without profit (Gen. 37:26–27). What Judah meant for evil, God meant for good. While the brothers profited from selling their brother, they profited far more from Joseph (unknown to them at the time) in the years to come when they needed grain (Gen. 42:3). Joseph had asked to see their youngest brother, but Benjamin had remained with Jacob in the Promised Land. Judah tried to convince Jacob to send Benjamin: "I will be a pledge of his safety. From my hand you shall require him. If I do not bring him back to you and set him before you, then let me bear the blame forever" (Gen. 43:9). Later, when Joseph ordered that a silver cup be secretly planted in Benjamin's sack, Judah offered himself in Benjamin's place: "Now therefore, please let your servant remain instead of the boy as a servant to my lord, and let the boy go back with the brothers" (Gen. 44:33). All became known as Joseph identified himself. And then Jacob and the rest of the family made the trek to Egypt. Before his death, Jacob spoke words of blessing over his children, saying to Judah: "The scepter shall not depart from Judah, nor the ruler's staff from between his feet, until tribute comes to him; and to him shall be the obedience of the peoples" (Gen. 49:10).

Jesus was a true and greater Judah. All that Jesus spoke and all that he did, he said and did for the good of his people. Whereas Judah offered himself in the place of Benjamin, Jesus offered himself in the place of us all (Mark 10:45). "In Judah we have a picture of the Surety and Substitute."[26] Judah was ready to lay his life down in order to please his father and protect his youngest brother. Jesus, who pleased his Father through laying down his life on the cross (John 10:17), is the Good Shepherd who protects us from condemnation. We are all Benjamin. Judah had said he would be a pledge for Benjamin's safety, and

---

25. See Link and Emerson, "Searching for the Second Adam," 130–32; Tim Gallant, "Judah's Life from the Dead: The Gospel of Romans 11," in Leithart and Barach, *Glory of Kings*, 51; Johnson, *Walking with Jesus*, 63.
26. A. M. Hodgkin, *Christ in All the Scriptures* (London: Pickering & Inglis, 1909), 15.

Jesus is our hope and peace and place of refuge. Jacob had promised that the scepter would not depart from Judah, and Jesus, who descended from Judah's tribe, rose from the dead to hold the scepter forever and receive the praise and obedience of the nations (Rom. 1:5).

Summary

The foundation for biblical typology is laid in Genesis. The attentive reader is able to notice multiple characters, events, places, and things that have christological significance. The impact of Adam is especially profound, for subsequent characters are reminiscent of him and thus function as types of Christ as he did. The Adamic shadow will continue to stretch over characters in later biblical books, and so the number of characters serving as types of Christ will increase. Earthly judgments and deliverances also anticipate future eschatological activity, specifically the future resurrection of the dead and the final judgment of the wicked. God's end-time new creation is foreshadowed in Genesis by the first heaven and earth, by the garden of Eden, and by the land of promise. As we progress further into Scripture, we will see the number of types increase as if they are fulfilling the creation mandate to be fruitful and multiply.

REFLECTION QUESTIONS

1. How is Abel a type of Christ?

2. How does the flood and ark relate to God's final judgment of the wicked?

3. Why should Isaac be considered a type of Christ?

4. Can you think of additional correspondences between the story of Joseph and the ministry of Jesus?

5. Can you think of other characters in Genesis who could be types of Christ?

What Types Are in Exodus?

The stories in Exodus tell the rise of Israel as a nation, the flight from Egypt, the arrival at Mount Sinai, the giving of the Law, the forming of a covenant with Israel, and the building of the tabernacle. An entire chapter is devoted to Exodus because, like Genesis, it is a deep well of types from which interpreters continue to draw.

Exodus 1–12

Moses

Born under a death threat to Hebrew male babies, Moses is spared by the providence of God in order to deliver the people of God (Exod. 1:22—2:10). He faced rejection and opposition from his own people (Exod. 2:14), yet God had set him apart for a mission of redemption. Moses performed signs and wonders by the power of God, and these miracles confirmed that Moses had been sent by God and that God was going to do what he promised: deliver the Israelite captives by an exodus out of Egypt (Exod. 7–12).

Jesus is the true and greater Moses, for he too escaped the threat of death imposed on babies by a villainous ruler (Matt. 2:13–18).[1] While crowds followed Jesus and listened to his teachings and benefited from his miracles, the religious leadership exhibited strong opposition to him (Mark 3:6; 14:1). Jesus faced rejection from his own people! Yet their plots against him would not succeed before the appointed hour of death, for God had sent his only Son on a mission of redemption. Jesus's signs and wonders confirmed his identity (John 5:36). Jesus had been sent to lead a new exodus.

---

1. See Benjamin Keach, *Preaching from the Types and Metaphors of the Bible* (1855; repr., Grand Rapids: Kregel, 1972), 976; Sidney Greidanus, *Preaching Christ from the Old Testament: A Contemporary Hermeneutical Method* (Grand Rapids: Eerdmans, 1999), 260, 327.

Israel

Israel was God's firstborn son (Exod. 4:22), a corporate child whom God delivered and nurtured. This corporate son was to inherit the promises of Abraham (Exod. 3:8). God brought Israel through the Red Sea waters of judgment and into the wilderness (Exod. 13–14). When they faced temptation, again and again they failed (Exod. 15–17). God gave them his law and made with them a covenant by blood (Exod. 19–24). Yet Israel could not keep the law, and its curses came upon their heads.

Jesus was the Son of God and the true heir of Abraham's promises (Gal. 3:16). At his baptism, he came through the waters to symbolize the victory he was going to accomplish. After his baptism, Jesus faced temptation in the wilderness—but, unlike Israel, Jesus prevailed over the Enemy and did not sin (Matt. 4:1–11).[2] In fact, Jesus kept all of God's law, never violating its precepts by his actions or words or thoughts. Jesus did what Israel could never do. He was the true light for the world (John 8:12). And at his death, a new covenant was formed by blood (Luke 22:20). The judgment of God, which he did not deserve, came upon his head in our place.

Plagues upon Egypt

After Israel had been in Egypt for more than four hundred years, God unleashed plagues upon Egypt that brought devastation to the land and humiliated its gods (Exod. 7–12). God was answering the wickedness of Egypt and preparing to deliver his people from captivity. Those judgments—which included transforming waters, striking animals, darkening the sun, and killing image-bearers—were like a de-creation happening in front of everyone that was both terrifying and unstoppable.

The plagues of Egypt foreshadow the final day of God's wrath, when the wicked are brought to account and must face the justice they had never feared or never thought would come. Earthly judgments, such as the one upon Egypt in the days of Moses, are historical evidence that God is serious about sin and has the power to overcome his enemies. As Goppelt says, "The OT miracles of punishment continue to show us that God is judging with forbearance. For us and for Christ, they are types of the future judgment."[3] And on the last day, his judgment will be terrifying and unstoppable.

The Passover Lamb

Heeding the words of God through Moses, Israelite families put lamb's blood on the doorframes of their homes (Exod. 12:21–23, 28). If the firstborn

---

2. See Dennis E. Johnson, *Walking with Jesus through His Word: Discovering Christ in All the Scriptures* (Phillipsburg, NJ: P&R, 2015), 61.
3. Leonhard Goppelt, *TYPOS: The Typological Interpretation of the Old Testament in the New* (Grand Rapids: Eerdmans, 1982), 75.

son was covered by sacrificial blood in this way, judgment would not fall on him when the tenth plague began. Israel would commemorate this event through the Feast of Passover each year (Exod. 12:24–27). Through Passover, the Israelites would remember when death passed over them because they were under the blood.

Jesus did not die on just any week of the year. Jesus's death on the cross occurred on Passover because Passover was a type that he fulfilled (Mark 14:1–2). Jesus was the slain lamb we needed. He was our Passover lamb (1 Cor. 5:7) and the lamb who would truly deal with sin through his sacrifice (John 1:29). And condemnation will not meet any who are covered by his blood, for he is the true and greater Passover sacrifice.[4]

Exodus 13–18

The Red Sea Deliverance

With the Egyptian army pursuing them, the Israelites had nowhere to go, with their backs to the Red Sea (Exod. 14:9–10). Moses called upon his people to stand firm and behold the salvation of God (Exod. 14:13). A mighty wind parted the sea, and the Israelites traveled on dry ground to the other side, flanked along the way by walls of water (Exod. 14:22). The Red Sea deliverance displayed the power of God to rescue his people all by himself.

And all by himself, Christ accomplished atonement on the cross. He parted the waters of judgment that we might pass through on the dry ground of justification. The Red Sea deliverance anticipates the redemption and ultimate vindication of God's people. Routed by the enemies of sin and Satan, we had no hope but the power of God Almighty. The exodus from Egypt and through the sea pointed to the new and greater exodus that Christ led.[5]

Manna

The years between Egypt and the Promised Land were years of miraculous provision every morning. God gave his people manna six mornings a week; the sixth morning had twice as much so that they didn't have to gather it on the Sabbath (Exod. 16:22–26). He did this for forty years (Exod. 16:35). The manna sustained them, and it showed God's care for them. Contrary to the fears they sometimes voiced, God had not brought them into the wilderness to see them all die.

The day came when God provided something better than the manna of Israel's past. Jesus said, "My Father gives you the true bread from heaven. For the bread of God is he who comes down from heaven and gives life to the world"

---

4. See Keach, *Types and Metaphors of the Bible*, 995–96. Edmund P. Clowney, *The Unfolding Mystery: Discovering Christ in the Old Testament* (Phillipsburg, NJ: P&R, 1988), 98.
5. See Greidanus, *Preaching Christ from the Old Testament*, 259.

(John 6:32–33). The world needs life, and it needs life that will last. Jesus is this bread of life. "I am the living bread that came down from heaven. If anyone eats of this bread, he will live forever. And the bread that I will give for the life of the world is my flesh" (John 6:51). Jesus is the true and greater manna from God.[6]

The Struck Rock

God provided not only food for the Israelites; he provided them drink as well. When they were fearful and grumbling due to their thirst, the Lord told Moses, "Behold, I will stand before you there on the rock at Horeb, and you shall strike the rock, and water shall come out of it, and the people will drink" (Exod. 17:6). So Moses was to strike the rock, and upon this rock the Lord would be standing. Strike the rock where the Lord was, and then water would flow? Moses did, water came, and the people drank (Exod. 17:6). God provided throughout their wilderness journeys. It was like the divinely blessed rock followed them wherever they went.

When Paul wrote to the Corinthians about their Israelite forebears, he said the Israelites "drank from the spiritual Rock that followed them, and the Rock was Christ" (1 Cor. 10:4). Christ was struck and nourished the people of God, just as the rock in Exodus 17 was struck and nourished the people.[7] Yet the rock that Moses struck could not provide the people with anything other than physical water. Jesus has living water that quenches the soul's thirst (John 4:14). Through the striking of the cross, the death of Christ secures everlasting life for his people.

The Raised Hands of Moses

On the way to Mount Sinai, the Israelites faced the hostile Amalekites. Joshua led a battle with them, while Moses and two others went to the top of a hill (Exod. 17:10). Moses held up his staff—the staff that worked signs and wonders in Egypt and that struck the rock that poured forth water—until his hands grew weary, after which his two companions held up his hands (Exod. 17:11–12). The Israelites were victorious as long as the staff was raised up by the hands of Moses. The battle ended, and the Israelites prevailed.

The victory over the Amalekites foreshadowed the victory of Christ.[8] Jesus ascended a hill and, with his outstretched hands, accomplished the greatest wonder of all: atonement for sinners to reconcile them to a holy God. Now the risen and ascended Savior reigns until he subdues all enemies under his feet (Ps. 110:1; Mark 12:36). He has all authority in heaven and on earth (Matt. 28:18). In him all things hold together, and his hands will not grow weary.

---

6. See Greidanus, *Preaching Christ from the Old Testament*, 260.
7. See Keach, *Types and Metaphors of the Bible*, 993–94; Johnson, *Walking with Jesus*, 63.
8. See Tertullian, *Against the Jews* 10; Sidney Greidanus, *Preaching Christ from the Old Testament*, 330–31.

Exodus 19–40

The Sabbath

Of all Ten Commandments in Exodus 20, the fourth commandment is the longest. God tells the Israelites to remember the Sabbath by resting from normal labor on the seventh day (Exod. 20:8–11). We were made to exercise dominion and to enjoy rest, yet sin has compromised our ability to fulfill this mandate. Israel was to keep the Sabbath holy in order to demonstrate their trust in the Lord and remember his creation of all things. In Genesis 1, God created the world in six days, and then in Genesis 2 he entered into rest on the seventh day. The rhythm of Israel's life would have a six-day pattern of labor because they were made to reflect the Lord and enter into his rest as well.

Sometimes Jesus healed on the Sabbath, showing that he came to bring what the Sabbath pointed to. The rest we need is one that overcomes the curse and the effects of sin. When Christ's miracles brought transformation and restoration on the Sabbath, his actions corrected the false notions of his contemporaries who believed that such miracles violated the fourth commandment (Mark 2:23–28; 3:1–6). The rest that creation needs is not the cessation of activity but the invasion and presence of peace and life. It is good news, then, that Jesus said, "The Son of Man is lord even of the Sabbath," for he is the source of this peace and life. As the Sabbath's Lord, Jesus both accomplished and gives what the Sabbath pointed to. He said, "Come to me, all who labor and are heavy laden, and I will give you rest" (Matt. 11:28; Heb. 4:9). As Ounsworth puts it, "The keeping of the Sabbath is being interpreted typologically, and once again we have a type that acts as a mediating term: as the Sabbath is formed for God's covenant people in the image of God's own primordial rest, so its purpose is to mould them into a people prepared to enter into that primordial rest when the covenant is brought to its fulfilment."[9]

The Feasts of Israel

The calendar of Israel oriented the life of the people toward God. In addition to the weekly Sabbath, they had multiple annual feasts to observe. In the first month of their year, Israelites would keep the Feast of Unleavened Bread, which was a weeklong feast starting after Passover (Exod. 23:15). Seven weeks later was the Feast of Harvest (or Pentecost), which celebrated the provision of God (Exod. 23:16a; Lev. 23:15–22). The firstfruits of the crops belonged to the Lord, and this offering symbolized the worth of Yahweh, as well as Israel's trust in his goodness. At the end of the fall harvest was the Feast of Ingathering (or Booths/Tabernacles), which marked and celebrated the provision of God in Israel's vineyards and orchards (Exod. 23:16b; Lev. 23:33–44).

---

9. Richard Ounsworth, *Joshua Typology in the New Testament* (Tübingen: Mohr Siebeck, 2012), 83.

Believers do not keep the feasts of Israel, because the Lord Jesus has fulfilled the cycle of festivals.[10] If anyone taught that life in the new covenant required the keeping of Jewish feasts, Paul's response was, "Let no one pass judgment on you in questions of food and drink, or with regard to a festival or a new moon or a Sabbath. These are a shadow of the things to come, but the substance belongs to Christ" (Col. 2:16–17). The shadows have given way to the Substance. Jesus is our unleavened Savior, who was without sin and gives life to the world. He is the firstfruits of the resurrection from the dead (1 Cor. 15:20) and the giver of the promised Spirit on the Day of Pentecost (Acts 2:1). Christ tabernacled among us, declaring at the Feast of Ingathering that he had living water for the thirsty and light for the world (John 7:37–39; 8:12). Israel's feasts were pictures of Christ's person and work.[11] They were shadows destined to fade when the Substance came.

The Tabernacle

Exiled from Eden, Adam and Eve left God's dwelling place (Gen. 3:24). But God would not allow sin to bring permanent disruption to his fellowship with man. Israel's construction of a tabernacle at the foot of Mount Sinai is a clear signal that God pursues sinners in order to dwell among them. God said, "And let them make me a sanctuary, that I may dwell in their midst" (Exod. 25:8).

Jesus is the true and greater tabernacle.[12] "When the Israelites brought the tabernacle to Moses, even if they didn't fully understand it, they were laying out the gospel. Long before Christ came into the world, God was using symbols to teach people about his saving work."[13] John opens his Gospel with language about the Word that was with God: "The Word became flesh and dwelt among us, and we have seen his glory, glory as of the only Son from the Father, full of grace and truth" (John 1:14). The Word *dwelt*—like a tabernacle (see Exod. 25:8). In fact, the phrase can be translated "the Word became flesh and tabernacled among us." The construction of the tabernacle in Exodus anticipated the day when God would dwell among them in Jesus Christ.

The Ark of the Covenant

Among the vessels and furniture to be built and placed in different parts of the tabernacle, the ark of the covenant would be the most significant. A box of wood, overlaid with gold and carried by poles, the ark of the covenant would be in the Most Holy Place and concealed by a curtain (Exod. 25:10–15). The inside of the ark would contain the tablets of the Ten Commandments, a jar

---

10. See Johnson, *Walking with Jesus*, 207–9.
11. Roy Gane, *Leviticus, Numbers*, NIV Application Commentary (Grand Rapids: Zondervan, 2004), 393.
12. See Keach, *Types and Metaphors of the Bible*, 983.
13. Philip Graham Ryken, *Exodus*, Preaching the Word (Wheaton, IL: Crossway, 2015), 1086.

of manna, and—eventually—Aaron's budded staff (Heb. 9:4). On the lid (or mercy seat) of the ark were two sculpted cherubim of gold (Exod. 25:18–20). The ark represented the presence of God and could not be touched by human hands (see 2 Sam. 6:7). Later in Israel's history, when Babylon destroyed the temple of Solomon, they raided the vessels and furniture, which included taking the ark of the covenant. Though Israel eventually returned from exile, the ark did not return with them and was never recovered.

The ark of the covenant points to Jesus Christ, who is God dwelling with humans.[14] He is the seat of mercy and bearer of God's testimonies. While the ark of the covenant was eventually lost to Israel, the arrival of Jesus Christ is the escalation of that artifact. Instead of acacia wood overlaid with gold, the Word became flesh and dwelled among us. And after his death on the cross, he was laid in an unused garden tomb, which became a Most Holy Place (John 19:41). After his resurrection, Mary wept at the empty tomb, seeing two angels sitting where his body had been, one at the head and one at the feet (John 20:11–12). Our true and greater ark, Jesus is the glory of God and place of mercy.

The Priesthood

The portable sanctuary would be transported and maintained by the Levites (Num. 3:5–39). From the Levites would be Israel's priesthood. These priests were mediators between God and the nation of Israel (Exod. 40:12–15). The priests depended on other tribes for food and finances. They facilitated the sacrifices offered at the tabernacle, so the priesthood was a vital office in the life of Israel. But the priests could not last in their office. They were sinners, and death took one after another.

When the writer of Hebrews discussed the priesthood, he contrasts Jesus with the former priests: "He holds his priesthood permanently, because he continues forever" (Heb. 7:24). Through his resurrection on the third day, Jesus can hold the office of priest forever.[15] He ends the need for priests, even a high priest.[16] Paul wrote, "There is one mediator between God and men, the man Christ Jesus, who gave himself as a ransom for all, which is the testimony given at the proper time" (1 Tim. 2:5–6). Jesus is the true and greater mediator, the priest sinners needed and the one they now have in the heavenly places. Jesus entered "into heaven itself, now to appear in the presence of God on our behalf" (Heb. 9:24). He is our sinless mediator.

---

14. See Keach, *Types and Metaphors of the Bible*, 984.
15. See David Schrock, "From Beelines to Plotlines: Typology That Follows the Covenantal Typography of Scripture," *Southern Baptist Journal of Theology* 21, no. 1 (Spring 2017): 44.
16. See Keach, *Types and Metaphors of the Bible*, 980–82.

Summary

When God raised up Israel in the book of Exodus, he raised up types as well that pointed to the person and work of Christ. The stories of Moses and Israel report experiences that become expectations, and these expectations take us to the Savior who is a greater Moses and true Israel. He is the Lord of the Sabbath and the greatest meaning of Israel's feasts. The tabernacle and priesthood were designed to typify the perfect sacrifice who would simultaneously be the priest we needed in the heavenly holy place. He is Immanuel, God with us—foreshadowed by the ark of the covenant. He is the bread of heaven and rock who was struck. He has led the greater exodus through the waters of judgment, and in him we have crossed from darkness to light.

REFLECTION QUESTIONS

1. What correspondences exist between Jesus and the people of Israel in the Old Testament?

2. How does the Passover relate to the work of Jesus upon the cross?

3. How does Jesus fulfill the feasts of Israel?

4. How does the tabernacle point to Jesus?

5. How does Jesus fulfill the priesthood of Israel?

QUESTION 19

What Types Are in Leviticus through Deuteronomy?

In the books of Leviticus through Deuteronomy, Israel receives more in-structions that regulated the lives of the priests and the people; the Israelites departed Mount Sinai for the Promised Land; they wandered in the wilder-ness for forty years; and eventually the new generation paused at Moab as Moses readied them for entrance into the Promised Land. During these forty years, the reader beholds deliverances and judgments, special occasions and key characters, promises and practices, all of which reach fulfillment in the person of Christ and his past and future work.

Leviticus

The Sacrificial System

The opening chapters of Leviticus explain various sacrifices the Israelites were to offer.[1] Some sacrifices were morning and evening. God says, "If his of-fering is a burnt offering from the herd, he shall offer a male without blemish. He shall bring it to the entrance of the tent of meeting, that he may be ac-cepted before the LORD" (Lev. 1:3). The sacrificial system indicated our need to be accepted by the Lord, yet it made clear that something had to be offered in our place.

Jesus fulfilled the sacrificial system. All the animals that were ever offered could not atone for sin. Why? Because "it is impossible for the blood of bulls and goats to take away sins" (Heb. 10:4). If the sacrifices had been sufficient

---

1. Roy Gane writes, "No single kind of sacrifice could adequately prefigure the richness of Christ's sacrifice, just as no single picture in an anatomy and physiology textbook can capture the full complexity of a living organism" (*Leviticus, Numbers*, NIV Application Commentary [Grand Rapids: Zondervan, 2004], 24–25).

to atone for sin, they would not need to have been continually offered. The work of Jesus upon the cross changed the sacrificial system by bringing it to an end.[2] Jesus offered himself once for all (Heb. 10:10). He was the Lamb of God who ended all sacrificial lambs (John 1:29). And then, when he had offered this "single sacrifice for sins, he sat down at the right hand of God" (Heb. 10:12). The sacrificial system was full of shadows, and after the cross the shadows were no more.

Aaron

Aaron, the elder brother of Moses, plays a crucial role in the events in Egypt and in the life of Israel's priests. In the first three plagues, Aaron holds the staff through which God worked wonders of blood, frogs, and gnats (Exod. 7:14–8:19), and Aaron served on multiple occasions as the mouthpiece of Moses (Exod. 3:14–16; 4:30; 16:9–10). God set apart Aaron and his sons to serve as priests (Exod. 28:1). They were consecrated for their priestly work (Lev. 8). Aaron would represent Israel in his role as their mediator.[3] When he presented offerings before the Lord after his consecration, the Lord accepted his sacrifices (Lev. 9). As Aaron served the people of Israel, he experienced their opposition and grumbling, like Moses did (Num. 14:2). Like Moses, Aaron never entered the Promised Land. Aaron and his son Eleazar climbed a mountain, and Moses removed the priestly vestments of Aaron and put them on Eleazar (Num. 20:24–28). Aaron's role as high priest came to an end.

Jesus is a true and greater Aaron.[4] Jesus is our elder brother who works wonders to deliver the people of God. And when he speaks, he speaks the words of God (John 17:8). He is not just God's mouthpiece; he is God himself speaking. Jesus was set apart for his work as our true mediator, the one who would accomplish what Aaron never could (Heb. 5:1–6). Aaron's work as a high priest was not free from corruption (Heb. 7:27; 9:7). Aaron himself was a sinner and needed a greater mediator. Only Jesus is our high priest who was without sin (Heb. 7:26–27). All that Jesus did was pleasing to God, including his sacrifice upon the cross as a propitiation for our sins. While Jesus died, his high priestly ministry continues because he rose from the dead (Heb. 7:23–25). The mediating work of Jesus will never be passed on to a successor. Being greater than Aaron, Jesus is our high priest forever.

---

2. See the *Epistle of Barnabas* 7–8; Benjamin Keach, *Preaching from the Types and Metaphors of the Bible* (1855; repr., Grand Rapids: Kregel, 1972), 987–93.
3. See Richard Ounsworth, *Joshua Typology in the New Testament* (Tübingen: Mohr Siebeck, 2012), 175.
4. See Keach, *Types and Metaphors of the Bible*, 980.

The Day of Atonement

Once a year, on the Day of Atonement, the high priest entered the taber-nacle (and later the temple) in order to go behind the veil into the Most Holy Place (Lev. 16). The high priest sprinkled blood that had been shed, for his own sins and the sins of the people (Lev. 16:11–17). After atoning for the Holy Place, the tabernacle, and the altar, the high priest would lay his hands on the head of a live goat and confess the sins of Israel (Lev. 16:21). This act symbol-ized the transfer of sin, and the goat went away into the wilderness.

Jesus, our mighty mediator, fulfilled the Day of Atonement.[5] At his death, he declared, "It is finished" (John 19:30). The death of Jesus was the ultimate day of atonement. "When the Aaronic High Priest passed through the veil into the Holy of Holies, taking with him the blood of sacrificial beasts for its cleansing, he participated in another shadowy image of what Christ would achieve."[6] Weeks after his resurrection, Jesus ascended to the right hand of the Father, entering "once for all into the holy places, not by means of the blood of goats and calves but by means of his own blood, thus securing an eternal redemption" (Heb. 9:12). The Most Holy Place in the tabernacle had repre-sented the greater and heavenly counterpart, into which Jesus entered with victory in his wake.

The Temple Veil

The temple veil, which was the last barrier into the Most Holy Place, con-cealed the ark of the covenant from view (Exod. 26:31–34). Only the high priest could pass through this veil, and he could only do so once a year, on the Day of Atonement (Lev. 16:14–15). The veil was a symbol of the disruption sin has brought to fellowship with a holy God. The veil reminds us that we are transgressors, and transgressors cannot abide in divine glory and live.

When suffering and crucifixion tore the body of Christ, the veil of the temple was torn at his death (Matt. 27:51). Atonement had been accom-plished but not through anything done at the physical temple. The temple veil was a type of Christ, torn for us so that we might have fellowship with the God who has drawn near to us.[7] We enter the holy of holies through the blood of Christ, "by the new and living way that he opened for us through the curtain, that is, through his flesh" (Heb. 10:20). Through the veil of his flesh, Christ has opened the way to come to God.

---

5. See the discussion in Ounsworth, *Joshua Typology in the New Testament*, 168–172; Dennis E. Johnson, *Walking with Jesus through His Word: Discovering Christ in All the Scriptures* (Phillipsburg, NJ: P&R, 2015), 213–14.
6. Ounsworth, *Joshua Typology in the New Testament*, 175.
7. See the discussion in Ounsworth, *Joshua Typology in the New Testament*, 157–65; Keach, *Types and Metaphors of the Bible*, 984.

The Year of Jubilee

Israel had multiple feasts and events to be counting and remembering throughout the year. After forty-nine years, Israel would prepare for the Year of Jubilee: "And you shall consecrate the fiftieth year, and proclaim liberty throughout the land to all its inhabitants. It shall be a jubilee for you, when each of you shall return to his property and each of you shall return to his clan" (Lev. 25:10). This fiftieth year was rightly a celebratory time! But a greater jubilee would come one day. In the book of Daniel, the practice of counting sevens is behind Gabriel's words about seventy sevens (Dan. 9:20–27).[8] Daniel learned about a time when God would atone for sin and bring in righteousness (Dan. 9:24).

Jesus came to bring the ultimate Year of Jubilee.[9] Upon the cross, Jesus made atonement for sin and brought in righteousness, just as Daniel had learned God would do. The Year of Jubilee in Leviticus 25 pointed to, and was fulfilled by, the redemptive work of Christ. The redemption of Christ accomplished the greatest freedom and warrants the most celebration. Daniel heard that an anointed one would be cut off and make a strong covenant (Dan. 9:26–27), and we know from the New Testament that Jesus was God's Anointed One who embraced the cross in order to form a new covenant. The obedience of the last Adam brought life and joy, justification and jubilee.

Numbers

The Death of the Wilderness Generation

When spies returned with a mixed report about the Promised Land, the majority of them expressed fear and unbelief (Num. 13:31–32). Their bad report provoked a rebellion among the Israelites, who grumbled against Moses, Aaron, and the Lord. Due to the wickedness of the people, the Lord determined that the Israelites would wander in the wilderness until the older generation died (Num. 14:32–34). That rebellious generation did not inherit the promises made to Abraham.

A far worse judgment lay in store for those who live in rebellion against the Lord. "Take care, brothers," the writer of Hebrews warns, "lest there be in any of you an evil, unbelieving heart, leading you to fall away from the living

---

8. In Leviticus 25, the Israelites were supposed to give the land rest every seven years (25:1–7). In this way, the Lord gave the land a Sabbath. And after seven cycles of seven years, the Israelites were to mark the Year of Jubilee, the fiftieth year. When Gabriel speaks about seventy sevens (Dan. 9:24), the angel's words are based on the number seven which structures Israel's agricultural life in Leviticus 25.

9. See Sidney Greidanus, *Preaching Christ from the Old Testament: A Contemporary Hermeneutical Method* (Grand Rapids: Eerdmans, 1999), 261; Johnson, *Walking with Jesus*, 207–10.

God" (Heb. 3:12). The author has just cited from Psalm 95, which uses the wilderness generation as an example of unbelief (Heb. 3:7–11; Ps. 95:7–11). There is an everlasting rest for the people of God, but an unbelieving heart will fall short of the new creation. If God judged the wilderness generation for their wickedness, how much more will those who reject the gospel face the wrath of the living God and not enter into the promised rest.

The Opening of the Earth

Despite the disapproval of the Lord for their murmuring, the Israelites continued to behave in rebellious ways. Korah, Dathan, and Abiram rose up against Moses and Aaron (Num. 16:1–3). Moses warned the group that they were actually assembling against the Lord. The Lord's judgment came upon Korah and company when the earth opened its mouth and consumed them (Num. 16:30–33).

Christ's final judgment will consume the wicked. None will withstand the wrath of the Lamb. Yet the righteous will not perish with the wicked, for the Lord knows how to preserve those who are his (2 Peter 2:4–10). The final judgment is an escalation of every earthly judgment. Those who gather against God's people are gathering against God himself and his Anointed One (see Acts 9:4–5). But who could succeed against the Lord? "He who sits in the heavens laughs; the Lord holds them in derision" (Ps. 2:4). Like Korah and his companions, those who oppose the Lord will learn that it is "a fearful thing to fall into the hands of the living God" (Heb. 10:31).

The Bronze Serpent

On another occasion when the Israelites spoke against God and Moses, the people asked, "Why have you brought us up out of Egypt to die in the wilderness? For there is no food and no water, and we loathe this worthless food" (Num. 21:5). The rebels faced an immediate judgment: fiery serpents began biting the people (Num. 21:6). Moses interceded for the people, and the Lord provided a remedy: "Make a fiery serpent and set it on a pole, and everyone who is bitten, when he sees it, shall live" (Num. 21:8). Moses obeyed, raised up a bronze serpent on a pole, and the bitten Israelites would live if they looked at it.

The provision of the bronze serpent was a type of Christ upon the cross.[10] Jesus's own words about the story link it to his coming death: "And as Moses lifted up the serpent in the wilderness, so must the Son of Man be lifted up, that whoever believes in him may have eternal life" (John 3:14–15). Sin is a serpent that has bitten all of us, and we are going to perish under the judgment of God unless we look in faith to the provision of the cross. Jesus has been lifted up for us, that all who look to him may have eternal life.

---

10. See the *Epistle of Barnabas* 12; Johnson, *Walking with Jesus*, 76–77.

The Zeal of Phinehas

If Phinehas is known for anything, he is known for taking God's law seriously. While Israel lived in Shittim, they committed sexual immorality with Moabite women (Num. 25:1), and the resulting idolatry angered the Lord (25:2–3). The Lord ordered punishments for these sins (25:4–5). Phinehas followed a transgressing Israelite into a place of intimacy, where the Israelite committed immorality with a Midianite woman. Phinehas was the instrument of judgment, spearing the couple whose sin found them out (Num. 25:7–8). The Lord commended the zeal of Phinehas, who was jealous with a divine jealousy for the Lord's glory (Num. 25:11–13).

But no one prized the glory of God like Jesus did. Jesus was a true and greater Phinehas, exhibiting a commitment in his heart and life to the law of God. While Phinehas turned the anger of God from Israel for a time (Num. 25:11), only Jesus could make propitiation for sin, satisfying the justice of God. Sinners deserved the wrath of God, and Jesus bore this wrath in their place. In his jealousy for God's glory, Christ became the offering acceptable to God so that sinners could live in him. Rather than pursuing sinners with a spear, Jesus received the spear into his own body.

Deuteronomy

The Prophet Like Moses

Before Moses died and the Israelites entered the Promised Land, he told them, "The LORD your God will raise up for you a prophet like me from among you, from your brothers—it is to him you shall listen" (Deut. 18:15). A prophet like Moses—this was a pattern that God laid down and one that future Israelites were to look for. Who would be the prophet like Moses? Of that prophet, God said, "I will put my words in his mouth, and he shall speak to them all that I command him" (Deut. 18:18). Joshua led after Moses, but Joshua wasn't the expected prophet. Jeremiah had been appointed as a prophet and even objected to this commission because of his inadequate speech (Jer. 1:6), but he wasn't the expected prophet either.

The book of Hebrews opens this way: "Long ago, at many times and in many ways, God spoke to our fathers by the prophets, but in these last days he has spoken to us by his Son, whom he appointed the heir of all things, through whom also he created the world" (Heb. 1:1–2). Jesus is the prophet like Moses, the Word of God who became flesh and revealed God. The apostles believed that Jesus fulfilled this typological expectation. Peter preached that "Moses said, 'The Lord God will raise up for you a prophet like me from your brothers. You shall listen to him in whatever he tells you.' . . . God, having raised up his servant, sent him to you first, to bless you by turning every one of you from your wickedness" (Acts 3:22, 26; cf. Matt. 17:5). An Old Testament prophet could say, "Thus says the Lord," but Jesus could simply speak—for every word from the mouth of Jesus was the word of God. He was the prophet like, and the prophet greater than, Moses.[11]

Covenant Blessings and Curses

When God gave the law to the Israelites, it came with blessings if obeyed and curses if disobeyed. Obedience would lead to flourishing in the land of promise, but disobedience could result in expulsion from the land of promise. The curse of exile would be by the hand of a foreign enemy whom God would raise up to judge his rebellious people. "And the LORD will scatter you among all peoples, from one end of the earth to the other, and there you shall serve other gods of wood and stone, which neither you nor your fathers have known" (Deut. 28:64; see Lev. 26:33).

The earthly blessings and curses of the Mosaic law are typological. They foreshadow the fullness of life and the fullness of destruction that await believers and unbelievers. The blessing of God is indicated in the invitation of Christ: "Come, you who are blessed by my Father, inherit the kingdom prepared for you from the foundation of the world" (Matt. 25:34). And the curse of God is evident in the command of Jesus: "Depart from me, you cursed, into the eternal fire prepared for the devil and his angels" (Matt. 25:41). In the Old Testament curses, exile from the land was a terrible consequence that portended a dreadful future. But an even worse exile is coming for the enemies of God. The historical judgments in the Old Testament are small glimpses of it.

Summary

Jesus united things in the Old Testament that had been kept separate throughout Israel's history. A priest was different from the tabernacle, which was separate from the sacrifices offered there. But Jesus is the perfect sacrifice as well as the tabernacle, and he is the high priest who offers himself. His torn flesh is the veil being ripped so that we might know the glory of God. The veil kept sinners out, but Jesus brings sinners in. He is the bronze serpent raised up so that we might live and not perish. He bore the covenant curses so that we could have the covenant blessings. He ushered in the age of atonement and jubilee, an age that will have no end.

---

11. See Johnson, *Walking with Jesus through His Word*, 64; Friedbert Ninow, *Indicators of Typology within the Old Testament: The Exodus Motif* (Frankfurt: Peter Lang, 2001), 146–48.

REFLECTION QUESTIONS

1. In what ways did the sacrificial system and Day of Atonement point to Christ?

2. How should we understand the Old Testament tabernacle/temple veil in light of the cross?

3. How does Jesus use the story about the bronze serpent in John 3:14–15?

4. Are there other historical judgments in Leviticus through Deuteronomy that foreshadow the final judgment of the wicked?

5. In what ways is Jesus a prophet like Moses?

What Types Are in Joshua through Ruth?

The books of Joshua through Ruth tell of Israel's entrance into the Promised Land and the dark years of rebellion that followed. All along, however, God was preparing a king who would rule the people. The years covered by these books were filled with conquest and compromise, rescue and ruin.

Joshua

Joshua

The man Joshua was Moses's assistant and successor (Num. 27:15–18). God told him to hold to the law and not turn from it to the right or to the left (Josh. 1:7). Joshua would lead the people into the land for conquest and inheritance. He would witness the power of God overcome cities and armies. His name meant "Yahweh is salvation," and he beheld the Lord's hand accomplish the promises made to the patriarchs. Before his death, he called the Israelites to renew their commitment to the Lord (Josh. 24).

Joshua and Jesus share the same name. The Hebrew name Joshua is equivalent to the Greek name Jesus. According to Ounsworth, "The future shapes the past, and that shaping is signalled to the Christian reader of the scriptures of Israel through the identity of names."[1] The angel told Joseph that Mary "will bear a son, and you shall call his name Jesus, for he will save his people from their sins" (Matt. 1:21). And Jesus will live up to his name. He is a true and better Joshua.[2]

---

1. Richard Ounsworth, *Joshua Typology in the New Testament* (Tübingen: Mohr Siebeck, 2012), 15.
2. See the *Epistle of Barnabas* 12; Justin Martyr, *Dialogue* 113; Rich Lusk, "Holy War Fulfilled and Transformed: A Look at Some Important New Testament Texts," in *The Glory of Kings:*

From his heart, he delighted in God's law, turning from it neither to the right nor the left. Jesus will lead the saints into the fulfillment of all God's promises.

The Scarlet Cord

In Jericho, a woman named Rahab hid Israelite spies because she believed the rumblings she had heard: that the God of the Hebrews was with his people and would give them the land of Canaan (Josh. 2:9–11). Her plea to the spies was that the coming judgment upon the land would pass over her and her household, "that you will save alive my father and mother, my brothers and sisters, and all who belong to them, and deliver our lives from death" (Josh. 2:13). The spies told her to "tie this scarlet cord in the window through which you let us down" (Josh. 2:18), and then the Israelites would pass over her home when they saw the scarlet cord.

The symbol of the scarlet cord was reminiscent of the Passover, and forward-looking to the cross. In Exodus, the Israelites were to put blood on the doorposts so that judgment would pass by (Exod. 12:23), and in Joshua, the family of Rahab would be spared from judgment because a scarlet cord was put in a window (Josh. 2:18). Like the Passover, the placing of the scarlet cord foreshadows the cross, where the blood of Christ brought atonement for sinners and thereby spared from judgment all who come to Christ in faith.

Entrance into the Promised Land

Under the leadership of Joshua, the Israelites finally entered the Promised Land. They crossed the Jordan River on dry ground and walked into Canaan (Josh. 3:14–17). Entrance into the land was the culmination of a long journey. The Israelites—now comprised of the second generation that grew up in the wilderness over four decades—were ready to receive their inheritance.

As significant as entering the Promised Land was, the entrance could be reversed by exile. Occupying the land was not a permanent situation. This entrance foreshadowed the new creation into which Jesus, the new and greater Joshua, will lead his people. "For the crossing of the Jordan and the subsequent renewal of the Mosaic covenant and conquest of the Land of Canaan was only a shadowy image of the true fulfilment of God's promises to Abraham and his descendants."[3] The Promised Land was flowing with milk and honey, but there is "a better country" in store for God's people (Heb. 11:16). Joshua was unable to provide the Israelites the "rest" they needed (Heb. 4:8). Our hope is for a better rest in a better land.

A Festschrift in Honor of James B. Jordan, eds. Peter J. Leithart and John Barach (Eugene, OR: Pickwick, 2011), 75, 90; Edmund P. Clowney, The Unfolding Mystery: Discovering Christ in the Old Testament (Phillipsburg, NJ: P&R, 1988), 134–35.

3.   Ounsworth, Joshua Typology in the New Testament, 175.

The Conquest of the Promised Land

The Promised Land was not vacant when the Israelites arrived. And hostile peoples within Canaan prepared to engage the people of God in battle. Inheriting the land would come through conquest. The Israelites were to exercise dominion over the enemies of God and subdue them (Josh. 1:14–15). Rulers were conquered, armies were routed, fortresses were brought down. In the southern and the northern parts of Canaan, the conquest by Israel unfolded (see Josh. 10–12).

When Jesus began his earthly ministry, he too had come for conquest, though his conquering was not of earthly armies and cities.[4] He performed signs and wonders against the powers of darkness and the effects of the curse. He came to conquer demons, the devil, disease, and death (Mark 1–3; 5). He did miracles in the southern part of the Promised Land and in the north, moving as a greater Joshua and true Israel. He came to exercise dominion, and nothing could resist his word. Winds ceased, demons left, sight returned, and death buckled. Greidanus notes that "Christ conquers Satan's stronghold (cf. Matt. 12:28–29; Rev. 20:2–3) and opens the way for his people into the new creation."[5] The conquest of Christ continues now through the proclamation of the gospel and building of his church.[6] At the right hand of God, he is King of kings and Lord of lords. All enemies will be put under his feet (1 Cor. 15:25).

Judges–Ruth

The Judges

In the last chapters of Judges, the author notes that there was no king in Israel, and so everyone did what was right in their own eyes (see Judg. 17:6; 18:1; 19:1; 21:25). The Israelites were in the Promised Land, but they did not have a leader. This period of Israel's history was characterized by rebellion, subjugation, repentance, and rescue: the people rebelled; God raised up an enemy to overcome them; the Israelites would then repent, and God would raise up a judge to deliver them. The judges were military leaders, predecessors to Israel's kings.

The role of judge is a type of Christ.[7] Jesus is the king whom the judges ultimately point to, and he is the rescuer that sinners need. The judges arrived on the scene when Israel's sin had reaped subjugation, and the judge came to save them. Judges were saviors and warriors. And in the fullness of time, Christ our warrior-judge came to deliver us by reaping what we had sown: the wrath of God.

---

4. See Lusk, "Holy War Fulfilled and Transformed," 80. Clowney, *Unfolding Mystery*, 133.
5. Sidney Greidanus, *Preaching Christ from the Old Testament: A Contemporary Hermeneutical Method* (Grand Rapids: Eerdmans, 1999), 341.
6. See the discussion in Ounsworth, *Joshua Typology in the New Testament*, 167.
7. See Greidanus, *Preaching Christ from the Old Testament*, 260.

Gideon

Gideon came from "the weakest" clan in Manasseh, and he was "the least" in his father's house (Judg. 6:15). Yet the angel of Yahweh declared that Gideon would strike the Midianites (Judg. 6:16). After an altar to Baal was broken, men of the town came out against Gideon, saying to his father, "Bring out your son, that he may die" (Judg. 6:30). Yet God was with Gideon, and "the Spirit of the LORD clothed Gideon" (Judg. 6:34). The Lord would save Israel by Gideon's hand (Judg. 6:36). When Gideon went against the Midianites, he had an army of a mere three hundred men (Judg. 7:6–8). Gideon had seventy sons, and one was named Abimelech (Judg. 8:30–31). The name Abimelech means "my father is king."

Despite the meaning of Abimelech's name, Gideon was not a king, but he foreshadowed the future king of God's people. Christ was clothed with the Spirit for all that God had set him apart to do. He was born in the small town of Bethlehem, and he grew up in Nazareth. Like Gideon, Jesus came from what seemed to be the least and the weakest of places. Could anything good come out of Nazareth (John 1:46)? The mission of Christ provoked opposition from others, but he persevered in what God gave him to say and do. His journey to the cross was characterized by weakness that seemed outmatched in every way by the resolve of the Jewish leaders and the zeal of the Roman soldiers, similar to how Gideon's army of three hundred seemed outmatched by the Midianites. Yet the apparent inequity only served to highlight God's power and wisdom. Though their numbers were unimpressive, Gideon's army was victorious (Judg. 7:19–25). And Christ, though apparently the latest victim of Roman crucifixion, became triumphant over all.

Samson

Not often in Scripture do we get a birth narrative of a character. Out of all the judges in the book of Judges, only Samson's story begins with a birth narrative. His mother had been barren, until an angel of the Lord appeared to her and said, "Behold, you are barren and have not borne children, but you shall conceive and bear a son" (Judg. 13:3). The angel told her, "No razor shall come upon his head, for the child shall be a Nazirite to God from the womb, and he shall begin to save Israel from the hand of the Philistines" (Judg. 13:5). The woman bore a son and called him Samson (Judg. 13:24). He was a mighty judge, overcoming enemies by unparalleled strength. Samson confided the importance of his hair to Delilah, who facilitated his defeat (Judg. 16:19–21). But the defeat was only temporary. His hair regrew, and he seized the opportunity to overcome the enemies of God. Grasping pillars nearby, he pulled the house down upon everyone inside, including himself (Judg. 16:22, 29–30). Incredibly, "the dead whom he killed at his death were more than those whom he had killed during his life" (Judg. 16:30).

With the New Testament Gospels of Matthew and Luke, we get birth narratives about Jesus (Matt. 1–2; Luke 1–2). We learn that his conception was miraculous and that he was set apart to accomplish salvation. While his enemies believed they finally defeated him, his "defeat" was only temporary. Through his death and resurrection, he was vindicated and victorious. Jesus, who fulfilled the role of a warrior-judge, was a true and greater Samson.[8] He took the pillars of sin and Satan and tore them down. Whereas Samson's death brought death to many, Jesus's death brought life to many.

The Kinsman-Redeemer

Loss and indebtedness could leave Israelites in terrible straits. According to Leviticus 25, a relative known as a "kinsman-redeemer" could bring relief to a relative's situation at cost to himself. He would act with a redemptive aim. Prior to Leviticus 25, only God had been called a redeemer (see Exod. 6:6). He redeemed the captive Israelites from the oppressive Egyptians. And in Leviticus 25 we learn that Israelites could imitate the Lord and redeem the situation of a family member. The book of Ruth tells the story of how a kinsman-redeemer brought relief and restoration to women facing destitution.

Jesus is the ultimate fulfillment of the kinsman-redeemer role.[9] He has looked upon the desperate situation of sinners and has acted with redemption. Paul says, "Christ redeemed us from the curse of the law by becoming a curse for us" (Gal. 3:13). Since a kinsman-redeemer sacrificed his own time and resources, we can affirm that Christ acted in the most sacrificial way possible, that he might redeem us. He laid down his own life, drinking the cup of God's justice. He who had no sin became sin for us. In Jesus's words to his disciples, "For even the Son of Man came not to be served but to serve, and to give his life as a ransom for many" (Mark 10:45). On the cross, Christ was our ransom, our kinsman-redeemer.

Boaz

Boaz was a redeemer from Bethlehem. He is the hero of the book of Ruth, stepping into the kinsman-redeemer role to aid Ruth and Naomi (Ruth 3:13; 4:9–10). Before marrying Ruth the Moabite, Boaz had already acted with kindness and generosity toward her (Ruth 2:15–16; 3:15). His actions showed that he kept the Law of Moses, but his behavior toward Ruth even surpassed what the Law required. He had an honorable reputation in the eyes of others, and he affirmed Ruth's integrity and dignity as well (Ruth 3:10–11, 14).

Jesus is a true and greater Boaz.[10] Jesus is our redeemer from Bethlehem, who kept the law of Moses and fulfilled it (Matt. 5:17). His earthly ministry was

---

8. See Benjamin Keach, *Preaching from the Types and Metaphors of the Bible* (1855; repr., Grand Rapids: Kregel, 1972), 977. Clowney, *Unfolding Mystery*, 13–15, 136–42.

9. See A. M. Hodgkin, *Christ in All the Scriptures* (London: Pickering & Inglis, 1909), 61.

10. See Mitchell L. Chase, "A True and Greater Boaz: Typology and Jesus in the Book of Ruth," *Southern Baptist Journal of Theology* 21, no. 1 (Spring 2017): 85–96.

characterized with kindness and generosity, acting in the best interests of others as he looked upon their needs and hardships (Mark 7:24—8:10). His integrity was unmatched. He, like Boaz, took a bride from among the nations, for the church (his bride) consists of every nation, tribe, and tongue (Rev. 7:9–14).

The Birth of Obed

The book of Ruth opens with Naomi being emptied through loss and grief and ends with Naomi being restored (Ruth 1:3–5; 4:14–15). The birth of Boaz and Ruth's child was the restoration of the family line that had ceased when Naomi's husband and sons died. The new child, named Obed, was a son and sign of hope. Women told Naomi, "He shall be to you a restorer of life and a nourisher of your old age, for your daughter-in-law who loves you, who is more to you than seven sons, has given birth to him" (Ruth 4:15). The end of the book is a genealogy. We learn that Obed fathered Jesse, and Jesse fathered David (Ruth 4:22).

In the days of the judges, God was preparing a king, and the story of Ruth contributes to that preparation (Ruth 1:1; 4:22). Jesus would be a redeemer from Bethlehem of Judah, and he descended from a line that, centuries earlier, crossed through Bethlehem and the family of Boaz (Matt. 1:5; Luke 2:4–7). The birth of Obed brought restoration and joy, and the birth of Jesus would bring that and much more.

Summary

Israel entered the Promised Land but lacked a king. The intervening years were dark, but God was still at work. The conquest had been crucial, but it did not remedy the hearts of the people. When the people strayed and repented, judges rose to deliver them—yet these temporary warriors could not establish a lasting hope for God's people. The types in the books of Joshua, Judges, and Ruth continued to light the path leading to Jesus. The people of God needed a Joshua who could lead them, a Samson who could defend them, and a Boaz who could redeem them. And when Jesus came, we got everything we needed.

REFLECTION QUESTIONS

1. What are the correspondences between Joshua and Jesus?

2. How can the scarlet cord in Rahab's window point to Christ?

3. How do the warrior-judges foreshadow the Savior?

4. Can you think of particular judges whose stories typify Christ?

5. Why should we consider Boaz a type of Christ?

What Types Are in 1 Samuel through 2 Chronicles?

The books of 1 Samuel through 2 Chronicles tell the rise of Israel's monarchy, the division of the kingdom, and the fall of the nation under a foreign power. The promises and covenants of God seem to be coming apart at the seams, but the abundance of types show us that God was at work the whole time, overtly and covertly, advancing his plan for the sake of the world.

1–2 Samuel

Samuel

The story about Samuel begins with his parents, specifically his barren mother Hannah. By the power of God, she and her husband conceived and gave birth to Samuel (1 Sam. 1:20). Ministering to the Lord under the supervision of Eli, Samuel learned to be a priest. A word from the Lord came by a man to Eli: "And I will raise up for myself a faithful priest, who shall do according to what is in my heart and in my mind. And I will build him a sure house, and he shall go in and out before my anointed forever" (1 Sam. 2:35). In addition to this, the Lord established Samuel as a prophet (1 Sam. 3:20). And furthermore, after the ark returned to Israel, Samuel was a judge in Israel the rest of his life (1 Sam. 7:15). Altogether, then, Samuel was a man who had multiple roles—prophet, priest, and judge.[1]

Jesus was born because of a miraculous conception (Luke 1:35). Like Samuel, Jesus held multiple roles. Jesus was the consummate prophet, perfect priest, and promised king (which the role of a judge foreshadowed). While the reader of 1 Samuel is prepared to see the boy Samuel as the fulfillment of the prophecy about a faithful priest (see 1 Sam. 2:35; 3:1–18), ultimately

---

1. See A. M. Hodgkin, *Christ in All the Scriptures* (London: Pickering & Inglis, 1909), 65.

Samuel is a type of Christ. Only Christ would be able to "do according to what is in my heart and in my mind" (1 Sam. 2:35). God was with Samuel as he grew, and God showed favor to Jesus as well (1 Sam. 3:19; Luke 2:40, 52). Incredibly, the Lord let none of Samuel's words "fall to the ground" (1 Sam. 3:19). And if Samuel's words were so sure and trustworthy, how much more trustworthy and sure were the words of Christ! No matter what Jesus spoke, his words never hit the ground.

The Capture and Return of the Ark

Philistines, the enemies of Israel, captured the ark of God and sent it around to different places in Philistia. No matter where the captured ark went, however, it caused havoc for the Philistines. In Ashdod, the Philistines discovered their god Dagon facedown with broken parts (1 Sam. 5:4). In Gath, men of the city developed tumors (1 Sam. 5:9). In Ekron, tumors broke out on men there too (1 Sam. 5:12). The exile of the ark was a journey that brought great panic and harm to the enemies of God. The Philistines finally sent the ark back to the Israelites (1 Sam. 6:11–15).

The capture and return of the ark was a type of Christ's death and resurrection. The ark represents God's presence, and Christ was the fullness of deity in bodily form (Col. 2:9). Though Christ's opponents believed that his arrest, suffering, and death were desirable and advantageous, in reality they were assaulting the Son of God and sowing judgment for themselves. Though Christ seemed to be conquered at the cross, he was actually conquering *through* the cross. Like the ark, Jesus returned vindicated—a return through resurrection (John 20:1–10). Moreover, his ascension mocked the dark powers (1 Peter 3:19). Jesus "has gone into heaven and is at the right hand of God, with angels, authorities, and powers having been subjected to him" (1 Peter 3:22).

David

David was a boy from Bethlehem who grew up to be king. The youngest of Jesse's sons, David seemed least likely to be a candidate for the monarchy. He was out shepherding sheep when Samuel showed up at the house (1 Sam. 16:11). But when Samuel saw young David, he anointed him, and suddenly the Spirit of the Lord was upon David from that day forward (1 Sam. 16:13). David was a man after God's own heart (see Acts 13:22). But like the couple in the garden of Eden, David saw something he desired yet should not have taken (2 Sam. 11:1–5). He was tempted and fell into sin.

Jesus was a true and greater David.[2] Born in Bethlehem, he was God's Anointed One, the Messiah, who would be king (Luke 2:1–7). David was his

---

2. See Sidney Greidanus, *Preaching Christ from the Old Testament: A Contemporary Hermeneutical Method* (Grand Rapids: Eerdmans, 1999), 251–52. Benjamin Keach, *Preaching from the Types and Metaphors of the Bible* (1855; repr., Grand Rapids: Kregel,

ancestor (Matt. 1:1–17). The Spirit was upon Jesus for his ministry (Matt. 3:16–17). Jesus spoke and did all that the Father gave him to say and do (John 5:19; 17:8). Unlike David, Jesus overcame all temptation and never sinned. Through his life of devotion, Jesus was truly a man after God's heart.

The Defeat of Goliath

Goliath was a Philistine who taunted the Israelites and dared anyone to fight him. David, the young man whom Samuel had anointed, stepped up to the challenge. Though Goliath mocked David's size and lack of proper weaponry (1 Sam. 17:42–43), David did not waver. He was incensed at Goliath's blasphemy, and he determined to defend God's honor (1 Sam. 17:45–47). David ran toward the giant warrior, removing a stone and slinging it into the Philistine's forehead (1 Sam. 17:49). The seed of the woman had triumphed over the seed of the serpent, with a head-crushing result (see Gen. 3:15).[3]

David's defeat of Goliath foreshadowed the victory of Christ over his enemies.[4] Jesus, the seed of the woman, had come to battle the serpent and conquer the powers of darkness (Mark 3:27; John 12:31). Though looking inept and unprepared, Jesus knew that the hour of his death would simultaneously be the fulfillment of his earthly mission (John 17:1). The victory at the cross surpassed the defeat of Goliath. We honor Christ, our mighty warrior, who crushed the head of his enemies.

Jerusalem

David endowed the city of Jerusalem with great significance. First, he defeated the Jebusite inhabitants, and second, he ordered that the ark be brought to Jerusalem (2 Sam. 5:6–7; 6:2–4, 16–17). Jerusalem would be known as the city of David (2 Sam. 5:9). Jerusalem was where the kings from David's line would reign, and it would be the place where Solomon built the temple (1 Kings 6–8). Jerusalem was known as Mount Zion and the city on a hill.

But the glory of Jerusalem would not last. Eventually the city was set ablaze by the Babylonians, with the temple and palace and houses destroyed (2 Kings 25). As great as Jerusalem was, it was also a sign of the city to come, the new

---

1972), 977–78; James M. Hamilton Jr., "The Typology of David's Rise to Power: Messianic Patterns in the Book of Samuel," *Southern Baptist Journal of Theology* 16, no. 2 (Summer 2012): 4–25.

3. See Peter J. Leithart, *A House for My Name: A Survey of the Old Testament* (Moscow, ID: Canon, 2000), 142; Hamilton, "Typology of David's Rise to Power," 4–25.

4. Edmund P. Clowney, *The Unfolding Mystery: Discovering Christ in the Old Testament* (Phillipsburg, NJ: P&R, 1988), 13–14. See Peter J. Leithart, "The Quadriga or Something Like It: A Biblical and Pastoral Defense," in *Ancient Faith for the Church's Future*, eds. Mark Husbands and Jeffrey P. Greenman (Downers Grove, IL: IVP Academic, 2008), 122–24.

Jerusalem.[5] While David and Solomon made Jerusalem great, better is "the city that has foundations, whose designer and builder is God" (Heb. 11:10). The earthly Jerusalem had renown far and wide, but better is "the city of the living God, the heavenly Jerusalem" (Heb. 12:22). Though Jerusalem was the city of David, who was a man after God's own heart, sin was within its walls and inside the hearts of its people. Better will be "the holy city, new Jerusalem, coming down out of heaven from God" (Rev. 21:2), where "death shall be no more, neither shall there be mourning, nor crying, nor pain anymore" (Rev. 21:4).

The Office of King

Israel had a series of kings from the tribe of Judah, descending from David. God promised a perpetual kingship. Through Nathan the prophet, God said to David, "When your days are fulfilled and you lie down with your fathers, I will raise up your offspring after you, who shall come from your body, and I will establish his kingdom. He shall build a house for my name, and I will establish the throne of his kingdom forever" (2 Sam. 7:12–13). God's promise was that a future son of David would enjoy an unending reign.

Jesus fulfilled the kingship. Paul told the Romans that Jesus "was descended from David according to the flesh" (Rom. 1:3). Matthew's Gospel began with the announcement that Jesus was "the son of David" (Matt. 1:1). As Jesus went toward Jerusalem on the first day of his passion week, people shouted "Hosanna to the Son of David!" (Matt. 21:9). A heavenly elder told John that Jesus is "the Lion of the tribe of Judah, the Root of David" (Rev. 5:5). One of John's visions of Christ was as a victor with the name "King of kings and Lord of lords" upon his thigh (Rev. 19:16). Based on the Old Testament promise to David, the sons of David foreshadowed the Son of David who would rule forever. The Old Testament doesn't name this Son, but the New Testament calls him Jesus.

1 Kings–2 Chronicles

Solomon

As David's son who became king, Solomon gave hope to the future of Israel. Solomon was wiser than any other king (1 Kings 3:12; 4:29–30), he exercised dominion in peace (1 Kings 4:24), he showed knowledge of plants and animals (1 Kings 4:33), and his reputation caused people from other nations to come hear his wisdom (1 Kings 4:34). "Like David, Solomon is a new and improved Adam."[6] He built a temple for God, fulfilling what his father David had wanted to do (1 Kings 5–8).

---

5. See T. Desmond Alexander, *The City of God and the Goal of Creation*, Short Studies in Biblical Theology (Wheaton, IL: Crossway, 2018), 38–42, 163–67.
6. Leithart, *House for My Name*, 153.

Solomon was a type of Christ. Once Jesus came, Solomon was no longer the wisest person who ever lived. Jesus, the Son of David, was "greater than Solomon" (Matt. 12:42). People throughout the Promised Land heard Jesus teach, and many expressed astonishment at his authority (Mark 1:27–28; 12:37). Like Solomon, Jesus would build a temple, with people of the church being "living stones" who are "built up as a spiritual house" (1 Peter 2:5). "Both in his glory and in his failures, Solomon points us to the greater Son of David, Jesus Christ."[7]

The Temple

The temple was better than the tabernacle, for the temple was fixed in one spot instead of portable; and it was located in Jerusalem, the chosen city (see 1 Kings 5–8). The temple communicated that God wanted to dwell with his people, and it also symbolized that sin was a barrier between sinners and a righteous God. The presence of the temple was what made Jerusalem a city set apart for God. No other city on earth had a sanctuary where God revealed his glory behind the veil concealing the Most Holy Place.

Jesus once spoke about the temple in a way that shocked his Jewish contemporaries: "Destroy this temple, and in three days I will raise it up" (John 2:19). The Jews objected that he could accomplish that feat in such a short span of time. But the temple existed for a typological purpose. Jesus "was speaking about the temple of his body" (John 2:21). Jesus said that "something greater than the temple is here" (Matt. 12:6). Tearing down the temple and raising it back up was imagery for the death and resurrection of Jesus.[8] And not only does the temple anticipate the Lord, it also anticipates his church. Because of our union with Christ through faith, temple language can be applied to us: the church is a temple (1 Cor. 6:19).

Elijah

Elijah was a prophet who spoke boldly and worked miracles. He raised a boy from the dead (1 Kings 17), called upon the Lord to rain down fire from heaven (1 Kings 18), parted the water of the Jordan River (2 Kings 2), and ascended to heaven (2 Kings 2). Not every prophet in the Old Testament was associated with wonders, so the plethora of wonders in Elijah's ministry is significant. Elijah's bold and authoritative words led to resistance from others, and Jezebel sought his life.

Jesus was a true and greater Elijah.[9] For Jesus's contemporaries, the resurrections he performed would naturally evoke the stories of Elijah. When

---

7. Leithart, *House for My Name*, 157.
8. See Leithart, *House for My Name*, 253–54.
9. See Leonhard Goppelt, *TYPOS: The Typological Interpretation of the Old Testament in the New* (Grand Rapids: Eerdmans, 1982), 71.

Jesus went into the waters of the Jordan, his Father spoke with delight and the Spirit descended in power. The many miracles in Jesus's ministry far exceeded those of Elijah's ministry. Like Elijah, Jesus spoke boldly and with authority, provoking resistance and opposition from those who didn't support what he said or what he did. While Elijah is a type of Christ, he also corresponds to John the Baptist, who was the forerunner of the Messiah (see Mal. 4:5; Matt. 11:14). Elijah and John both wore a garment of hair and a leather belt (2 Kings 1:8; Mark 1:6), and they both were opposed by a royal figure (1 Kings 19; Mark 6:19–25). But the end of Elijah and John's lives are not parallel. Elijah ascended to God, and in this sense Elijah is a type of Christ, for Jesus ascended to the right hand of God (Heb. 1:3).[10]

Elisha

Elisha had an even greater ministry than his predecessor Elijah. He had asked Elisha, "Please let there be a double portion of your spirit on me" (2 Kings 2:9). After Elijah ascended, Elisha parted the Jordan River and crossed over (2 Kings 2:12–14). While Elijah raised one person from death, Elisha had two resurrections associated with him (2 Kings 4:18–37; 13:21). He also remedied a poisonous pot of stew (2 Kings 4:40–41) and multiplied twenty loaves of bread for a hundred people (2 Kings 4:42–44). By following Elisha's instructions, a Gentile named Naaman was healed of leprosy.

Jesus was a true and better Elisha.[11] As Elisha was greater than his predecessor, Jesus was greater than his forerunner. John the Baptist had to decrease as Jesus increased (John 3:30). Jesus raised more people from the dead than Elisha (Mark 5:38–43; Luke 7:11–17; John 11:38–44), he multiplied fewer loaves to a greater number of people (John 6:1–15), and he healed people from leprosy (Mark 1:40–45). His miracles were upon both Jews and Gentiles, and his wonders surpassed any miracle-working prophet of the Old Testament.

Hezekiah

Hezekiah was a son of David and ruled in Jerusalem, but he became ill and neared the point of death (2 Kings 20:1). Hezekiah prayed to the Lord, and the Lord answered his prayer by sparing him from death: "Behold, I will heal you. On the third day you shall go up to the house of the LORD, and I will add fifteen years to your life" (2 Kings 20:5–6). This third-day deliverance meant a longer reign as king in Judah.

---

10. See Keach, *Types and Metaphors of the Bible*, 979; Matthew Barrett, *Canon, Covenant and Christology: Rethinking Jesus and the Scriptures of Israel*, New Studies in Biblical Theology, vol. 51 (Downers Grove, IL: IVP Academic, 2020), 131–34.
11. See Keach, *Types and Metaphors of the Bible*, 979; Hodgkin, *Christ in All the Scriptures*, 76–77.

Jesus, the promised Son of David, came not merely to the point of death but entered death itself. And he experienced a third-day deliverance (1 Cor. 15:4). Jesus is a true and greater Hezekiah. Jesus's healing was resurrection in a glorified body, the firstfruits of the coming resurrection for us all (1 Cor. 15:20). Jesus's third-day deliverance did not simply extend his reign; it solidified his reign eternally. By overcoming death, Jesus possesses indestructible life.

Josiah

Josiah, the king of Judah in Jerusalem, did what was right in the eyes of the Lord, walking in the good ways of David (2 Chron. 34:1–2). As a young man, he sought the God of David, and he determined to purge the idols from Judah, for he was zealous for God's glory. His focus on cleansing the land also involved repairing the temple (2 Chron. 34:8). When the book of the Law was discovered in the temple, Josiah read it and realized the wrath of God that was coming because of disobedience to God's Law (2 Chron. 34:15, 19, 21). Josiah committed to keep God's commandments with all his heart and soul (2 Chron. 34:31). This obedience included the keeping of Passover (2 Chron. 35:1, 16–17).

As a young man, Jesus honored God and had zeal for God's glory. He lived in a manner pleasing to God and did what was right (Mark 1:11). The wonders of Christ conquered the land and the effects of sin. He loved God's law and delighted in it as he kept it (Matt. 5:17). He loved God with all his heart and soul. Jesus is a true and better Josiah. He traveled to Jerusalem for Israel's feasts, including Passover. The day came, in fact, when he did not merely keep Passover—he fulfilled it (1 Cor. 5:7). For all the good that Josiah achieved for the people, he was still a king who died. Jesus is our king who lives.

Jehoiachin

The horrors of foreign opposition reached a threshold in the reign of King Jehoiachin of Judah. Jehoiachin surrendered himself to King Nebuchadnezzar and became his prisoner (2 Kings 24:11–12). During this time, Nebuchadnezzar raided and carried off the treasures of God's temple and the king's palace (2 Kings 24:13). Jehoiachin went into captivity and exile, from Jerusalem to Babylon (2 Kings 24:15). But Jehoiachin's life took an unexpected turn when Evil-merodach became king of Babylon. The new king released Jehoiachin from prison and gave him a seat above the other seats of kings who were in Babylon as well (2 Kings 25:27–28). Jehoiachin took off his prison garments, dining the rest of his life at the king's table (2 Kings 25:29–30).

Jesus is a true and greater Jehoiachin. While glories and treasures were lost under Jehoiachin, glories and treasures were regained under Christ—only better. He purchased a people from every nation, tribe, and tongue, securing their eternal atonement and pardon (Rev. 7:9–14). Jesus had been taken captive and led outside the city of Jerusalem to die upon a rugged cross. But on the third day, things took an expected turn: the body of Christ was freed from the clutches of death, and Christ removed his grave garments. As joint heirs with Christ through faith, we will eat with him from the table of the Lord (Matt. 8:11; Mark 14:25).

Cyrus

When the Israelites dwelled in Babylonian captivity for decades, at last the end of exile was near. God "stirred up the spirit of Cyrus king of Persia" (2 Chron. 36:22), who would be God's appointed deliverer. Cyrus conquered Babylon (see Dan. 5), and he permitted the Israelite exiles to return to the Promised Land (2 Chron. 36:23).

Cyrus would not be the last man of liberation for God's people. Cyrus was a type of Christ. In the first century AD and from the village of Nazareth, there emerged a man who said he had come to bring freedom for the captives (Luke 4:16–24). Jesus was the great emancipator, freeing slaves from sin and bringing them out of darkness into his marvelous light (1 Peter 2:9). While Cyrus was the political deliverer the people needed, Jesus was the true Savior the people needed.

Summary

The books of 1 Samuel through 2 Chronicles tell the rise of kings and prophets, and we see the importance of Jerusalem and the temple that was built there. The spiraling of God's people toward destruction is a discouraging storyline to follow, but 2 Chronicles ends with Cyrus, a figure of hope. Through many years, the promises and hopes seemed bleak. But not even the exile meant all hope was lost. These types remind us that God does some of his best work in the dark.

REFLECTION QUESTIONS

1. How can the capture and return of the ark of the covenant function as a type?

2. How does David's defeat of Goliath connect to the person and work of Christ?

3. Given the importance of the city of Jerusalem, what does it foreshadow?

4. How are the ministries of Elijah and Elisha typological?

5. How does Cyrus the Persian serve as a type of Christ?

What Types Are in Ezra through Esther?

The books of Ezra, Nehemiah, and Esther bring the Old Testament narrative to a close. Israel has returned from exile and rebuilt the temple, yet the hearts of the people need to be built up and strengthened. In fact, not every exile returned to the Promised Land. While Cyrus had granted permission to return, some Israelites chose to remain outside the land. During the years spanning these books, key characters and events anticipated the person and work of God's Messiah.

Ezra–Nehemiah

The Return from Exile

When Cyrus decreed that the Israelites were freed from captivity, he permitted them to return to the Promised Land and rebuild Jerusalem and the temple (Ezra 1:2–3). The freedom from Babylonian captivity was a new exodus, like the exodus that led them out of Egyptian captivity (Exod. 12). In Ezekiel 37, the return from exile was like resurrection from the dead, because the exile from the land had been the death of the nation.

The greatest return from exile was the redemptive work of Jesus upon the cross and his victory of resurrection. His death would bring liberation to sin's captives.[1] His resurrection would bring hope to those bound in the darkness of despair. As much as the return from Israel's exile was an exodus, the work of Jesus was the launching of the greatest exodus from the deepest exile (Luke 9:31).[2] Exile began in the early chapters of Genesis, when Adam and Eve were

---

1. See A. M. Hodgkin, *Christ in All the Scriptures* (London: Pickering & Inglis, 1909), 90–91.
2. In Luke 9:31, Moses and Elijah appeared with Jesus and "spoke of his departure, which he was about to accomplish at Jerusalem." The word "departure" is *exodus*.

sent from the garden sanctuary (Gen. 3:24). But Jesus's death and resurrection were good news to spiritual exiles that God had made a way to reconcile sinners to himself fully, finally, and forever.

Zerubbabel

The man who led the first wave of returning exiles back to Jerusalem was Zerubbabel (Ezra 2:1–2). Leading the exiles out of Babylonian captivity is reminiscent of Moses's work in Exodus when he led the Israelites out of Egyptian captivity. Zerubbabel was another Moses, leading another exodus, heading to God's Promised Land. It was time to rebuild the temple. Zerubbabel joined in the work of building the altar to offer burnt sacrifices on it (Ezra 3:2), and then builders laid the foundation of the temple (Ezra 3:10–11). Zerubbabel is not just a leader in rebuilding the temple; he is also from David's line. Zerubbabel is a son of David. God said, "I will take you, O Zerubbabel my servant, the son of Shealtiel, declares the LORD, and make you like a signet ring, for I have chosen you, declares the LORD of hosts" (Hag. 2:23).

Zerubbabel is a type of Christ.[3] Jesus is the Son of David who descended from Zerubbabel and fulfilled the promise of 2 Samuel 7:12–13. Jesus is also a Son of David who builds a temple. Not only is his body a temple which will undergo destruction through death and then rebuilding through resurrection, Jesus will build his temple, the church, and the gates of hell will not prevail against him (Matt. 16:18; 1 Peter 2:5). Jesus is the signet ring of the Lord, chosen as the cornerstone for God's end-time temple. Like Zerubbabel, Jesus leads an exodus as the greatest return commences through the proclamation of the gospel to the ends of the earth.

Ezra

Ezra was a priest of Levi's tribe, though first he lived in Babylon. He decided to go to the Promised Land, to Jerusalem (Ezra 7:8–9). His desire was threefold: to study the law of the Lord, to do the law of the Lord, and to teach the law of the Lord (Ezra 7:10). When he traveled to the land of Israel, thousands of exiles joined him on the journey. Ezra was grieved over the idolatrous marriages he saw (Ezra 9:2–3), and he interceded for the people (9:6–15). The book "presents Ezra as a new Moses and the return from exile as a new Exodus. Of course, like the rest of Israel's history, these stories are not intended to say that salvation has finally and fully arrived, but that these

---

3.   See Aubrey Sequeria and Samuel C. Emadi, "Biblical-Theological Exegesis and the Nature of Typology," *Southern Baptist Journal of Theology* 21, no. 1 (Spring 2017): 25; Benjamin Keach, *Preaching from the Types and Metaphors of the Bible* (1855; repr., Grand Rapids: Kregel, 1972), 979.

leaders and events in Israel's history point forward to the climactic event of salvation that comes in the person and work of Jesus Christ."[4]

Jesus is our true and greater Ezra.[5] He journeyed from heaven to earth, coming to proclaim God's word and the kingdom to all who would hear him. The heart of Christ loved the law of God, and he did not come to abolish it but to fulfill it (Matt. 5:17). Jesus came to lead the exiles home, doing so through the cross and the empty tomb. During his earthly ministry, Jesus saw the wickedness and unbelief of sinners as he traveled. Ezra was grieved by what he saw in Jerusalem, and Jesus expressed sorrow over that beloved city as well: "O Jerusalem, Jerusalem, the city that kills the prophets and stones those who are sent to it! How often would I have gathered your children together as a hen gathers her brood under her wings, and you would not?" (Matt. 23:37). Yet Jesus was and is our mighty intercessor and effective priest. Jesus prays and mediates for us, and the Father will not turn away his Son.

Nehemiah

A contemporary of Ezra, Nehemiah desired to journey to the Promised Land. Nehemiah was a cupbearer to the Persian king, and one day he asked permission to go bring restoration to the city of Jerusalem (Neh. 1:3–5; 2:1–8). Specifically, Nehemiah wanted to rebuild the broken walls around the city. Nearly a hundred years earlier, the first wave of Israelites had returned from exile. But the walls still lay in ruins. Nehemiah faced conspiracy and opposition against his work (Neh. 4–6), but he and his fellow builders persevered. Out of love for the Israelites, Nehemiah confronted their sin, especially their idolatrous marriages and corrupt priests (Neh. 13).

Jesus, despite conspiracy and opposition levied against him, persevered in the work of redemption he came to do (Mark 3:6). Jerusalem would be the focus of his work at the climax of his earthly ministry (Mark 11:1). Like Nehemiah, Jesus came not to be served but to serve (Mark 10:45). Jesus came because of a world oppressed by the ravages of sin and the curse. Jesus came to the perishing that they might be saved, for he saw their sin and their helpless estate.

Rebuilding of the Walls

One purpose of a city's walls was protection. When the Babylonian army had demolished the walls around Jerusalem, the city's vulnerability was seen and exploited. Over a century after Cyrus the Persian permitted Israelite exiles to return to their land, the ruined walls still needed to be rebuilt. The state

---

4. See Peter J. Link Jr. and Matthew Y. Emerson, "Searching for the Second Adam: Typological Connections between Adam, Joseph, Mordecai, and Daniel," *Southern Baptist Journal of Theology* 21, no. 1 (Spring 2017): 138.

5. See Hodgkin, *Christ in All the Scriptures*, 93–94.

of the walls symbolized the state of the people in the land: the people needed to be rebuilt as well, from the inside out. The task of Nehemiah was not easy, but he and his team completed the walls in fifty-two days (Neh. 6:15).

The rebuilding of Jerusalem's walls is an act of restoration and renewal, and ultimately it is a type of Christ's achievement upon the cross and the hope of new creation when he returns. We are broken because of sin, and creation groans for its redemption (Rom. 8:20–22). We have seen how Jesus spoke of his own body being torn down and rebuilt like a temple (John 2:19–21), and the same truth, by analogy, is in view with the walls. Christ has come to bring restoration and resurrection, and stories like Nehemiah's work of restoration leaves us hoping for all things to be made new.

Esther

Esther

Esther was a Jew who was providentially positioned to intervene for her fellow Jews. Her older cousin Mordecai told her, "For if you keep silent at this time, relief and deliverance will rise for the Jews from another place, but you and your father's house will perish. And who knows whether you have not come to the kingdom for such a time as this?" (Esther 4:14). Esther agreed to consider how her position could result in deliverance for her people. She said, "And if I perish, I perish" (Esther 4:16). She approached her husband (the king) on the third day, and she was spared from death (Esther 5:1). She invited the king and Haman to two banquets, where at last she exposed Haman's plot (Esther 5:1–8; 7:1–6). Through Esther's courage and actions, the plans against the Jews were foiled.

Jesus is a true and greater Esther.[6] He did not remain silent or dispassionate when the world was under the just condemnation of God (John 3:16–17). He came to save sinners. In the providence of God, he laid down his life and perished according to plan, but he experienced a third-day deliverance. Because of his courage and actions, he made atonement once for all, foiling the plots of his foes and vindicating his name through resurrection.

Mordecai

The plot against the Jews began with Haman's animosity toward Mordecai (Esther 3:2–6). Haman eventually planned to hang Mordecai on gallows that were being speedily constructed (Esther 5:14). But in an unexpected turn of events, the king ordered Haman to reward Mordecai with royal treatment: "Hurry; take the robes and the horse, as you have said, and do so to Mordecai the Jew, who sits at the king's gate. Leave out nothing that you have mentioned" (Esther 6:10). Haman dressed Mordecai in royal robes, put him on a horse the

---

6. See Hodgkin, *Christ in All the Scriptures*, 93–94, 101.

king had ridden, and led Mordecai through the city, proclaiming, "Thus shall it be done to the man whom the king delights to honor" (Esther 6:11).

Mordecai is a type of Christ.[7] Though the enemies of Jesus sought his destruction, their plans against him led to the highest status of honor for him, for God has given Jesus the name that is above every name (Phil. 2:9–11). While Mordecai was donned with royal garments, Jesus is the true King of kings who has all authority in heaven and earth (Matt. 28:18). When the Roman soldiers mocked Jesus with purple robes and a crown of thorns, these actions were communicating the deeper truth of his identity (Mark 15:16–20). Just as the book of Esther ended with the greatness of Mordecai, who "sought the welfare of his people and spoke peace to all his people" (Esther 10:3), the earthly ministry of Christ ends with his vindication and greatness. He, above all others we know, seeks our welfare and speaks peace to us.

The Defeat of Haman

The plot of Haman was not only to kill Mordecai but to eradicate the Jewish people (Esther 3:6). But the Lord used Mordecai and Esther to expose Haman's treachery, and Haman was hanged on the gallows he prepared for Mordecai (Esther 7:10). Haman, the villain of the story, was defeated. He is called "the Agagite" (Esther 3:1), which is a reference to King Agag of the Amalekites. The Amalekites were enemies of God's people (see Exod. 17; 1 Sam. 15) and thus the seed of the serpent.[8] Haman's defeat showed, once again, the victory of God over the seed of the serpent.

Haman's defeat also foreshadows the day when God has subjected all enemies under the feet of Christ (see 1 Cor. 15:25). All who gather against God's Anointed One will fail in their efforts to overcome him (Ps. 2:1–6). When we read about Haman's plans collapsing and coming back onto his own head, we can look forward to the day when justice will reign and the seed of the serpent will be fully and finally crushed (Rom. 16:20; 2 Peter 3:13).

The Deliverance of the Jews

In the book of Esther, God's people were under the threat of death (Esther 3:13). The resolution in the book was not just the defeat of Haman but the deliverance of the Jewish people (Esther 8–9). They marked their deliverance by establishing a new feast, the Feast of Purim, which they would keep during the last month of their calendar (Esther 9). The Israelites now began and ended their year with feasts remembering God's deliverance: Passover in the first month and Purim in the last.

The deliverance of God's people foreshadows the ultimate vindication of the saints over their enemies. Every earthly deliverance is a sign of hope that

---

7. See Link and Emerson, "Searching for the Second Adam," 132–39.
8. See Hodgkin, *Christ in All the Scriptures*, 100.

the wicked will face the justice of God. The Lord's Supper is the feast of the saints by which we corporately remember the redemption that purchased our deliverance (1 Cor. 11:25–26). And we look forward to the second coming of Christ, when he will deliver dead believers through their resurrection and then confirm, at the final judgment, their justification (Rom. 8:31–34; 1 Cor. 15:20). Deliverance is our present and our future.

Summary

Ezra, Nehemiah, Esther, and Mordecai are some of the types that are featured after Israel's return to the land, and these characters are involved in events like the rebuilding of Jerusalem's walls, the defeat of Haman, and the deliverance of the Jews from annihilation. In these books at the end of the Old Testament narrative storyline, these types picture, in one way or another, the person of Christ and his past or future work.

REFLECTION QUESTIONS

1. How is Ezra a type of Christ?

2. How does Nehemiah and his work relate to the cross of Christ and the new creation?

3. How is Esther a type of Christ?

4. How is Mordecai a type of Christ?

5. Can you think of other characters or events in Ezra, Nehemiah, or Esther that point to the person and work of Christ?

What Types Are in Job through Song of Solomon?

With the books of Job through the Song of Solomon, the reader is no longer primarily in biblical narratives.[1] Rather we are steeped in poetry and wisdom literature. Yet these books contribute to the christological hope of the Old Testament. There are pictures and patterns that point to Christ.

Job

The Righteous Sufferer

The opening verse of the book of Job calls the man "blameless and upright, one who feared God and turned away from evil" (Job 1:1). When Job faced the loss of livestock and children, he remained steadfast in his praise of God (Job 1:21). Even after his own health was assaulted, he refused to curse the Lord (Job 2:7–10). His suffering was severe and lengthy. His friends, who initially seemed sympathetic and comforting (Job 2:11–13), turned against him and accused him of wickedness (Job 3–31). Tempted and tried, Job hoped for his vindication, confident he would see the Lord for himself in victory (Job 19:25–27).

Jesus is the true and greater Job, for Jesus too was a righteous sufferer,[2] and he was the only sufferer who had no sin (1 Peter 1:19; 2:21).[3] Jesus was blameless and upright, fearing God and turning from evil. No matter what he

---

1. Readers will notice that Job does contain narration at its beginning and end. The book, however, is almost entirely poetic.
2. See Sidney Greidanus, *Preaching Christ from the Old Testament: A Contemporary Hermeneutical Method* (Grand Rapids: Eerdmans, 1999), 261; Leonhard Goppelt, *TYPOS: The Typological Interpretation of the Old Testament in the New* (Grand Rapids: Eerdmans, 1982), 100–106.
3. See Toby J. Sumpter, "Father Storm: A Theology of Sons in the Book of Job," in *The Glory of Kings: A Festschrift in Honor of James B. Jordan*, eds. Peter J. Leithart and John Barach (Eugene, OR: Pickwick, 2011), 128.

faced, no matter who opposed him, Jesus never turned from the Father and so remained steadfast in faith and courage. Though Peter denied him, Judas betrayed him, the disciples scattered, and the religious leaders plotted against him, Jesus never cursed God. Tempted and tried, Jesus entered his suffering and death with the hope of resurrection (Mark 8:31).

The Vindication of Job

The earthly sorrows of Job eventually led to blessing. What he had lost was restored, and the false accusations against him were cast down. The vindication, which Job had wanted, finally came. The restoration of his fortunes was twice as much as he had before the great loss (Job 42:10). His latter days were more blessed than his beginning (Job 42:12). Job's friends learned from the Lord himself of their false words against their friend. In fact, they needed Job's forgiveness and intercession—which he graciously provided (42:10). The book ends this way: "And Job died, an old man, and full of days."

The vindication of Job is a picture of our hope in Christ. God will restore what sin has ruined because of our union with Christ, who was rejected by his own people yet resurrected by his Father. Whatever he lost, glorification brought back in greater measure—and the same will be true for us. In this world we will have trouble, but Christ has overcome the world (John 16:33). To live is Christ, and to die is gain (Phil. 1:21). Our latter days, then, will be more blessed than our beginning. Right now our light and momentary troubles are producing a glory that we will experience at Christ's return (2 Cor. 4:17). We will die, but in him and because of him, we will live—full of days forever.

Psalms

The Suffering King

The most common type of psalm is lament, and many of these laments are by David. In Psalm 3, for example, David spoke of the opposition and persecution he faced: "O Lord, how many are my foes! Many are rising against me; many are saying of my soul, there is no salvation for him in God" (Ps. 3:1–2). He prays, "Be gracious to me, O Lord, for I am languishing; heal me, O Lord, for my bones are troubled. My soul also is greatly troubled. But you, O Lord—how long?" (Ps. 6:2–3). And "My God, my God, why have you forsaken me? Why are you so far from saving me, from the words of my groaning?" (Ps. 22:1). David was a king who suffered, and this set a pattern that the Son of David would resume and fulfill.

Jesus was a suffering king, and he quoted from suffering psalms.[4] On the cross Jesus said, quoting David, "My God, my God, why have you forsaken

---

4. See Richard P. Belcher Jr., *The Messiah and the Psalms: Preaching Christ from All the Psalms* (Scotland: Mentor, 2006), 31–41, 67–97.

me?" (Matt. 27:46; see Ps. 22:1). Greidanus points out, "In giving expression to his pain, his anguish, his trust in God, the king may be a type of Christ, as we recognize retrospectively when Jesus utters these same words when he relives these experiences at an even more intense level."[5] The words of David fit perfectly upon the lips of Jesus, the true and greater David and ultimate suffering king. At the bottom of the cross, soldiers gambled for his garments, an action which, according to John 19:24, fulfilled Psalm 22:18: "They divide my garments among them, and for my clothing they cast lots." While hanging on the cross, Jesus said, "I thirst" (John 19:28), which was from Psalm 69:21 (another psalm of David). Crowned with thorns, the King of kings suffered opposition, rejection, violence, and death.

The Victorious King

The book of Psalms not only preserves the prayers of a suffering king, it gives us the words of a victorious king as well. David writes, "All my enemies shall be ashamed and greatly troubled; they shall turn back and be put to shame in a moment" (Ps. 6:10), and "For the LORD is righteous; he loves righteous deeds; the upright shall behold his face" (Ps. 11:7). The hostility of the psalmist's enemies was not the final word. The final word was vindication and victory. Speaking of the king, Psalm 72 says, "May he have dominion from sea to sea, and from the River to the ends of the earth! . . . May all kings fall down before him, all nations serve him!" (Ps. 72:8, 11).

The victorious king of the Psalms is a type of Christ.[6] The enemies of the risen King shall tremble before him. Every knee will bow, and every tongue will confess that Jesus Christ is Lord (Phil. 2:10–11). David said with hope, "Surely goodness and mercy shall follow me all the days of my life, and I shall dwell in the house of the LORD forever" (Ps. 23:6), but those words are true of Jesus in a surpassing way. Goodness and mercy proceed from the heart of our Savior. He is seated at the right hand of God in the heavenly sanctuary (Heb. 1:3; 9:24). David sang, "Lift up your heads, O gates! And be lifted up, O ancient doors, that the King of glory may come in" (Ps. 24:7). In the fullness of God's revelation, the King of glory is Jesus.

Proverbs–Ecclesiastes

The Wise Son

Solomon hoped his son would be wise: "Hear, my son, your father's instruction, and forsake not your mother's teaching, for they are a graceful garland for your head and pendants for your neck" (Prov. 1:8–9). The father wanted a wise son, who would treasure what he had been taught and who

---

5. Greidanus, *Preaching Christ from the Old Testament*, 261.
6. See Belcher, *Messiah and the Psalms*, 31–41, 58–61.

would live out the fear of the Lord. Would the son recognize that wisdom was better than silver and more precious than hidden treasures (Prov. 2:4)?

Jesus held to the teachings of his mother and father. He treasured wisdom and walked in the fear of God. He grew and was "filled with wisdom" (Luke 2:40). When he was twelve years old, he amazed the people in the temple with his understanding and answers (Luke 2:47). "And Jesus increased in wisdom and in stature and in favor with God and man" (Luke 2:52). If we want to get insight into the moral life of Christ from Old Testament texts, the book of Proverbs unfolds the life of the wise son, which he lived.[7] Wisdom characterized Christ's relationships, speech, plans, conversations, and work. He did not follow the path of folly. The Son honored his Father who sent him. Jesus said, "For whatever the Father does, that the Son does likewise" (John 5:19), and "I always do the things that are pleasing to him" (John 8:29).

Wisdom

When God created the world, he used wisdom to do it. With the rhetorical device of personification, Solomon puts words in the mouth of wisdom. Wisdom says, "Ages ago I was set up, at the first, before the beginning of the earth. When there were no depths I was brought forth, when there were no springs abounding with water" (Prov. 8:23–24). Creation came after wisdom. Before the mountains and the earth (Prov. 8:25–26), before the heavens and the deep (8:27–29), Wisdom was the delight of the Lord always (8:30–31). Without Wisdom, nothing was made that has been made. In the beginning there was already Wisdom, and Wisdom was with God.

While wisdom was personified in Proverbs 8, something deeper and truer can be said of the Lord Jesus, the eternal Son of God.[8] All things were created by him and for him, and in him all things hold together (Col. 1:16–17). He, the everlasting Word, was in the beginning with God, and without the Word nothing was made that has been made (John 1:1–3). Wisdom said, "For whoever finds me finds life and obtains favor from the LORD" (Prov. 8:35), and of Christ it is said, "In him was life, and the life was the light of men" (John 1:4). Wisdom of Proverbs 8 was a type of Christ,[9] "in whom are hidden all the treasures of wisdom and knowledge" (Col. 2:3). Christ Jesus "became to us wisdom from God, righteousness and sanctification and redemption" (1 Cor. 1:30).

The Wise Teacher

In the book of Proverbs, Solomon is the wise teacher. He observes life and provides instruction for his son and for all who will hear Wisdom's call.

---

7. See Jonathan Akin, *Preaching Christ from Proverbs* (Bradenton, FL: Rainer, 2014), 39–49.
8. See Akin, *Preaching Christ from Proverbs*, 19, 65–93.
9. See Bruce K. Waltke, *The Book of Proverbs*, vol. 1, *Chapters 1–15*, New International Commentary on the Old Testament (Grand Rapids: Eerdmans, 2004), 130–31.

Through similes and metaphors, through pithy parallelisms and strings of im-
peratives, Solomon is teaching the reader of Proverbs. Sinners need instruction, for many walk the way of folly. The author of Ecclesiastes, too, steps into
the arena and calls for the crowd to heed what he sees under the sun. The wise
teacher aims his words especially to the young (Eccl. 11:9; 12:1, 12). This wise
teacher has seen it all and done it all, so his words bear the weight of age and
experience. In the end, everything can be summed up like this: fear God and
keep his commandments (Eccl. 12:13).

When Jesus claimed that "something greater than Solomon is here"
(Matt. 12:42), he was putting himself forward as the Son of David with greater
wisdom than Israel's wisest king.[10] Jesus was the Wise Teacher par excellence.
He lived before the sun and became flesh under the sun. He proclaimed the
kingdom of God and called people to repent (Mark 1:15). He taught crowds
of Jews and Gentiles, and he taught secrets of the kingdom in parables (Mark
4). During his passion week, Jesus responded with wisdom to hostile groups
(Mark 11–12). One man, a scribe, was impressed with Jesus and affirmed the
truthfulness of what he taught (Mark 12:32). Jesus himself raised questions for
the people to ponder, and "the great throng heard him gladly" (Mark 12:37).
Jesus's claims about his own teaching indicated the Wise Teacher that he indeed was: "Everyone then who hears these words of mine and does them will
be like a wise man who built his house on the rock" (Matt. 7:24). Jesus did not
direct his disciples to build their lives on some other foundation; he directed
them to himself. Whoever refused his words was a fool, and the house of their
life would fall when the flood of judgment arrived. Jesus was the consummate
Wise Teacher, and recognizing that truth was a matter of life and death.

Song of Solomon

The Husband

Solomon wrote a song about a man and woman who get married and
enjoy the delights of intimacy together in covenant. The man wooed her in the
springtime of love and flourishing (Song 2:10–14). He pursued her, though
she thought she was unlovely and nothing special (Song 1:6; 2:1). Their relationship is characterized by faithfulness and tenderness. He is her Beloved,
the Shepherd of her heart (1:7; 2:8).

The covenant of marriage is used outside this Song to represent the relationship between God and his people, so we are not surprised that the beauty
and poetry of this Song has a transcending and typological aim (see Eph.
5:32).[11] The husband (a character written by the son of David, Solomon) is a

---

10. See Waltke, *Book of Proverbs*, 1:131–32.
11. See James M. Hamilton Jr., *Song of Songs: A Biblical-Theological, Allegorical, Christological
    Interpretation*, Focus on the Bible (Fearn, Ross-shire, Scotland: Christian Focus, 2015).

type of Christ, and Christ is the beloved of his church and the shepherd of his people (John 3:29; 10:14). By his merciful sacrifice in laying down his life, the Lord Jesus has formed a new covenant in which we are sealed forever under his atoning work. The husband in the Song of Solomon describes the beauty of his wife, which is flawless and captivating (Song 4:1–15). And in a greater way, Christ's love for the church is cleansing and sanctifying. He "gave himself up for her, that he might sanctify her, having cleansed her by the washing of the water with the word, so that he might present the church to himself in splendor, without spot or wrinkle or any such thing, that she might be holy and without blemish" (Eph. 5:25–27).

The Bride
The bride in the Song is pursued by the son of David (Song 1:1; 3:9–11). Joined in covenant with him, her garden is unlocked and her fountain unsealed (Song 4:12–15). She is a bride whose mouth is flowing with milk and honey (Song 4:11; 5:1). On the wedding night, she and her husband are naked and unashamed (4:1–5:1). Her claim upon him is clear, and it is mutual: "My beloved is mine, and I am his" (Song 3:16). The fire of their love cannot be quenched, for its flame is the flame of the Lord (Song 8:6–7). The woman is secure in her union with the son of David.

The earthly ministry of Jesus is, in a true sense, the Son of David's pursuit of his bride—the church. The bride of the Song of Solomon is a type of the church's union with Christ.[12] In the new covenant, we are united to our shepherd (John 10:16). We can say with full assurance, "My beloved is mine, and I am his." And once we are united to Christ through faith, nothing will ever separate us from his love (see Rom. 8:31–39). The fire of God's everlasting love for the church cannot be quenched, not by our many sins nor by our weak faith nor by any evil forces. Why? For "love is strong as death" (Song 8:6). Or, given all that transpired centuries after this Song was written, love is strong as resurrection from the dead.

Summary
The Old Testament pictures the suffering and vindication of Christ, and we see such pictures in the motifs of the righteous sufferer and the suffering king as well as the motifs of restoration and victory that follow the suffering. Long before Jesus embraced the cross on his way to the crown, the way had been prepared in a shadowy sense by characters like Job, David, and others. Not only is Jesus the shepherd who laid down his life, he is the shepherd who guides and guards his people with wisdom. He is the wise Son of his Father, and he is also the wise teacher who surpassed Solomon. Jesus is the solid rock for people to build their lives upon, so that the crash of judgment does not

---

12. See A. M. Hodgkin, *Christ in All the Scriptures* (London: Pickering & Inglis, 1909), 131.

break them. Christ's people are secure because his relationship with them is covenantal, pictured by the covenant of marriage and thus by the Song of Solomon. Jesus is the beloved of the bride, the church. And he will never leave us or forsake us.

REFLECTION QUESTIONS

1. How does Job picture the suffering and vindication of Christ?

2. In what ways does the book of Psalms show types of Christ?

3. How do the books of Proverbs and Ecclesiastes point to Christ?

4. In the Song of Solomon, how is the husband a type of Christ?

5. In the Song of Solomon, how does the wife point to the church's union with Christ?

What Types Are in Isaiah through Malachi?

From Isaiah to Malachi, we will survey our final group of types. The books of Isaiah through Ezekiel, each part of the Major Prophets, will be handled together, for most of the types in their section can be found in one form or another in each of these prophets. Daniel will be treated separately, followed by a section on the twelve Minor Prophets.

Isaiah–Ezekiel

The Office of Prophet

God raised up prophets to confront his rebellious people with his word, a word that promised blessing if the people obeyed and judgment if the people disobeyed (Lev. 26; Deut. 28). The prophets had similarities to the foremost prophet in their history, Moses. Like Moses, there were prophets who performed signs. Like Moses, the words of the prophets were to guide and guard the people into right worship and obedience. Moses was the law-giver (Exod. 19–24), and the prophets after him were law enforcers by virtue of their calls to follow God's commands and turn from unrighteousness (2 Kings 17:14). But also like Moses, the prophets would face rejection (Acts 7:52–53). The office of prophet pointed forward to the One who would perfectly carry out this role.[1]

Jesus fulfilled the office of prophet by embodying the very word of God. John says the Word became flesh in the incarnation (John 1:14). When Jesus spoke, God was speaking (John 17:8). To reject Jesus was not merely to reject God's messenger but to reject God himself. Before being martyred, Stephen

---

1. G. K. Beale, *Handbook of the New Testament Use of the Old Testament: Exegesis and Interpretation* (Grand Rapids: Baker Academic, 2012), 16.

surveyed Israel's rejection of God's messengers and then said, "Which of the prophets did your fathers not persecute? And they killed those who announced beforehand the coming of the Righteous One, whom you have now betrayed and murdered" (Acts 7:52). Jesus is the culminating revelation of God, the one by whom God has spoken in these last days (Heb. 1:1–2). Jesus was more than a prophet, yes, but he was not less.

The Birth of a Son

In the days of King Ahaz, the king trembled when he heard that Syria aligned with the northern kingdom and posed a threat to him (Isa. 7:1–2). But the Lord sent Isaiah to quell the king's fear (Isa. 7:3–4). Part of Isaiah's message was that the plans of the king's enemies would not come to pass (Isa. 7:7). God would thwart their scheme. God told Ahaz, "Ask a sign of the LORD your God," but Ahaz refused (Isa. 7:11–12). The Lord gave the king a sign anyway: "Behold, the virgin shall conceive and bear a son, and shall call his name Immanuel. He shall eat curds and honey when he knows how to refuse the evil and choose the good. For before the boy knows how to refuse the evil and choose the good, the land whose two kings you dread will be deserted" (Isa. 7:14–16). The sign was the birth of a son. Moreover, the son would be born in the days of Ahaz. The word "virgin" (Isa. 7:14) can also be translated "young woman," and so, in the context of Isaiah 7, the sign of a child's birth was an expectation fulfilled in Isaiah's day.[2] While the son is unnamed in Isaiah 7, his birth would be a sign of God's presence with God's people.

The hope of a promised son is reminiscent of Genesis 3:15, the birth of Isaac, and other passages in the Old Testament, too. In Isaiah 7, the promised son motif is a type of Christ, for the birth of the Christ is the ultimate fulfillment of a sign of God's presence. When Matthew reports the angel's words, the angel instructed Joseph to name the promised son "Jesus" (Matt. 1:21). The young woman, Mary, gave birth just as the angel had said. Matthew tells us, though, that the birth of the promised son fulfilled more than just the angel's words: "All this took place to fulfill what the Lord had spoken by the prophet: 'Behold, the virgin shall conceive and bear a son, and they shall call his name Immanuel' (which means, God with us)" (Matt. 1:22–23). Matthew was seeing a typological fulfillment in Isaiah 7 with the birth of our Lord.[3] Could there ever be a greater sign of Immanuel than for God, in Christ, to dwell with us?

---

2. Beale, *New Testament Use of the Old Testament*, 16n44.
3. Beale, *New Testament Use of the Old Testament*, 16n44. See also James M. Hamilton, "The Virgin Will Conceive: Typological Fulfillment in Matthew 1:18–23," in *Built upon the Rock: Studies in the Gospel of Matthew*, eds. John Nolland and Dan Gurtner (Grand Rapids: Eerdmans, 2008), 228–47.

Jeremiah

Set apart by God as a young man, Jeremiah would be a mouthpiece for the Lord to the southern kingdom of Judah (Jer. 1:6). He called the surrounding land to repent, using the Lord's words: "Return, faithless Israel" (Jer. 3:12). He warned that God's judgment would fall and that the temple would be destroyed (Jer. 22:5). Yet, despite all his words and pleas, Jeremiah faced an unrepentant Jerusalem (Jer. 5). He faced rejection and persecution (Jer. 20). He was cast into a cistern, though later drawn out (Jer. 38:1–13). He was taken outside Jerusalem to Egypt, against his will (Jer. 43).

Jesus is a true and greater Jeremiah.[4] Jesus was set apart for the work of God, to proclaim the kingdom and call for repentance (Mark 1:15). He, like Jeremiah, warned of the temple's coming destruction (Mark 13). But, like Jeremiah, Jesus faced unrepentance in the land, specifically a hardened Jerusalem (Matt. 23:37–38). The city of David, which should have been ready and willing to receive their king, rejected the Son of David. He faced suffering and persecution and ultimately death (Mark 14–15). While Jeremiah proclaimed a future day when a new covenant would be formed (Jer. 31), Jesus did not merely reiterate this hope—he accomplished it (John 19:30).

The Suffering City

In Lamentations, the city of Jerusalem is in ruins. Smoke rises, people wail, and enemies rejoice. Jerusalem is suffering because of the faithfulness of God, who promised the curse of judgment and exile if the people violated the Mosaic covenant and refused to repent. Among all of Israel's lovers, "she has none to comfort her" (Lam. 1:2). Not only could Israel's idols not satisfy, they could not save. Jerusalem's shame and filth had been exposed (Lam. 1:8). God poured out judgment "without mercy," and "in his wrath" he broke down the strongholds of his people (Lam. 2:2). The people had aligned themselves against the Lord, and that meant judgment.

The suffering city was a type of God's future judgment upon the wicked at the return of Christ. Who can stand to resist him on that day? His wrath will be poured out, and without mercy, he will decimate the false securities and idols of the nations. The shame and horror of sin will be more real on that day than on any other. All that dwells in the dark will be brought into the piercing light of God's righteousness. The enemies of God will search in vain for any comforters. As for the faithless and the lawless and the idolaters, "their portion will be in the lake that burns with fire and sulfur, which is the second death" (Rev. 21:8). Not only does the destruction of Jerusalem anticipate the final judgment, it looks toward the arrival of the city of God, when the new

---

4. See Peter J. Leithart, *A House for My Name: A Survey of the Old Testament* (Moscow, ID: Canon, 2000), 198–99, 242; A. M. Hodgkin, *Christ in All the Scriptures* (London: Pickering & Inglis, 1909), 167.

Jerusalem comes out of heaven from God, "prepared as a bride adorned for her husband" (Rev. 21:2).

The Vine

God delivered Israel out of Egypt, guided them through the wilderness, and brought them into the Promised Land (Exod. 12–17; Josh. 1–3). One way the prophets depict God's grace toward Israel is that he dug a vineyard, planted it with choice vines, and looked for good fruit (Isa. 5:1–2). But the fruit was not good! The vine did not produce what was pleasing, and the vineyard was corrupt. The message was about Israel's spiritual condition. God had planted them in the Promised Land, but they turned against him and opposed his law and rejected his prophets.

Based on Jesus's own claims, he is "the true vine" (John 15:1). His claim unmistakably connects to the Old Testament. Jesus is the true Israel, displaying in his heart and life the fruit that Old Testament Israel failed to produce. Jesus is the true and better vineyard, whose life was characterized by delight in God's law and obedience to the Father (Matt. 5:17). In himself, Jesus was raising up a new Israel who would inherit a new Jerusalem because of promises sealed by a new covenant.

Destruction of the Temple

In the Old Testament, the land of Israel was the most important place in the world, Jerusalem was the most important city in that land, and the temple was the most important spot in that city. Given the prominence of the temple, it is no wonder that the destruction of the temple by the Babylonians was such a tragic and sorrowful time for the people of Israel. God had told Solomon to build the temple (1 Kings 6–8), but God's judgment eventually involved the temple's demise (2 Kings 25).

Jesus applied temple imagery to his body. Jesus told the Jews, "Destroy this temple, and in three days I will raise it up" (John 2:19). Destroying a temple, in their memory at least, was divine judgment. What could Jesus be referring to? They protested his statement: "It has taken forty-six years to build this temple, and will you raise it up in three days?" (John 2:20). The temple was the place where God manifested his presence, but Jesus was Immanuel—God with us. Jesus was greater than the temple (Matt. 12:6). Jesus's crucifixion was like a temple destruction. But the temple of his body would not remain in ruins.

Daniel

Daniel

During the beginning of Judah's captivity, Daniel was among the youth who were taken into exile (Dan. 1:1–4). But despite temptation and pressure, Daniel refused to defile himself (Dan. 1:8). He was faithful to the Lord in a foreign land, like Joseph. Daniel exceeded his contemporaries in his wisdom and understanding (Dan. 1:20). And on occasions when his life seemed to be in the hands of others, God showed him favor through promotions and vindications (Dan. 1:20–21; 2:48–49; 5:29; 6:28).

Daniel was a type of Christ.[5] Though tempted to sin, Jesus remained steadfast in obedience and trusted the word of God from his heart (Matt. 4:1–11). While the land of Israel—under Roman occupation—was steeped in spiritual exile and captivity, Jesus refused to defile himself. His life was marked by faithfulness, even greater than that of noble Daniel. Jesus was wiser than his contemporaries, greater than the ancient King Solomon himself (Matt. 12:42). The Jewish leaders, and eventually the Romans, conspired against the Lord's Anointed, but their schemes did not ultimately succeed, for they planned to destroy Jesus forever (Mark 14:1–2). Instead, they only killed him. Jesus had embraced the cross for the joy set before him, passing from temporary death into indestructible life through resurrection.

Friends in the Fire

God knows how to save his people. When Shadrach, Meshach, and Abednego refused to bow to the golden statue at the sound of the music, they did so while knowing the consequence of death in a fiery furnace (Dan. 3:4–7, 13–18). King Nebuchadnezzar ordered that they be thrown in, bound and fully clothed (Dan. 3:19–21). Yet when the king looked into the furnace to see the rebels' fate, he saw them unbound and walking around, along with a fourth figure in the fire (Dan. 3:25). The three Hebrew friends emerged from the furnace without any burnt clothing or singed hair or smell of smoke (Dan. 3:27).

The rescue of the three faithful friends was a type of Christ's rescue of sinners through the cross and final judgment.[6] In union with Christ, we are forever secure and not condemned (Rom. 8:1). God knows how to save his people. Jesus has already gone into the furnace of judgment for us on the cross, once for all. There upon the cross, Jesus made full atonement, and everyone who calls upon the Lord will be saved. And those who are saved now will be saved later too, for God's verdict of justification will not be reversed on the day of judgment when the nations are gathered before the throne (Matt. 25:31–34). In Christ and by his righteousness alone, we pass through the furnace of God's judgment and come out unharmed, without the smell of wrath upon us.

---

5. See Peter J. Link Jr. and Matthew Y. Emerson, "Searching for the Second Adam: Typological Connections between Adam, Joseph, Mordecai, and Daniel," *Southern Baptist Journal of Theology* 21, no. 1 (Spring 2017): 137–38.
6. See Hodgkin, *Christ in All the Scriptures*, 184.

The Lion's Den

Daniel's devotion made him an easy target. In the newly established Persian Empire, some leaders wanted to tarnish his reputation because they were jealous of the king's regard for him (Dan. 6:1–5). After persuading the king to agree to sign a document that would, by implication, pressure Daniel into compromising his allegiance to God (Dan. 6:6–9), Daniel maintained devotion to the Lord—just as they expected he would do (6:10–11). The penalty for violating the royal decree was being cast into a den of lions. Despite the king's reluctance that Daniel suffer this fate, the king ordered that Daniel be held accountable (Dan. 6:14–16). Daniel was thrown into the den, a stone was rolled over the entrance, the den was secured with the king's seal, and Daniel's death was certain (Dan. 6:17). But the next morning, the king rushed to the den, the stone was rolled away, and Daniel emerged victorious and delivered from death (Dan. 6:19–23). Those who planned Daniel's demise were themselves thrown into the den and instantly devoured by the lions (Dan. 6:24).

Likewise, the Lord Jesus would not compromise his mission or his obedience. This devotion put him on a collision course with the Jewish leaders, who convinced the Romans that Jesus was a political threat (Mark 15:1–15). And political threats get crucified. Despite Pilate's reluctance, he ordered that Jesus be killed (Mark 15:15). After his crucifixion, Jesus was laid in a borrowed tomb, a stone was rolled over its opening, and Roman soldiers secured the scene with their presence and a royal seal (Matt. 27:59–66). The rescue of Daniel foreshadowed the resurrection of Jesus.[7] While Daniel was spared from death, Jesus was delivered after death. The stone was rolled away, for Jesus was victorious. Those who opposed Christ, and those who oppose him now, will face the judgment of God if they do not repent and trust in Christ as their Savior and Redeemer. The jaws of God's wrath will consume them in justice.

The Minor Prophets

Gomer's Marriage and Redemption

Hosea's wife, Gomer, was an unfaithful woman (Hos. 1:2). And her actions led to a situation where she needed to be redeemed. Hosea bought his wife, which means he paid the price for her redemption, and he brought her home to dwell with him (Hos. 3:2–3). Within the book of Hosea itself, the marriage and redemption of Gomer pointed beyond her and her husband. The actions of Hosea represented God's heart toward the people (Hos. 2:14–23; 3:1). God was in covenant with Israel, and he would pursue them even though they were unfaithful. Though Israel went after other lovers, God would redeem them.

---

7. Mitchell L. Chase, "Daniel," in *ESV Expository Commentary*, vol. 7, *Daniel–Malachi* (Wheaton, IL: Crossway, 2018), 84–85.

The marriage and redemption of Gomer foreshadows the mercy shown to sinners through the cross of Christ. Jesus was our redeemer, establishing a new covenant for rebels and lawbreakers (Mark 10:45; Luke 22:20). His kindness leads us to repentance, and we unfaithful people are brought into his family and into a right standing with God that we do not deserve. The beautiful picture of Hosea's love escalates to the good news of the gospel. We are Gomer, Christ is Hosea, and he redeems us out of our spiritual debts and slavery.

Destruction of Nations

Throughout the writings of the prophets, more places than just Jerusalem receive warnings about future judgment. Israel's neighbors should not boast of security. Tyre and Sidon, as well as all the regions of Philistia, are put on notice (Joel 3:4, 7–8). Egypt and Edom will be made desolate (Joel 3:19). Damascus, Gaza, Ammon, and Moab will be held accountable to the righteous God who rules the world (Amos 1:2—2:3). Anytime one of Israel's neighbors faced God's judgment, it was a "day of the Lord" for them.

The historical judgments on the nations foreshadow the ultimate day of the Lord coming at the return of Christ. The "day of Jesus Christ" (Phil. 1:6) will be vindication for God's people, but it will mean wrath for those who are enemies of the cross (Phil. 3:18–19). The judgment of God will fall upon the wicked when Jesus "comes on that day to be glorified in his saints, and to be marveled at among all who have believed" (2 Thess. 1:10). Christ will sit "on his glorious throne. Before him will be gathered all the nations, and he will separate people one from another as a shepherd separates the sheep from the goats" (Matt. 25:31–32).

Jonah's Deliverance

God's word came to the prophet Jonah, but Jonah didn't want to obey it. He fled and boarded a boat, and God sent a storm (Jonah 1:1–4). Jonah's stubbornness and disobedience endangered the lives of all the pagan sailors (Jonah 1:4–6). After pinpointing Jonah by casting lots, the sailors threw him overboard at his request (Jonah 1:15). God prepared a fish that swallowed Jonah for three days and three nights, and then it spit him out onto dry land (Jonah 1:17; 2:10).

When some scribes and Pharisees requested a sign from Jesus, he told them, "An evil and adulterous generation seeks for a sign, but no sign will be given to it except the sign of the prophet Jonah. For just as Jonah was three days and three nights in the belly of the great fish, so will the Son of Man be three days and three nights in the heart of the earth" (Matt. 12:39–40). Jonah's descent was due to his own sin, but the descent of Jesus was due to his substitutionary work bearing the world's sin. The descent of Jonah was followed by a third-day deliverance, and Jesus's death would be followed by a third-day deliverance too.[8] Jesus said, "Behold, something greater than Jonah is here" (Matt. 12:41). Jesus, the true and greater Jonah, entered the depths of judgment at the cross.[9] Then, just as he prophesied, the Son of Man rose from the dead.

The Rebuilt Temple

After the Israelite exiles returned to the Promised Land, they began to rebuild the temple. But the work soon ceased. The ministries of Haggai and Zechariah reinvigorated the people to attend once again to the house of the Lord (Hag. 1:4–8). The temple of Solomon had been raided and destroyed by the Babylonians decades earlier, and finally the temple would be rebuilt and its activities reinstituted. Yet the rebuilt temple was not as magnificent as the first temple. Haggai spoke the word of the Lord: "The latter glory of this house shall be greater than the former, says the LORD of hosts. And in this place I will give peace, declares the LORD of hosts" (Hag. 2:9). What would fulfill that hope for greater glory?

The rebuilt temple was a type of Christ's person and work, for his body was the temple that would be destroyed and, in three days, rise again (John 2:19–22). The resurrection was the "rebuilding" of Jesus's body, and his glorified state ensured that he could never die again. The glorified existence of the risen Jesus is how the "latter glory of this house shall be greater" than the former temple under Solomon. He *is* the temple of greater glory. And in him, we—the church—are stones being built together as a dwelling place for the presence of God (1 Cor. 6:19; 1 Peter 2:4–5). The temple that God built is greater in glory and duration than anything built by Solomon or rebuilt by the returned exiles.

Summary

When we read through the writings of the prophets, they have prophecies and narratives and characters that picture the person and work of Christ. Jesus is God's perfect prophet and promised Son, who both *reveals* God and *is* God among his people. He is the true vine and faithful redeemer. He was delivered from the den of death, and he will bring all his people through the furnace of God's wrath because of their union with him. Jesus, the Son of Man, is greater than Jonah, for he was not delivered from death but *through* it, emerging vindicated and victorious. The cross and resurrection were the

---

8. See Nicholas P. Lunn, "'Raised on the Third Day according to the Scriptures': Resurrection Typology in the Genesis Creation Narrative," *Journal of the Evangelical Theological Society* 57, no. 3 (2014): 524–25.
9. See Benjamin Keach, *Preaching from the Types and Metaphors of the Bible* (1855; repr., Grand Rapids: Kregel, 1972), 979; Matthew Barrett, *Canon, Covenant and Christology: Rethinking Jesus and the Scriptures of Israel*, New Studies in Biblical Theology, vol. 51 (Downers Grove, IL: IVP Academic, 2020), 131.

destruction and rebuilding of the temple of his body, which lives in unrivaled glory now and forever.

REFLECTION QUESTIONS

1. How does the "sign" prophecy in Isaiah 7 function as a type?

2. How does the destruction of the temple point to the death of Christ?

3. How does the deliverance of Shadrach, Meshach, and Abednego prepare for the greater deliverance that the saints enjoy in Christ?

4. How does the deliverance from the lions' den point to the work of Christ?

5. Why did Jesus see the story of Jonah as a type?

Questioning Allegory

Understanding Allegory

What Is Allegory and Allegorical Interpretation?

In the history of exegesis there is perhaps no term more controversial than *allegory*."[1] That sentence is the right place to begin this chapter, because readers may already assume a certain definition of allegory, and they may also have determined the usefulness or illegitimacy of allegorical interpretation. But those precise points—what allegory is and whether it should be practiced—are disputed. Is allegorical interpretation merely a fanciful technique whereby the interpreter downplays the historicity of the Scripture for the sake of reading into a passage whatever subjective and (allegedly) deeper meaning he prefers to see there?

One Thing and Something Else

An allegory is a passage that says one thing in order to say something else.[2] An example would be Isaiah 5, where the language about destroying a vineyard is really about God's coming judgment on Israel. The prophecy was told as an allegory. The term "allegory" itself means to "speak other." Cicero says that allegory is "a manner of speech denoting one thing by the letter of the words, but another by their meaning."[3]

If a passage is an allegory, sometimes the meaning is not immediately apparent or explicitly stated (though it may be; see Isa. 5:7). Rather, an allegory invites the reader beneath the surface to discern a deeper significance

---

1. John J. O'Keefe and R. R. Reno, *Sanctified Vision: An Introduction to Early Christian Interpretation of the Bible* (Baltimore: Johns Hopkins University Press, 2005), 89 (emphasis original).
2. See Benjamin Keach, *Preaching from the Types and Metaphors of the Bible* (1855; repr., Grand Rapids: Kregel, 1972), 192.
3. Cicero, *Rhetorica ad Herennium*, trans. Harry Caplin, Loeb Classical Library (Cambridge, MA: Harvard University Press, 1954), 4.34.46.

in the words used in the passage. And the interpretive key to the allegory, which will take the reader from one thing to something else, will not be impossible for readers to discern. In fact, an allegory embeds meaning in such a way that the meaning can be unearthed through attention to the immediate context, to a larger corpus of material, and/or to shared symbols that have been identified elsewhere.

We need to distinguish an allegory from allegorical interpretation. The former is the passage itself, and the latter is a way of reading that passage. An allegory must be read allegorically in order to honor the intent of the literary device. Allegorical interpretation treats a passage as if it contains deeper meaning(s) than what appears on the surface of the words themselves. Allegory is a way of *writing*, and allegorical interpretation is a way of *reading*. More controversial is the notion of reading a passage allegorically that may have not been written as an allegory by the human author. Though caution is required here, we may acknowledge that the divine author interweaves the stories of Scripture in such a way that the canonical meaning and significance of a passage may surpass (though not contravene or nullify) the awareness and intent of the human author.

Back to the Greeks

When scholars write about the history of allegorical interpretation, they consistently point to the Hellenistic world. According to Bray, "Allegory began in the Hellenistic world as a means of interpreting the Homeric poems."[4] The mythology of the gods was not morally ambiguous. The stories were filled with violence and sexual escapades. In order to downplay the outrageous behavior of the gods, interpreters insisted on deeper meanings to these myths. "As far back as the sixth century BC, Greek authors allegorized Homer and Hesiod and the stories about the gods, largely for the purpose of removing the rampant immorality present in the pantheon and ensuring that nothing unworthy of the gods was believed."[5] In allegorized myths, the deities or other figures were interpreted as representing cosmological forces or abstract values.[6]

Allegorical interpretation made the stories about the gods sound more palatable and commendable. The allegorization made the myths "philosophically respectable and morally justifiable."[7] One of the earliest Greek writers, Pherecydes of Syros (c. 550 BC), began to view the words of Zeus to Hera in a

4.   Gerald Bray, "Allegory," in *Dictionary for Theological Interpretation of the Bible*, ed. Kevin J. Vanhoozer (Grand Rapids: Baker Academic, 2005), 35.

5.   Keith D. Stanglin, *The Letter and Spirit of Biblical Interpretation: From the Early Church to Modern Practice* (Grand Rapids: Baker Academic, 2018), 22–23.

6.   Rita Copeland and Peter T. Struck, introduction to *The Cambridge Companion to Allegory*, eds. Rita Copeland and Peter T. Struck (New York: Cambridge University Press, 2010), 6.

7.   K. J. Woollcombe, "The Biblical Origins and Patristic Development of Typology," in *Essays on Typology*, Studies in Biblical Theology 22 (Naperville, IL: A. R. Allenson, 1957), 50.

nonliteral sense, and by the end of the fourth century BC, "the allegorical and etymological interpretation of Homer was in full swing."[8]

Following the fourth century BC, allegorization was associated with the Stoics, and Chrysippus of Soli (280–207 BC) was a major advocate of it.[9] In the third century BC, Alexandria became the hub of Homeric scholarship. Near the end of the second century BC, a Jew named Aristobulus began to allegorize parts of the Old Testament. This practice paved the way for Philo, who was born near the end of the first century BC and whose life overlapped with Jesus and the apostles. He died in his seventies around AD 50. Philo became one of the most important Jewish allegorists to have ever lived. According to Woollcombe, "Philo offered his allegorized Pentateuch to the Hellenistic world, and thereby prepared the way for the application of a transformed Stoic exegesis to the whole Bible."[10] Like Greek philosophers before him, he allegorized sacred texts in order "to say nothing unworthy of God."[11]

In addition to its advocates, allegorization had its critics too. In the first century BC and first century AD, authors like Cicero and Plutarch criticized allegorization as implausible and even blasphemous.[12] And yet this criticism of allegorization could be accompanied by a celebration of allegory when it was used "to uncover the symbolic structure of religious texts and practices."[13] Given the sacredness of Holy Scripture, we can understand why allegorical interpretation became not only practiced but encouraged. "Ways of reading that could see Christ in the Old Testament were a part of early Christian culture; by the time of the first century, there were plenty of Hellenistic and Jewish antecedents congenial to this type of interpretation."[14]

Hearing the Concerns

Allegorical interpretation, then, goes back more than twenty-five hundred years. And during these years, several concerns have dominated the critics. First, allegorizing is an abuse of the literal sense. If an author writes something that is not an allegory, and then an interpreter allegorizes the writing, the author's intent has been both ignored and distorted. Second, allegorizing treats a deeper meaning as more important than the literal sense. Why shouldn't the simple literal sense of the author be treated as more important than the allegorizing of the interpreter? Third, allegorizing opens wide

---

8. Woollcombe, "Patristic Development of Typology," 50–51.

9. Woollcombe, "Patristic Development of Typology," 51.

10. Woollcombe, "Patristic Development of Typology," 51.

11. Stanglin, *Letter and Spirit of Biblical Interpretation*, 23.

12. Lewis Ayres, "'There's Fire in That Rain': On Reading the Letter and Reading Allegorically," in *Heaven on Earth? Theological Interpretation in Ecumenical Dialogue*, eds. Hans Boersma and Matthew Levering (Hoboken, NJ: Wiley-Blackwell, 2013), 36.

13. Ayres, "'There's Fire in That Rain,'" 36.

14. Stanglin, *Letter and Spirit of Biblical Interpretation*, 22.

the gate for subjectivity that cannot be restrained. If an interpreter suggests a deeper meaning for a passage, who is to say, objectively, the meaning is that instead of something else?

These three concerns are understandable, and they exist for good reasons. We don't want interpreters treating Scripture in ways that are motivated by avoiding embarrassment from the text, as those who allegorized Greek myths were embarrassed by the surface sense of the poetry and the activities of the gods. The dilution of Scripture for the sake of cultural acceptability is a road to disaster and endless reinterpretations.

We also know from the history of biblical interpretation that allegorical readings have reached conclusions that seem exegetically indefensible. For instance, in his book *City of God*, Augustine said the dimensions of Noah's ark represent the proportional dimensions of the human body and, specifically, Christ's body, such that the door on the side of the ark represents the spear-wound in the side of Jesus.[15] Or consider Augustine's interpretation of the parable of the good Samaritan. In Luke 10:30–35, Jesus told of a man going from Jerusalem to Jericho who was overcome by robbers and then passed over by a priest and a Levite, only to be helped by a Samaritan who had compassion on him, cared for his wounds, and arranged for his lodging and provision. Augustine's interpretation of this parable is a famous example of why interpreters feel hesitant about allegorical readings. Augustine says the victim was Adam, Jerusalem was the heavenly Jerusalem, Jericho is the moon, the thieves are the devil and his angels, the stripping of the man is his loss of immortality, binding his wounds is the restraint of sin, and the place of lodging is the church.[16] So if there arises within the interpreter a hesitancy to tread down this same path, we should want to affirm that instinct.

There is a danger that allegorical interpretation may misunderstand the passage or offer conclusions that distract from the point of the passage. An interpreter might rely on his own subjective imagination in order to impute creative yet unwarranted conclusions that cannot be exegetically and canonically defended. So, yes: there are dangers to be acknowledged in the venture of allegorical readings. But there is also a danger about these dangers, and that would be stiff-arming the strategy of allegorical reading in every case.

We must acknowledge the prominence of allegorical interpretation throughout church history. Allegorizing was not some aberration. Were these Christian interpreters seeking to deny the historical value of Scripture when they sought a deeper sense in the passage? Augustine was certainly not denying the historicity of Noah's ark, even though he spoke of a deeper meaning of the ark and its door as the body and side of Christ. An interpreter may justifiably take issue with Augustine's allegorical reading of the good Samaritan

---

15. Augustine, *City of God* 15.26.
16. Augustine, *Questions on the Gospels* 2.19.

parable. But should the enterprise of allegorical interpretation be abandoned just because of undesirable readings or abuses?

What if Christian interpreters practiced allegorical interpretation when it could be textually grounded in God's canonical revelation? And if allegorical interpretation needs to be supported by textual reasons, how is it different from typology?

Allegory and Typology

Typology and allegory are not synonymous, but they are related. Both are examples of seeing significance in a text that is beyond the text itself. Unlike a type, an allegory does not have to be historical. For instance, allegories might appear in visions or parables that are not meant to be taken literally. Unlike an allegory, a legitimate type depends upon correspondences and patterns in redemptive history that link to, and escalate toward, the antitype. According to John J. O'Keefe and R. R. Reno, "Allegory is more fluid and ambitious. It seeks patterns and establishes diverse links between scripture and a range of intellectual, spiritual, and moral concerns."[17] Allegorical interpretation will often yield timeless truths and moral exhortations.

While typology and allegory are examples of figural reading, a distinction between the terms is valuable. Patristic interpreters may not have explicitly distinguished between the interpretive practices of typology and allegory, but there is no virtue in maintaining an ambiguity where greater precision is possible. Typological exegesis discerns organic connections and development across redemptive history and through progressive revelation. The patterns of the Old Testament—particularly with persons, events, and institutions, but also with offices, places, and things—find their fulfillment christologically in the person and past or future work of Jesus. Allegorical interpretation views the text under consideration as having a deeper meaning, understanding the text to "say other" than what the words read.

Summary

Allegory is a controversial term, and allegorical interpretation is a controversial practice. An allegory is a passage with a deeper meaning. In allegorizing a text, the reader must look past the initial sense of the words for what lies beneath, "explaining a work, or a figure in myth, or any created entity, as if there were another sense to which it referred, that is, presuming the work or figure to be encoded with meaning intended by the author or a higher spiritual authority."[18] Legitimate concerns exist about seeking deeper meanings in texts, but perhaps its use could be justified if the proposed allegorical interpretation—like typology—could be established with scriptural warrant.

---

17. O'Keefe and Reno, *Sanctified Vision*, 21.
18. Copeland and Struck, introduction to *Cambridge Companion to Allegory*, 2.

REFLECTION QUESTIONS

1. What is allegorical interpretation?

2. Why did some Greek philosophers treat stories of their gods in an allegorical manner?

3. What concerns have been raised about allegorizing texts?

4. Why was Philo significant?

5. Is there a difference between allegory and typology?

What Are the Theological Assumptions of Allegory?

Whenever the early church interpreted the Old Testament allegorically, they did so with a shared set of assumptions undergirding their practice. While not every allegorist drew the same conclusions about an image or the details of a narrative, the eight assumptions in this chapter were what shaped their allegorical instincts.

One Story in Two Testaments

Without denying the reality of human authorship, the Great Tradition has always insisted upon the divine authorship of Holy Scripture. And the two Testaments are united in their aim—to prepare for and proclaim the Lord Jesus Christ. The unity of the Testaments "was a key assumption for all patristic exegetes."[1] The sweep of God's progressive revelation unfolds the divine drama of redemption. "Because scripture tells this story, and because it points always forward to include us within that story, it seems to follow naturally that Christians should read scripture as both a trustworthy account of God's dealings with the cosmos, and as a world of signs."[2]

Apart from the unity of Scripture, an embedded deeper sense is not of divine design at all but rather mere coincidence and fanciful imagination. With a divine author superintending the progressive revelation in the Old and New Testaments, organic connections are not only reasonable but expected. Through allegorical interpretations, the early church fathers were showing the

---

1. Hans Boersma, *Scripture as Real Presence: Sacramental Exegesis in the Early Church* (Grand Rapids: Baker Academic, 2017), 39.
2. Lewis Ayres, "'There's Fire in That Rain': On Reading the Letter and Reading Allegorically," in *Heaven on Earth? Theological Interpretation in Ecumenical Dialogue*, eds. Hans Boersma and Matthew Levering (Hoboken, NJ: Wiley-Blackwell, 2013), 33–34.

interconnectedness of God's Word. Through verbal associations and other avenues, allegorists could take a Bible passage and speak of deeper meanings pertaining to Christ and Christian doctrine.

Hermeneutical Keys

The realities of Christ and his church unlock the Old Testament, like keys unlocking a chest of treasure. The Old and New Testaments belong together and serve to mutually interpret one another. The christological realities, proclaimed in the New Testament, serve as bright lights to shine into the shadows of the Old. Apart from the hermeneutical insights taught by Christ and practiced by his apostles, the Old Testament does not reach its culmination or fulfillment. Therefore, "the reason the church fathers practiced typology, allegory, and so on is that they were convinced that the reality of the Christ event was already present (sacramentally) within the history described within the Old Testament narrative."[3]

Reading the Old Testament with a christological lens was not a wholly subjective enterprise. While critics of allegory may fear that the practice has zero constraints and will inevitably descend into absurdities without accountability for the interpreter, there is an impressive amount of overlap in the allegorical interpretations offered by the church fathers. Their reading of Scripture was shaped by their conviction that Christ is the goal of the Old Testament and that the rule of faith provides important doctrinal boundaries within which Christians can handle the sacred text. It is simply not the case that the early fathers read into the text whatever they wanted to see. Carter points out, "The allegorical approach views the text as having more than one meaning, but not an unlimited number of meanings and certainly not mutually contradictory ones."[4]

The Imitation of Paul

When it comes to allegorical interpretation in the early church, the writers were not afraid to say that the apostle Paul set an example to follow when he interpreted figures and images in the Old Testament.[5] The most famous text they used to prove their point was Galatians 4:24: "Now this may be interpreted allegorically."[6] Paul proceeded to interpret Abraham's two sons and two wives, teaching that a deeper meaning exists in the historical events and people of Abraham's life.

---

3. Boersma, *Scripture as Real Presence*, 12.
4. Craig A. Carter, *Interpreting Scripture with the Great Tradition: Recovering the Genius of Premodern Exegesis* (Grand Rapids: Baker Academic, 2018), 6.
5. Boersma, *Scripture as Real Presence*, 79.
6. John J. O'Keefe and R. R. Reno, *Sanctified Vision: An Introduction to Early Christian Interpretation of the Bible* (Baltimore: Johns Hopkins University Press, 2005), 90.

Also influential on the church fathers were Paul's words in 1 Corinthians 10:1–4: "For I do not want you unaware, brothers, that our fathers were all under the cloud, and all passed through the sea, and all were baptized into Moses in the cloud and in the sea, and all ate the same spiritual food, and all drank the same spiritual drink. For they drank from the spiritual Rock that followed them, and the Rock was Christ." A thread of "spiritual" participation runs through his Old Testament references. The words of Paul became an invitation to imitation.

The Literal Sense as Foundation

Many early church fathers may have had allegorical instincts, but they did not abandon consideration of the literal sense. This point is especially important, for many readers suspect that allegorists had little to no regard for the literal sense of the biblical text. In fact, as Hans Boersma notes, "One of the most common accusations against the scriptural interpretation of the church fathers is that by allegorizing the biblical text, they failed to take seriously the literal meaning and, along with it, the history it recounts."[7] To the contrary, the consistent practice of the church fathers was to affirm the literal sense. They paid attention to questions of authorial intent, the text's literal meaning, and the historicity of biblical narratives.[8] For instance, Augustine, who was no stranger to allegory, wrote that "when we read in the divine books such a vast array of true meanings, which can be extracted from a few words, and which are backed by sound Catholic faith, we should pick above all the one which can certainly be shown to have been held by the author we are reading."[9]

The literal sense was the foundation for any higher sense that they discerned. The literal sense was important, but it did not exhaust the meaning of a passage. Allegorical interpretation acknowledged that Scripture consisted of multiple parts, like people. Just as people have a body as well as nonmaterial aspects, Scripture has a literal sense as well as nonliteral senses. And in order to pursue any deeper meaning to a passage of Scripture, an interpreter needs to first attend to its literal sense.

The Avoidance of Absurdity

The literal sense was foundational for interpreters within the Great Tradition, but there were times when a reader felt driven to allegorical interpretation due to the apparent nonhistorical nature of a passage. If affirming the literal sense of a text seemed absurd and to transgress the bounds of reason,

---

7. Boersma, *Scripture as Real Presence*, 27.
8. Boersma, *Scripture as Real Presence*, 29.
9. Augustine, *The Literal Meaning of Genesis*, trans. Edmund Hill, The Works of Saint Augustine: A Translation for the 21st Century I/13, ed. John E. Rotelle (Hyde Park, NY: New City, 2002), 1.21.41 (pp. 188–89).

an allegorical interpretation became not only preferable but necessary.[10] This move might seem reminiscent of the Greek interpreters of Homeric myths, who offered allegorical interpretations in order to sanitize the immoral behavior of the gods. So if the church fathers found the literal sense of a biblical text untenable and then allegorized it, were they treating the Bible like pagans treated Greek myths?

The allegation does not hold up to scrutiny. First, unlike the allegorists of Homeric myths, the church fathers generally affirmed the literal sense. The church fathers were not simply engaging in pagan allegorizing. "In contrast to Hellenistic interpreters of Homer, the church fathers treated salvation history as indispensable."[11] Second, they appealed to the example of Paul in order to show biblical precedent for reading Scripture with layers of meaning. Nevertheless, as John O'Keefe and R. R. Reno note, "An interpretive move that directs attention away from the literal sense is, of course, a dangerous game. Allegorical readings, especially of obscure or offensive texts, are prone to spin out of control. . . . Not surprisingly, the history of Christian exegesis has been marked by warnings against and resistance to allegory."[12]

The Desire for Edification

Allegorical interpretation could be desirable when the literal sense of a text did not appear edifying to the reader. This move is not intended to minimize the historicity of a passage but, instead, to maximize the helpfulness of a passage. For instance, in Gregory of Nyssa's work *The Life of Moses*, he addresses the priestly vestments in Exodus 28. Gregory says the Urim and Thummim are doctrine and truth, and he interprets other features of the vestments as things the soul should pursue for the sake of a pure life.[13] The allegorical interpretation of the priestly vestments is driven by Gregory's assumption that "all of scripture somehow aids in the development of the Christian life," and so this reading strategy "allowed him to locate his life as a Christian more deeply in seemingly useless passages of the Bible."[14]

In reading Gregory's *The Life of Moses*, his affirmation of the literal sense is clear. When he puts forward deeper meanings to the text, he was not trying to set the spiritual sense against the literal sense. As O'Keefe and Reno explain, "Gregory is content with the biblical account of Moses's life—so much so that modern readers find him hopelessly naïve in his trust of the historical accuracy of the biblical material—but he is also eager to draw out the spiritual level of meaning. His allegorical interpretation of Moses's life supplements

---

10. See the explanation in O'Keefe and Reno, *Sanctified Vision*, 91–92.
11. Boersma, *Scripture as Real Presence*, 23.
12. O'Keefe and Reno, *Sanctified Vision*, 93.
13. Gregory of Nyssa, *The Life of Moses* 2.189.
14. O'Keefe and Reno, *Sanctified Vision*, 22.

and extends the literal sense by establishing its correspondence to the life of faith. The purpose of the allegorical reading is to transform a canonical story into a narrative applicable to Christian practice."[15]

A Virtuous Ear

To encounter Scripture is to hear the voice of the living God. And the more prepared the ear for hearing, the more meaningful the encounter with God's Word. A sensitive ear comes from a holy life, and so the virtue of the interpreter was crucial to the task of interpretation. Since the Bible was not like any other book, it shouldn't be approached like any other book. Allegorical interpretation was not for those who didn't take the text or the Lord seriously. Rather, the pursuit of deeper meaning in the text was to be an overflow of the interpreter's pursuit of wisdom and virtue.

A devoted life and deeper readings go together as an inextricable pair. According to Stanglin, "An unbeliever, almost by definition, fails to see and believe the basic assumptions grounding biblical interpretation: that Scripture is inspired and Christ is its scope. Biblical interpretation calls for humility, a desire to be formed morally, willingness to listen, and openness to spiritual illumination and understanding. The greater the character, virtue, and holiness of the interpreter, the further the interpreter can progress in spiritual interpretation."[16]

Virtue Formation

Not only was virtue important for the act of interpretation, virtue was important for the aim of interpretation. Reading a text allegorically would often lead to discerning truths to believe and moral virtues to pursue. To read the Word of God with faith was to be changed by the living God of the text. A goal of allegorical interpretation was not elitism but holiness and humility. The incarnate Word was enjoyed and honored and embraced in the written Word. And since the incarnate Christ is the embodiment of all virtue, faithful reading became formative reading, as God renews and transforms his people through Holy Scripture.

Boersma writes, "This emphasis on virtue keeps us from treating Holy Scripture as if it were merely a book that presents us with fascinating literature from a bygone age or that gives us invaluable information for studying the history of religion."[17] The living Word of Scripture summons us to commune with the living Word—Christ—to share in the blessed life of God, under his rule and for his glory. In Gregory of Nyssa's *Homilies on the Beatitudes*, he

---

15. O'Keefe and Reno, *Sanctified Vision*, 100–101.
16. Keith D. Stanglin, *The Letter and Spirit of Biblical Interpretation: From the Early Church to Modern Practice* (Grand Rapids: Baker Academic, 2018), 75–76.
17. Boersma, *Scripture as Real Presence*, 20.

explains that since God is the subject of Scripture, and since God himself is virtue, the subject matter of Scripture is also virtue that leads to sharing more deeply in the life of God.[18]

Summary

The practice of allegorical interpretation rested on multiple assumptions. Contrary to caricatures about the practice of the church fathers, they did not insert purely arbitrary meanings into biblical texts. They cared deeply about the details of the text, and they sought the edification and virtue formation of the reader. "The scriptures were the divinely ordained means for entering into the mysteries of salvation, and for this reason, the fathers assumed that the words, episodes, and images of scripture must have an 'other speaking' power, an allegorical sense that could direct the reader from worldly realities to the heavenly reality."[19] Their default position to the literal sense was to affirm it, though they viewed it as the foundation for allegorical interpretation.

REFLECTION QUESTIONS

1. Why is the unity of the Old and New Testaments a necessary assumption to allegorical interpretation in the Great Tradition?

2. How did the writings of Paul seem to justify allegorical interpretation?

3. Did allegorists make it a practice to deny and ignore the literal sense of a passage?

4. On what occasions might an allegorist reject the literal sense of a passage?

5. How does allegorical interpretation relate to the concept of virtue?

---

18. Boersma, *Scripture as Real Presence*, 19–20.
19. O'Keefe and Reno, *Sanctified Vision*, 93.

Allegory in Church History

How Was Allegory Practiced in the Early Church?

During the period of the early church (AD 100–450), allegorical interpretation was a common feature in the writings of the church fathers. Not every writer allegorized to the same degree or drew the same conclusions, but this particular way of reading Scripture was prominent in the first several centuries of Christianity.

The Right Reading of Israel's Scripture

The Old Testament is Christian Scripture. Such a conviction drove the church fathers into the text in order to show the presence of Christ in it. Their christological preoccupation was the defining feature of patristic interpretation: "knowing the identity of Jesus Christ is the basis for right reading of the sacred writings of the people of Israel."[1] Allegorizing passages in the Old Testament was a way of showing that the meaning of Genesis through Malachi could not be rightly understood apart from God's revelation in Christ.

In one of his letters, Ignatius of Loyola (AD 35–108) wrote, "To my mind it is Jesus Christ who is the original documents. The inviolable archives are his cross and death and his resurrection and the faith that came by him."[2] According to Irenaeus (AD 140–202), Christ is the "treasure which was hid in the field" of Scripture.[3] And as Augustine (AD

---

1. John J. O'Keefe and R. R. Reno, *Sanctified Vision: An Introduction to Early Christian Interpretation of the Bible* (Baltimore: Johns Hopkins University Press, 2005), 28.
2. Ignatius, *To the Philadelphians* 8.2, in Justin S. Holcomb, *Know the Heretics* (Grand Rapids: Zondervan Academic, 2014), 19.
3. Irenaeus, *Against Heresies* 4.26.1, in Karlfried Froehlich, *Biblical Interpretation in the Early Church*, Sources of Early Christian Thought (Philadelphia: Fortress, 1984), 44.

354–430) put it, "the New is in the Old concealed, and the Old is in the New revealed."[4]

Adding to the Literal Sense

Most of the time, the church fathers did not deny the literal sense when they sought a deeper one. This point is very important when we consider that their hermeneutics are often compared to the pagans who allegorized Homeric myths. A key distinction between the groups is that the church fathers affirmed the historicity of Scripture. As de Lubac puts it, "The reflections of an Irenaeus or an Origen—as of a John Chrysostom, an Augustine, or a Gregory the Great—upon the Scripture transport us into a completely different region than that to which we are led by the reflections of a Plutarch on the myth of Osiris or a Porphyry on the Cavern of the nymphs."[5] Allegorizing for the church fathers, then, was not about escaping historicity. Instead, allegorizing was adding to and building upon the literal sense of the text. The divine authorship of Scripture was reason for them to believe that the words of the human author did not exhaust the meaning of the passage.

Augustine, who was no stranger to allegorical interpretation, viewed the spiritual sense as adding to, and not negating, the literal sense. For instance, in his comments on 1 Corinthians 10:1–11, Augustine believed that the book of Exodus told the history of Israel yet also foretold (through allegory) the future of God's people.[6] When Augustine wrote about the resurrection of Lazarus, he said, "Though we hold with complete faith that Lazarus was revived in accord with Gospel history, nevertheless I do not doubt that he also signifies something in allegory. Nor again, when a fact is allegorized, do people lose faith in the actual accomplishment of the deed: when Paul explains that the allegory of the sons of Abraham is the two Testaments, why should anyone suppose either that Abraham did not exist or that he did not have two sons?"[7] Notice Augustine's conviction that allegorical interpretation did not automatically deny the literal sense of a biblical passage. And also notice that he appealed to Paul's use of Genesis in Galatians 4, observing that Paul affirmed the historicity of the very account that also had a greater meaning.

---

4. Augustine, *Questions on the Heptateuch* 2.73, quoted in Pamela Bright, ed. and trans., *Augustine and the Bible: The Bible through the Ages* (Notre Dame, IN: University of Notre Dame Press, 1999).

5. Henri de Lubac, *Medieval Exegesis: The Four Senses of Scripture*, vol. 2, trans. Mark Sebanc (Grand Rapids: Eerdmans, 2000), 2:17–18.

6. Augustine, *De utilitate credenda*, sec. 8.

7. Augustine, *Eighty-Three Different Questions* 65, as quoted in Henri de Lubac, *Medieval Exegesis: The Four Senses of Scripture*, vol. 2, trans. Mark Sebanc (Grand Rapids: Eerdmans, 2000), 2:7.

The Origen of Allegory

But what about Origen (AD 184–253)? Surely he's the out-of-control allegorizer who doesn't take the text of Scripture seriously, right? Perhaps to the surprise of readers, Origen did take the text of Scripture seriously. In fact, one of his great achievements was the Hexapla, an edition of the Old Testament in six columns. Origen believed the testimony of the miraculous in Scripture, and he affirmed the historicity of most biblical narratives, though exceptions were passages like Genesis 1–2 and the book of Revelation.[8] But "it is important to keep in mind that in most of Origen's biblical exegesis, a literal reading of the text accompanied his allegorical interpretation."[9] In fact, Origen "often found the biblical text to be historically reliable, morally edifying, and doctrinally sound on the literal level. It was the basis for the spiritual meaning."[10]

With Origen, and his predecessor Clement, a school of exegesis was developing out of Alexandria. But Origen did have his detractors. For example, Eusebius cites words from Porphyry, who considered Origen's exegesis a kind of absurdity.[11] Origen was aware of contemporaries who were concerned with his methods. He said, "One should not suspect us of thinking that the Scripture does not contain real history, or that the precepts of the Law were not to be fulfilled to the letter, or that what has been written about the Savior has not sensibly taken place. . . . The truly historical passages are many more numerous than those that are to be taken in a purely spiritual sense."[12] While Theodore of Mopsuestia associated Origen's exegesis with the denial of history, people like Pamphilus and Eusebius defended Origen against that charge, citing lengthy passages from Origen in which he affirmed the historicity of biblical characters and events.[13] Origen believed Scripture was like the human body, containing multiple aspects to it. The body of the text was its literal sense, the soul its moral sense, and the spirit its highest sense that reveals the mysteries of God.

The Enrichment of the Saint

One function of allegorical interpretation was to exhort and enrich the saint toward virtuous living. The early fathers' allegory "consistently assumed that scriptural texts were ordained by God as a map for navigating from

---

8. Hans Boersma, *Scripture as Real Presence: Sacramental Exegesis in the Early Church* (Grand Rapids: Baker Academic, 2017), 29.
9. Boersma, *Scripture as Real Presence*, 30.
10. Keith D. Stanglin, *The Letter and Spirit of Biblical Interpretation: From the Early Church to Modern Practice* (Grand Rapids: Baker Academic, 2018), 62.
11. Eusebius, *Ecclesiastical History* 6.19.4–5.
12. Origen, *On First Principles* 4.3.4, as quoted in de Lubac, *Medieval Exegesis*, 2:15.
13. Peter W. Martens, "Origen against History? Reconsidering the Critique of Allegory," in *Heaven on Earth? Theological Interpretation in Ecumenical Dialogue*, eds. Hans Boersma and Matthew Levering (Hoboken, NJ: Wiley-Blackwell, 2013), 57.

sin to righteousness."[14] The saints were especially focused on how the Bible strengthened their faith, hope, and love. The "goal of exegesis" was not merely worldly knowledge but divine wisdom that would stimulate and shape virtue. For Gregory of Nyssa, "the life of Moses is not just a biography; his sandals are not just coverings for his feet. His life can be read as a map for every Christian engaged in the ascetic pursuit of virtue."[15]

If the literal sense of the text seemed like a stumbling block to the reader, then interpreters were further motivated to allegorize because edification was immensely desirable and sometimes only an allegorical interpretation seemed to edify. Origen explains:

> The divine wisdom has arranged for there to be certain stumbling blocks or interruptions of the narrative meaning, by inserting in its midst certain impossibilities and contradictions, so that the very interruption of the narrative might oppose the reader, as it were, with certain obstacles thrown in the way. By them wisdom denies a way and an access to the common understanding; and when we are shut out and hurled back, it calls us back to the beginning of another way, so that by gaining a higher and loftier road through entering a narrow footpath it may open for us the immense breadth of divine knowledge.[16]

This gain from allegorical interpretation was divine knowledge. For Gregory of Nyssa and for the Great Tradition as a whole, "the goal of exegesis . . . is not worldly knowledge but divine wisdom."[17]

The Defense of Scripture

The early church fathers faced false teachers and heretics. The rise of gnosticism had proponents like the Valentinians, who emphasized the spiritual and denigrated the physical. In the AD 150s and 160s, Valentinians were writing and commenting on New Testament texts,[18] and these efforts meant that the early church fathers wrote in an environment where the defense of Scripture was necessary. Multiple writers pushed against the Valentinian exegesis that was promoting gnostic interpretations. These anti-Valentinian writers included Irenaeus, Clement of Alexandria, Origen, and Tertullian.

---

14. O'Keefe and Reno, *Sanctified Vision*, 106.
15. O'Keefe and Reno, *Sanctified Vision*, 103.
16. Origen, *On First Principles* 4.2.9.
17. O'Keefe and Reno, *Sanctified Vision*, 139.
18. Lewis Ayres, "'There's Fire in That Rain': On Reading the Letter and Reading Allegorically," in Boersma and Levering, 36.

In *Against Heresies*, Irenaeus was concerned about these Valentinian exegetes. "Time and again Irenaeus suggests his opponents do not know how to punctuate a sentence, how to identify in whose person a particular text is spoken, how to interpret a term by its use elsewhere in scripture, how to recognize a figure of speech or a quirk of personal style, or how to read a statement in its immediate context."[19] While Irenaeus and other church fathers practiced allegorical interpretation, they defended the Scripture against gnostics whose exegesis was deemed heretical. Tertullian even wrote a work entitled *Against the Valentinians*. According to Irenaeus, the gnostics erred by bringing Scripture's plain teaching into question on the basis of their idiosyncratic interpretation of obscure passages.[20] If an interpreter claimed a deeper meaning to Scripture, it must "supplement rather than contradict its plain meaning."[21]

The Schools of Alexandria and Antioch

Out of Alexandria, a group of allegorists had been teaching a spiritual sense to Scripture. Famous for allegorical interpretation, this group is referred to as the School of Alexandria. In response to the Alexandrian emphasis on the spiritual sense of the biblical text, a group of interpreters from Antioch emphasized the literal sense. This latter group, comprising the School of Antioch, criticized the excesses that they observed from the Alexandrian allegorists. For instance, the Antiochene interpreter Theodore of Mopsuestia (AD 350–428) believed that allegorists were twisting Scripture, diminishing the historical nature of Scripture, and wrongly justifying their practice by appealing to the apostle Paul who did not compromise the integrity of salvation history.[22] In his ninth homily on the Hexaemeron, Basil of Caesarea (330–379) penned what Jaroslav Pelikan describes as "one of the most vigorous criticisms of allegorical exegesis to come from any orthodox Christian theologian in the fourth (or any other) century."[23] Basil criticized the allegorist's lack of interpretive control, and he linked the desire for allegorizing to a dissatisfaction with the Bible's plain meaning.[24]

When the Alexandrian and Antiochene schools are viewed in historical hindsight, the difference between them is not allegory versus the literal sense.

---

19. Ayres, "'There's Fire in That Rain,'" 37.
20. Joseph Trigg, "The Apostolic Fathers and Apologists," in *A History of Biblical Interpretation*, vol. 1, *The Ancient Period*, eds. Duane F. Watson and Alan J. Hauser (Grand Rapids: Eerdmans, 2003), 330. See Irenaeus, *Against Heresies* 2.27.1
21. Trigg, "Apostolic Fathers and Apologists," 330.
22. Ian Christopher Levy, *Introducing Medieval Biblical Interpretation: The Senses of Scripture in Premodern Exegesis* (Grand Rapids: Baker Academic, 2018), 19.
23. Jaroslav Pelikan, *Christianity and Classical Culture: The Metamorphosis of Natural Theology in the Christian Encounter with Hellenism* (New Haven, CT: Yale University Press, 1995), 226. See Homily 9:101.
24. Christopher Hall, *Reading Scripture with the Church Fathers* (Downers Grove, IL: InterVarsity, 1998), 87.

That dichotomy is a caricature. While the Antiochene School was concerned that the Alexandrian allegorists were overshadowing the literal sense, the Antiochenes still employed a spiritual sense. And while the Alexandrian School faced criticism for their allegorical interpretations, they still affirmed the literal sense. Boersma urges a caution: "We should not exaggerate the differences either between Origen and Chrysostom or between the Antiochene and the Alexandrian interpretive approaches."[25] Diodore of Tarsus, an Antiochene interpreter, wrote in the prologue to his *Commentary on the Psalms* that "we will not disparage anagogy and the higher *theoria*. For history is not opposed to *theoria*. On the contrary, it proves to be the foundation and the basis of the higher senses."[26] Diodore didn't want any higher sense to comprise the underlying sense of the text. But his interpretive method still made room for a higher sense to the biblical text. In the big picture, "most of the Alexandrians and Antiochenes have much more in common with each other than either group has with the Enlightenment."[27]

Cassian and the Quadriga

The early church fathers considered the biblical text to have historical and spiritual senses. A man named John Cassian (360–435) further divided the spiritual sense: "There are three kinds of spiritual knowledge, the tropological, the allegorical and the anagogical."[28] Counting the historical sense, the threefold division of the spiritual sense established a four-sense grid for the biblical text. This fourfold sense was known as the Quadriga, and it made a lasting impact in the years to come. The historical sense was the surface (or visible) meaning of the text, the allegorical sense was the christological meaning and focused on what should be believed, the tropological sense was the moral instruction and focused on what the reader should do, and the anagogical sense was future-oriented and focused on the reader's hope.

Cassian appealed to the book of Proverbs for the various senses that could be discerned in the biblical text. Solomon wrote, "Have I not written for you thirty sayings of counsel and knowledge, to make you know what is right and true, that you may give a true answer to those who sent you?" (Prov.

---

25. Boersma, *Scripture as Real Presence*, 77.
26. As quoted in Karlfried Froehlich, *Biblical Interpretation in the Early Church* (Philadelphia: Fortress, 1984), 85. The word *theoria* is equivalent to a higher sense of insight, building on the *historia* of the text. As Stanglin points out, "The favorite Antiochene term for going beyond the letter was *theoria* (insight), which was used earlier by the Alexandrians Clement and Origen to describe their own practice of allegory" (*Letter and Spirit of Biblical Interpretation*, 67).
27. Craig A. Carter, *Interpreting Scripture with the Great Tradition: Recovering the Genius of Premodern Exegesis* (Grand Rapids: Baker Academic, 2018), 95.
28. John Cassian, *Conferences* 14.8, as quoted in Denys Turner, "Allegory in Christian Late Antiquity," *Cambridge Companion to Allegory*, eds. Rita Copeland and Peter T. Struck (New York: Cambridge University Press, 2010), 72.

22:20–21). In the LXX, rather than the verse being a rhetorical question about "thirty sayings," the verse was translated as a command to "write . . . three times," which seemed to substantiate the discernment of three spiritual senses of the biblical text. To illustrate the use of the Quadriga, Cassian wrote about the four senses of Jerusalem: historically, Jerusalem is the city of the Jews; allegorically, it is the church of Christ; tropologically, it is the human soul; anagogically, it is the city of God which is in heaven.[29] Cassian also appealed to the apostle Paul for the biblical precedent of construing literal narratives in the Old Testament as allegories for revelation in the New Testament.[30]

Summary

The subject of allegorical interpretation in the early church is rich with examples and complexity. While some interpreters seemed to allegorize texts in a way that diminished the historical sense, other interpreters emphasized the historical sense yet also allowed for a higher or spiritual meaning as well. If a general statement can be made about the approach of the church fathers, they considered any spiritual sense to be in addition to the literal sense. Allegorical interpretation aimed at the edification of the reader. This kind of reading was understood to rightly unpack the Scriptures of Israel, for the unity and divine authorship of the Bible ensured an interconnectedness, which allegorizing revealed to the interpreter. By the end of the early church era, the historical and spiritual senses of Scripture had become four: the historical sense and three spiritual senses, forming the Quadriga. And the Quadriga would endure for the centuries to come.

REFLECTION QUESTIONS

1. Why is it not accurate to say that the church fathers denied the historicity of the biblical text for the sake of allegorical interpretation?

2. What was Origen's view of the literal sense and of allegorical interpretation?

3. How was allegorical interpretation intended to enrich the saint?

4. What were the differences between the Alexandrian and Antiochene schools of interpretation?

5. How did John Cassian apply the Quadriga to the city of Jerusalem?

---

29. John Cassian, *Conferences* 14.8.
30. Denys Turner, "Allegory in Late Christian Antiquity," in *The Cambridge Companion to Allegory*, eds. Rita Copeland and Peter T. Struck (New York: Cambridge University Press, 2010), 74.

How Was Allegory Practiced in the Middle Ages?

The period of the Middle Ages covers approximately a thousand years (450–1450). During these centuries, the practice of allegorical interpretation not only continued but increased. And of the Alexandrian and Antiochene schools, the Alexandrian School dominated the landscape with its (over)emphasis on spiritual meaning.

Multiple Senses—Again

In the Great Tradition, exegetes viewed the text of Scripture as containing both letter and the spirit, both historical and spiritual meanings. The spiritual sense had been subdivided into the allegorical, tropological, and anagogical senses. Together with the literal or historical sense, these three spiritual senses formed the Quadriga. There was continuity, then, between the end of the early church era and the beginning of the Middle Ages.

The benefit of the multiple senses in Scripture was the recognition of Scripture's fullness and the edification of the saint. According to Gregory the Great (who died in 604), allegorical interpretation gave the soul "a kind of mechanism by which it is raised to God."[1] Through this "mechanism," the interpreter would see the relationship between the Old and New Testaments, that the former contained the latter. Gregory said, "The book of sacred eloquence has been written allegorically on the inside, historically on the outside; inside, in terms of the spiritual understanding, and outside, through the simple sense of the letter."[2]

---

1. Denys Turner, *Eros and Allegory: Medieval Exegesis of the Song of Songs* (Collegeville, MN: Cistercian, 1995), 217–18.
2. As quoted in Henri de Lubac, *Medieval Exegesis: The Four Senses of Scripture*, vol. 2, trans. Mark Sebanc (Grand Rapids: Eerdmans, 2000), 8.

The Foundational Sense

The first part of the Quadriga is the historical sense, known as the *littera* or *historia*. In the Middle Ages, the aim of allegorical interpretation was not to ignore or deny the literal sense. Rather, the literal sense was the foundation for the higher senses that followed. Henri de Lubac explains that "in Scripture itself, one professes that there is no dissociation of the two senses. The spirit does not exist without the letter, nor is the letter devoid of the spirit. Each of the two senses is in the other—like the 'wheel within the wheel.' Each needs the other. With those two they constitute 'the perfect science.'"[3]

Out of love for and devotion to Scripture, the Christian exegetes of the Middle Ages pursued the fullest meaning of the biblical text, aided by the Quadriga. These interpreters did not have a one-to-one correspondence with the ancient pagan allegorists who tried to veil the outrageous actions of the gods by allegorizing Homeric myths. Instead, the medieval interpreters believed that the divine inspiration of Scripture justified deeper senses in the text, for divine intent transcends and envelops and clarifies the intent of the human author. The "letter," or foundational sense of the text, matters but is not the endpoint of exegesis. From the letter, the exegete moves to the spiritual meaning—its allegorical, tropological, and anagogical senses. De Lubac writes, "To tell the truth, from the start [these three senses] constitute really only one. The spiritual sense is also necessary for the completion of the literal sense, which latter is indispensable for founding it; it is therefore the natural term of divine inspiration, and, as Bossuet will say, 'pertains to the original, principal plan of the Holy Spirit.' *Christus in littera continetur. The spirit is not outside the history.* They are given together, inseparably, through the fact of a single inspiration."[4]

The Impact of Origen and Augustine

The interpretive methods of Origen influenced later exegetes. Some people imitated him, others criticized him, but his influence was so profound that subsequent interpreters had to deal with him in one way or another. In the Latin Middle Ages, Origen was the most read of all the ancient Greek authors, being constantly cited.[5] As an example, his commentary on the Song of Solomon established the mystical interpretation of the book, an interpretation that became incorporated into the tradition of the church.[6] De Lubac's words summarize the church father's influence: "Throughout the radical transformations or slow evolutions that take place from the fifth century to

---

3. De Lubac, *Medieval Exegesis*, 2:26.
4. De Lubac, *Medieval Exegesis*, 2:26.
5. Henri de Lubac, *Medieval Exegesis: The Four Senses of Scripture*, vol. 1, trans. Mark Sebanc (Grand Rapids: Eerdmans, 1998), 165.
6. De Lubac, *Medieval Exegesis*, 1:170–71.

the thirteenth, the reading and constant use of the translations of Origen constitute one of the elements that assure a continuity."[7]

Augustine's reading of Scripture also made a far-reaching impact. Though
he belonged to the era of the church fathers, his treatment of the biblical text
was studied and followed in the Middle Ages. In fact, Augustine is arguably
the most influential theologian of church history. In particular, "the influence
of Augustine's *On Christian Doctrine* on hermeneutical matters is everywhere
to be seen."[8] In addition to his allegorical interpretations, he valued the historical sense of Scripture, even writing a book entitled *The Literal Meaning
of Genesis*. His works were widely read and influential. Gerald Bonner says,
"The influence of Augustine on the later biblical exegesis of the Latin Middle
Ages was enormous."[9] According to Keith Stanglin, "Augustine's thought—
doctrinal, moral, philosophical, psychological, political, and otherwise—as
distilled and dispersed by subsequent generations of admirers, set the tone for
the Western medieval church."[10]

Aquinas and the Literal Sense

The most influential theologian in the Western church, after Augustine,
is Thomas Aquinas (1225–74).[11] It is Aquinas's view of the literal sense that
marked such a difference in light of earlier interpreters. While critics of medieval interpreters will typically lament an underemphasis on the literal sense,
they cannot rightly charge Aquinas with such a thing. Not only did Aquinas
emphasize the literal sense, he considered the allegorical sense (labeled such
by earlier interpreters) to be embedded in the literal sense.[12]

In his work *Summa Theologiae*, Aquinas addresses the multiple senses
that had been pursued in the Great Tradition. For Aquinas, the literal sense
is the plain sense of Scripture, and since the plain meaning of the text can
be conveyed through features such as figures and metaphors and parables,
"the literal sense is the plain meaning of Scripture in its historical and literary
context."[13] While Aquinas affirms that Scripture can have multiple senses, he
believed that no higher sense is disassociated from, or outside the purview
of, the literal sense. He recognizes that allowing multiple senses can produce

---

7. De Lubac, *Medieval Exegesis*, 1:172.
8. Iain Provan, *The Reformation and the Right Reading of Scripture* (Waco, TX: Baylor
   University Press, 2017), 200.
9. Gerald Bonner, "Augustine as Biblical Scholar," in *The Cambridge History of the Bible*, vol.
   1, *From the Beginnings to Jerome*, eds. P. R. Ackroyd and C. F. Evans (New York: Cambridge
   University Press, 1975), 561.
10. Keith D. Stanglin, *The Letter and Spirit of Biblical Interpretation: From the Early Church to
    Modern Practice* (Grand Rapids: Baker Academic, 2018), 81.
11. Stanglin, *Letter and Spirit of Biblical Interpretation*, 103.
12. Craig A. Carter, *Interpreting Scripture with the Great Tradition: Recovering the Genius of
    Premodern Exegesis* (Grand Rapids: Baker Academic, 2018), 99.
13. Stanglin, *Letter and Spirit of Biblical Interpretation*, 104.

interpretive confusion, so he reiterates that valid spiritual senses flow from what is signified by the literal sense and thus are an extension of the literal sense.[14] With all his writing about the importance of the literal sense, Aquinas does not reject the legitimate pursuit of spiritual senses.

Nicholas and the Double Literal Sense

Nicholas of Lyra (1270–1349) argued that the spiritual senses of Scripture presupposed the literal sense. So while allegorical interpretation was permitted, it should not stray from the literal sense, just like the foundation of a building should not be removed, lest the building collapse.[15] Allegorical interpretation must not be the first concern of an interpreter. Rather, the priority in reading Scripture is to start with understanding the literal sense.[16]

When an interpreter considered a meaning beyond the human author's intent, this consideration would be part of what Nicholas called the "double literal sense." As Stanglin explains, "The double literal sense seems to be Nicholas's way of emphasizing that the spiritual senses must be based on the literal sense. With the double literal sense, the letter of Scripture contains many senses."[17] Nicholas shared a poem that had originated with Augustine of Dacia (c. 1260):

> The letter teaches what happened,
> The allegory what you should believe,
> The moral sense what you should do,
> The anagogy what you should hope.[18]

His use of this poem confirms his approval of the Quadriga, for he even illustrates the fourfold sense with John Cassian's example of Jerusalem, though Nicholas observes that not every biblical passage contains all four senses.[19]

Summary

Allegorical exegesis flourished in the Middle Ages. Relying on the interpretive methods like the Quadriga, readers pursued multiple senses in the biblical text. Even though there were interpreters who emphasized the literal sense as foundational for all other senses, it was easy for readers to embrace mystical and allegorical readings that bypassed, or disengaged from, the literal sense. So theologians like Thomas Aquinas and Nicholas of Lyra highlighted the literal sense and insisted that any higher senses be grounded in

---

14. Stanglin, *Letter and Spirit of Biblical Interpretation*, 104–5.
15. Stanglin, *Letter and Spirit of Biblical Interpretation*, 106.
16. Nicholas of Lyra, "Prologus secundus," in *Patrologia Latina* 113:29C.
17. Stanglin, *Letter and Spirit of Biblical Interpretation*, 107.
18. Nicholas of Lyra, "Incipit prologus," in *Patrologia Latina* 113:28D.
19. Stanglin, *Letter and Spirit of Biblical Interpretation*, 107.

this foundational sense. While they did not reject allegorical readings, their emphasis upon the *historia* of the text would help curb the abuses of spiritual interpretation. Increased significance was given to the literal-grammatical sense. In fact, "the literal sense was enjoying something of a renaissance on the eve of the Reformation."[20]

REFLECTION QUESTIONS

1. What is meant by the *historia* or *littera* of a text?

2. How was Origen influential on later interpreters?

3. How was Augustine influential on later interpreters?

4. What was Thomas Aquinas's view of multiple senses in Scripture?

5. What was Nicholas of Lyra's double literal sense?

---

20. Stanglin, *Letter and Spirit of Biblical Interpretation*, 111.

How Was Allegory Practiced in the Early Modern Era?

During the early modern era (1450–1650), allegorical interpretation received strong criticism. The emphasis on the literal sense by medieval interpreters—like Thomas Aquinas and Nicholas of Lyra—carried over into the preaching and writing of the Reformers. The transition from the Middle Ages to the Reformation "was not, certainly, a transition from precritical to modern 'critical' exegesis. . . . It was a transition, however, from a precritical approach that could acknowledge spiritual senses of the text *beyond* the literal sense to a precritical approach that strove to locate spiritual meaning entirely *in* the literal sense."[1]

Erasmus and Fanciful Reading

As Erasmus (1466–1536) evaluated previous interpreters, he saw an overzealous use of allegorical interpretation. He insisted upon the literal sense as the basis for any spiritual meaning and criticized those who preferred fanciful allegory. But his criticism was not a rejection of finding spiritual meaning in biblical texts. In his fifth rule for Christian living, the principle is to pursue the spirit and not the flesh, and he applies this principle to biblical interpretation.[2] Seeking the spiritual in Scripture presupposes that the words of the text include "body and soul," that is, "a literal and mystical sense."[3]

In his *Handbook of the Christian Soldier*, he writes about the importance of seeking the spiritual meaning in Scripture: "If you read unallegorically of

---

1. Richard A. Muller, "Biblical Interpretation in the Era of the Reformation: The View from the Middle Ages," in *Biblical Interpretation in the Era of the Reformation*, eds. Richard A. Muller and John L. Thompson (Grand Rapids: Eerdmans, 1996), 14 (emphasis added).
2. Keith D. Stanglin, *The Letter and Spirit of Biblical Interpretation: From the Early Church to Modern Practice* (Grand Rapids: Baker Academic, 2018), 120.
3. Stanglin, *Letter and Spirit of Biblical Interpretation*, 120.

222 **Question 29** How Was Allegory Practiced in the Early Modern Era?

the infants struggling within the womb, the right of primogeniture sold for a mess of pottage, the fraudulent seizing of a father's blessing ahead of time, David's slaying of Goliath with a sling, and the shaving off of Samson's locks, then it is of no more importance than if you were to read the fiction of the poets."[4] Erasmus complained about his present-day theologians who either practically despised allegory or treated it with indifference.[5]

Strong Words from Luther

Martin Luther (1483–1546), never a man to hide his thoughts on a matter, spoke frankly about allegorical readings of Scripture. In a lecture on Genesis, Luther said, "Allegory is a sort of beautiful harlot, who proves herself especially seductive to idle men."[6] And, slightly less subtly, "Allegories are empty speculations, and as it were the scum of holy scripture."[7] With such denunciations, we would imagine Luther kept his distance from allegorical interpretation. Philipp Melanchthon sounded like Luther by writing that "any discourse which does not have a single and simple meaning teaches nothing for certain."[8]

The early exegetical work of Luther—when he was still a monk for the Roman Catholic Church and after he embraced the true gospel with reformational unction—evidenced a use of the Quadriga. In an exposition of Psalm 4, he said, "The present psalm is understood first of all concerning Christ, who calls and is heard; then allegorically, concerning the church, His body; and finally, in a tropological sense, concerning any holy soul."[9] Here Luther used multiple senses, except the anagogical. Luther's christological reading is equivalent to the literal sense. "While Luther's commitment to a christological reference remained constant, his disquiet about Quadriga and allegorical interpretation in general intensified over the next few years."[10]

Despite Luther's reaction against allegorical interpretation, his practice in preaching was less stringent. In fact, when reading Luther's words about allegory, context is everything, for he still used allegory sometimes in his own exegesis of Scripture.[11] In Genesis 2:7, God "formed the man of dust from

---

4. Erasmus, *Handbook of the Christian Soldier*, in *Collected Works of Erasmus*, 66:68.

5. Stanglin, *Letter and the Spirit of Biblical Interpretation*, 121. See Erasmus, *Handbook of the Christian Soldier*, 66:34–35.

6. Martin Luther, *Luther's Works*, ed. Jaroslav Pelikan (St. Louis: Concordia Publishing House, 1955–86), 5:347.

7. Martin Luther, as quoted in Brian Cummings, "Protestant Allegory," in *The Cambridge Companion to Allegory*, eds. Rita Copeland and Peter T. Struck (New York: Cambridge University Press, 2010), 177.

8. Philipp Melanchthon, *Elementa rhetorices* (Lyon: Sebastian Gryphius, 1539), 76.

9. Luther, *Luther's Works*, 10:52.

10. Mark D. Thompson, "Biblical Interpretation in the Works of Martin Luther," in *A History of Biblical Interpretation*, vol. 2, *The Medieval through the Reformation Periods*, eds. Alan J. Hauser and Duane F. Watson (Grand Rapids: Eerdmans, 2009), 308.

11. Cummings, "Protestant Allegory," 179.

the ground and breathed into his nostrils the breath of life, and the man became a living creature." About this verse, Luther said, "And here by a very beautiful allegory, or rather by an anagoge, Moses wanted to intimate dimly that God was to become incarnate."[12] By preferring a different term than allegory, Luther makes a distinction to separate himself from the baggage that was connected to "allegory." He viewed a spiritual—or allegorical—reading as legitimate when it could be shown to work intrinsically, with Scripture itself intending the allegory.[13]

For Luther, the plain sense of Scripture was the true meaning. Allegorical readings ran the risk of obscuring the pure meaning of the Bible's language. According to the reformer, "The historical account is like logic in that it teaches what is certainly true; the allegory, on the other hand, is like rhetoric in that it ought to illustrate the historical account but has no value at all for giving proof."[14] Luther engaged in much allegorizing when he was a monk with the Roman Catholic Church, but his writings as a Protestant advocated the clear and simple sense of the biblical text.[15] Biblical passages "are to be retained in their simplest meaning ever possible, and to be understood in their grammatical and literal sense unless the context plainly forbids."[16]

Allegorical interpretation, while possible for interpreters, was not something Luther recommended. Experienced exegetes might seek spiritual meaning in the text, but "unless someone has a perfect knowledge of Christian doctrine, he will not be successful at presenting allegories."[17] The notion that only experienced interpreters should attempt allegorical interpretation echoes Gregory of Nyssa and others who assumed that such a method was not for everyone.[18]

John Calvin and Wayward Allegory

In his *Institutes of the Christian Religion*, John Calvin (1509–1564) wrote about allegorical interpretation in six different passages. Carter summarizes the content of the passages:

> All six are refutations of doctrinal error. Three are arguments against Roman Catholic doctrines: one opposes medieval semi-Pelagianism, another argues against transubstantiation, and one opposes required oral confession to priests. Two of the other passages defend infant baptism, one with

---

12. Luther, *Luther's Works*, 1:87.
13. Cummings, "Protestant Allegory," 179.
14. Luther, *Luther's Works*, 1:233.
15. See Martin Luther, *Table Talks*, #5285.
16. Luther, *Luther's Works*, 6:509.
17. Luther, *Luther's Works*, 26:433.
18. Stanglin, *Letter and Spirit of Biblical Interpretation*, 123–24.

regard to Anabaptists in general and one with regard to Michael Servetus in particular. The sixth passage is one in which Calvin condemns Servetus for denying the ontological reality of the three persons of the Trinity. What is striking about these passages is that he does not say that his opponents are wrong because of their use of the allegorical method of biblical interpretation. . . . His point is that his opponents have interpreted Scripture *poorly* and used allegory in the *wrong way*, which is why they got the result wrong.[19]

To be precise in the relationship between John Calvin and allegorical interpretation, the former was opposed to the waywardness of the latter. He wrote, "Allegories ought not to go beyond the limits set by the rule of Scripture, let alone suffice as the foundation for any doctrines."[20] His words are not a rejection of the method but, rather, a concern about allegories transcending certain limits. Calvin's preaching and writing show that he is not opposed to spiritual meaning in the biblical text, but he is opposed to the abuse of Scripture under the so-called rubric of "spiritual interpretation." For him, what was previously regarded as an allegorical meaning would be included within the literal sense of the text.[21] A christological interpretation was rooted in and encompassed by the "plain sense" of the text.

If Calvin weighed a "deeper" interpretation for a text, it was never the result of rejecting the plain sense. For example, about Moses removing his sandals at the burning bush, Calvin said, "If any prefer the deeper meaning (*anagoge*) that God cannot be heard until we have put off our earthly thoughts, I object not to it; only let the natural sense stand first, that Moses was commanded to put off his shoes, as a preparation to listen with greater reverence to God."[22] And when Calvin considered Paul's words in Galatians 4, he wrote, "As in circumcision, in sacrifices, in the whole Levitical priesthood, there was an allegory, as there is an allegory in the house of Abraham; but this does not involve a departure from the literal meaning."[23] For Calvin, the plain sense of Scripture embraced what had previously been called the literal and spiritual senses.[24]

---

19. Craig A. Carter, *Interpreting Scripture with the Great Tradition: Recovering the Genius of Premodern Exegesis* (Grand Rapids: Baker Academic, 2018), 185.
20. John Calvin, *Institutes of the Christian Religion*, ed. John T. McNeill, trans. Ford Lewis Battles, 2 vols., Library of Christian Classics (Philadelphia: Westminster, 1960), 2.5.19.
21. Carter, *Interpreting Scripture with the Great Tradition*, 99.
22. John Calvin, *Commentaries on the Four Last Books of Moses arranged in the Form of a Harmony*, vol. 1, trans. Charles William Bingham, Calvin's Commentaries (Grand Rapids: Baker, 2005), 64.
23. John Calvin, *Galatians*, trans. William Pringle, Calvin's Commentaries, reprint of the Calvin Translation Society edition (Grand Rapids: Baker, 2005), 136.
24. Carter, *Interpreting Scripture with the Great Tradition*, 176.

While Calvin emphasized the historical and grammatical features of a passage as well as authorial intent, Stanglin cautions us against viewing Calvin as an early proponent of historical-critical exegesis. He says, "Calvin's exegetical practice may reflect the long transition between medieval and modern critical exegesis, but in nearly every respect, he is closer to medieval than to modern exegesis, and he should be interpreted in the former context. All of Calvin's guiding hermeneutical principles, including the stress on authorial intent, are, as we have seen, typical of patristic and medieval biblical interpretation."[25] Calvin's exegesis showed substantial continuity with the medieval tradition rather than a clean break with the past, and he interpreted Scripture in consultation with great interpreters from church history like Chrysostom and Augustine.

William Perkins and the Only Sense

The literal sense was emphasized in the works of William Perkins (1558–1602). In his book *The Art of Prophesying*, he wrote about the fourfold interpretive method (the Quadriga). He said the fourfold method ought to be "exploded" and rejected.[26] He says, with words that capture the tenor of Protestant hermeneutics, "There is one onelie sense, and the same is the literall"[27]—one sense only, the *literal*.

Given the way Perkins spoke about the literal sense, was there a place for allegorical interpretation? According to Perkins, and perhaps surprisingly, yes. An allegory was a specialized type of the literal sense, just as anagogical and tropological meanings were "applied" forms of the single literal sense.[28] So, by speaking of a single literal sense, Perkins is not thereby denying allegorical readings. As with other Protestants, the literal sense has broadened enough to envelop the allegorical. The three spiritual senses of the Quadriga were understood to be "not senses" but "applications" or uses of Scripture.[29]

The concern of Perkins is clear: speaking about multiple senses results in uncertainty of meaning. According to Stanglin, "The assertion of only one sense is the common Protestant reaction to the perceived chaos of spiritual senses not properly linked to the literal sense."[30] But Perkins was open to nonliteral readings of the biblical text. He said that if a literalistic reading is "against common reason, or against the analogy of faith, or against good manners [morals], they are not then to be taken properly, but by figure."[31]

25. Stanglin, *Letter and Spirit of Biblical Interpretation*, 139.
26. William Perkins, *The Arte of Prophecying, or, A Treatise concerning the Sacred and Onely True Manner and Methode of Preaching* (London: Felix Kyngston, 1607), C4v.
27. Perkins, *Arte of Prophecying*, C5r.
28. Cummings, "Protestant Allegory," 184.
29. William Perkins, *A Commentarie or Exposition, vpon the Fiue First Chapters of the Epistle to the Galatians* (Cambridge: John Legate, 1604), XXIr.
30. Stanglin, *Letter and Spirit of Biblical Interpretation*, 143.
31. Perkins, *Galatians*, 305.

Turretin and Uninspired Allegory

Like other reformers, Francis Turretin (1623–1687) spoke of Scripture as having a single sense, and any spiritual meaning was rooted in this literal sense. Since senses were not multiple, interpretation would not be as chaotic. "The importance of the perspicuity of Scripture is evident in Turretin's claim that the sense is single and straightforward."[32] The spiritual senses—which had been previously considered the allegorical, tropological, and anagogical— were understood to be extensions of, applications of, the literal sense.

Turretin is not enthusiastic about allegorical interpretations offered by uninspired interpreters.[33] He believed that certainty about allegorical inter- pretations is possible when a biblical author is doing the allegorizing, but otherwise we are left with the uncertain allegorical interpretations that ac- company the uninspired interpreter. But if an allegorical interpretation is used for the purpose of illustration, then it is suitable as long as the interpreter does not rely on it as proof of a doctrine.[34] Turretin, and Perkins before him, disliked the Quadriga with its multiple senses. Instead, Turretin embraced a fuller sense of the literal sense, which allowed for christological readings of the Old Testament.[35] If the New Testament confirmed a particular allegorical reading of an earlier text, that reading was valid. But in general, for Turretin, Origen's allegorical instincts were not a method that should be followed.

Summary

Christian interpreters in the early modern era rethought the Quadriga that was so dominant during the Middle Ages. The rising Protestant posi- tion was to subsume the spiritual senses—the allegorical, tropological, and anagogical—under the literal sense, emphasizing the single and plain sense of Scripture, which could then have spiritual illustrations or applications. Reformers like Luther and Calvin spoke strong words against allegorical fan- cies, but they did not wholly reject the use of allegory. Christian interpretation during the early modern era was in continuity with convictions of previous interpreters within the Great Tradition. While the Middle Ages saw a shift toward the *littera* of the text, "Luther, Calvin, and their contemporaries did not simply trade allegory for literal interpretation. They strengthened the shift to letter with increased emphasis on textual and philological study, and then proceeded to find various figures and levels of meaning."[36]

---

32. Stanglin, *Letter and Spirit of Biblical Interpretation*, 145.
33. Stanglin, *Letter and Spirit of Biblical Interpretation*, 145.
34. Stanglin, *Letter and Spirit of Biblical Interpretation*, 145.
35. Stanglin, *Letter and Spirit of Biblical Interpretation*, 146.
36. Muller, "Biblical Interpretation in the Era of the Reformation," 12.

REFLECTION QUESTIONS

1. Was Erasmus open to multiple senses in Scripture?

2. Why did Luther have strong words against allegorical interpretation?

3. Where did Luther believe the text's true meaning resides?

4. What did Calvin mean by the "plain sense" of a text?

5. What kind of allegorical interpretations would Turretin permit?

How Was Allegory Practiced in the Enlightenment?

Significant changes occurred in biblical interpretation during the era of the Enlightenment (1650–1800), particularly impacting Bible scholars and their respective academic institutions. While the unity of the Testaments and the divine inspiration of the text were two of the treasured values in premodern exegesis, those values experienced a fracture amid the dominance of humanism.

The Aim of Objectivity

The enlightened position became the following: to assume the divine authorship of Scripture was to compromise the objectivity of the interpreter. People like Thomas Hobbes (1588–1679) rejected the notion that visible things truly related to invisible things. "For Hobbes, then, a proper reading of Scripture is one that is freed from ecclesial constraints and one that abandons the metaphysical notion that earthly things are linked to heavenly things. Having rejected the sacramental link between heaven and earth, Hobbes turned the reading of Scripture into a purely natural exercise of historical scholarship."[1]

A so-called pursuit of objectivity meant this: if the inspiration of Scripture was set aside, and if Scripture could simply be read and studied like any other book, then the interpreter has the best chance of understanding the text. But if biases like divine inspiration and theological unity are permitted to color the eyes of the interpreter, then the true meaning of the text will be unfortunately tainted—maybe lost altogether—in the interpretive task. Baruch Spinoza (1632–1677) believed that the true meaning of Scripture was achieved through human reason and not by any church

---

1. Hans Boersma, *Scripture as Real Presence: Sacramental Exegesis in the Early Church* (Grand Rapids: Baker Academic, 2017), 7.

tradition or authority. Hans Boersma explains, "Human reason has the ability to investigate history, and so Scripture should be read historically rather than allegorically. As a result, Spinoza claimed that Scripture must be treated like any other ordinary, visible thing: it must be analyzed empirically, and one must not allow higher, invisible realities to determine one's natural understanding of the Bible."[2]

Like a rock thrown into a pond, the pursuit of objectivity has a ripple effect. One of the effects is the inadmissibility of allegorical interpretation. If the Bible must be studied like any other piece of literature, with no theological presuppositions that would influence the interpreter, then allegorical interpretation cannot survive such an approach. Allegorizing a biblical text relies on the notion that the text is ultimately *God's* Word for us, and that the divine design has embedded meaning that speaks to the realities of Christ and his church. But if human authorship establishes the limit for what the interpreter can conclude, then obviously human authors are subject to inconsistencies, contradictions, and errors. With the kind of objectivity being pursued by people like Hobbes and Spinoza, there is no room for allegorical readings of texts. Such readings would be viewed as subjective conclusions that wrongly assume a divine design and unity to Scripture and that recklessly exceed the bounds of the human author's intent.

Calling Out the Myth

Historical hindsight helps us to see that total objectivity is a myth. No interpreter is unbiased, every conclusion about the Bible is reached within an individual's worldview (whatever it may be), and the Bible's self-testimony (and the position of the Great Tradition) is that the Bible is certainly *not* like any other book. Interpreters who try to understand Scripture by first ignoring the testimony *of* Scripture and the testimony *about* Scripture have embarked on a kind of scholarship that is something other than Christian.

Christian scholarship is not against reason, and the Great Tradition is bursting with examples of interpreters paying thoughtful attention to the text. Human reason is not dispensable in the interpretive task. But, as John Webster said, "God is not summoned into the presence of reason; reason is summoned before the presence of God."[3] Human reason is not the final arbiter of truth. Sin has affected our human faculties, with reason not exempted. In order to understand the meaning of Scripture, the interpreter ultimately needs more than grammatical and historical tools. The interpreter needs eyes to see and ears to hear. "Holy Scripture is the result of a divine movement; it is generated not simply by human spontaneity but by the moving power of the Holy Spirit.

---

2. Boersma, *Scripture as Real Presence*, 8.
3. John Webster, *Holiness* (Grand Rapids: Eerdmans, 2003), 17.

That moving power so orders these human, textual acts of communication that they may fittingly serve the publication of the knowledge of God."[4]

Before and after the Enlightenment

Interpretation during the years of the Enlightenment starkly contrasts with how premodern Christian interpreters treated the biblical text. Spinoza was among the first interpreters "to look behind the biblical text for historical origins, arriving at positions that adumbrated viewpoints commonly associated with the later higher biblical criticism of nineteenth-century German scholarship."[5] As Richard Muller and John Thompson put it, "unlike the historical-critical exegesis of the eighteenth, nineteenth, and twentieth centuries, the older exegesis (whether of the patristic, medieval, or Reformation eras) understood the *historia*—that is, the story that the text is properly understood to recount—to be resident in the text and not under or behind it."[6]

In other words, according to the Great Tradition, the way to understand the meaning of the biblical text is not by going behind the text. The canonical text must be the focus of the interpreter. If, instead, the canonical text is viewed to be the final stage of composition that must be deconstructed in order to get at the real or intended meaning, then the Great Tradition has been on the wrong path all along. Allegorical interpretation—being founded upon the literal sense and then seeking to make innerbiblical connections that testify of Christ and edify the church—would be a severe deviation from sound interpretation. The premodern exegetes believed that "the meaning of a text is governed by the scope and goal of the biblical book in the context of the scope and goal of the canonical revelation of God. In other words, Christian exegetes traditionally have assumed that a divine purpose and divine authorship unite the text of the entire canon."[7]

Hans Frei observes that "once literal and historical reading began to break apart, figural interpretation became discredited both as a literary device and as a historical argument."[8] The Great Tradition believed that God's plan was embedded in Old Testament signs and symbols and types, and these elements were fulfilled in Christ and his church in the centuries that followed these patterns and prophecies. Yet the philosophical cracks within biblical studies had effects deep and wide, for they "strained credulity beyond the breaking point by the suggestion that sayings and events of one day referred predictively to

---

4. Webster, *Holiness*, 18.
5. Boersma, *Scripture as Real Presence*, 9.
6. Richard A. Muller and John L. Thompson, "The Significance of Precritical Exegesis: Retrospect and Prospect," in *Biblical Interpretation in the Era of the Reformation*, eds. Richard A. Muller and John L. Thompson (Grand Rapids: Eerdmans, 1996), 339.
7. Muller and Thompson, "Significance of Precritical Exegesis," 340.
8. Hans W. Frei, *The Eclipse of Biblical Narrative: A Study in Eighteenth and Nineteenth Century Hermeneutics* (New Haven, CT: Yale University Press, 1974), 6.

specific persons and events hundreds of years later."[9] From a historical-critical perspective, typological exegesis and allegorical interpretation were absurd. Interpreting the Bible with the Great Tradition can only be done with a supernatural worldview. The problem in the Enlightenment was that human reason became the alternative to a supernatural worldview.[10]

The Exegesis of the Puritans

Though allegorical interpretation suffered under the naturalistic assumptions of the Enlightenment's approach to the Bible, the Puritans were an exception to these assumptions and affirmed the divine inspiration and unity of Scripture. The Puritans believed interpreters should honor the literal sense of the text. They noted various types within the Old Testament, but they were reluctant to employ allegorical interpretation. Thomas Gataker (1574–1654) laid out the Puritan sentiment when he said, "We dare not allegorize the Scriptures, where the letter of it yields us a clear and proper Sense."[11] But there were occasions when an allegorical reading was preferable. For example, in his interpretation of the Song of Solomon, James Durham (1622–1658) affirmed the literal sense of the Song but believed this sense incorporated "figures and allegories" that the Spirit intended, pointing to the communion between Christ and his church.[12]

Jonathan Edwards (1703–1758) exhibited a deep reverence for Scripture. He affirmed the unity of the Testaments and the interconnectedness of God's revelation. He shared an outlook that "was strikingly akin to that group of late seventeenth- and early-eighteenth-century thinkers who have been characterized as 'theocentric metaphysicians,'" people who saw any new science as compatible with God's intimate and moment-by-moment involvement with creation.[13] Edwards was a patient exegete, devoting many hours to studying a text's grammatical and historical meaning. But his commitment to the literal sense did not exclude employing a spiritual reading of the text.[14]

---

9. Frei, *Eclipse of Biblical Narrative*, 6.

10. Craig A. Carter, *Interpreting Scripture with the Great Tradition: Recovering the Genius of Premodern Exegesis* (Grand Rapids: Baker Academic, 2018), 88.

11. As quoted in Leland Ryken, *Worldly Saints: The Puritans as They Really Were* (Grand Rapids: Zondervan, 1986), 145.

12. Joel R. Beeke and Mark Jones, *A Puritan Theology: Doctrine for Life* (Grand Rapids: Reformation Heritage Books, 2012), 34.

13. George M. Marsden, *Jonathan Edwards: A Life* (New Haven, CT: Yale University Press, 2003), 73–74.

14. David Barshinger, "'The Only Rule of Our Faith and Practice': Jonathan Edwards's Interpretation of the Book of Isaiah as a Case Study of His Exegetical Boundaries," *Journal of the Evangelical Theological Society* 52, no. 4 (December 2009): 823.

The Full Force of Change

The critical assumptions of the latter 1600s achieved a powerful effect in the 1700s. Iain Provan writes, "It is the eighteenth century above all that is associated with the title 'the Age of Enlightenment.' Among its most famous names we must include Voltaire (Francois-Marie Arouet, 1694–1778), David Hume (1711–1776), Jean-Jacques Rousseau (1712–1778), Adam Smith (1723–1790), and Immanuel Kant (1724–1804)."[15]

By the 1700s, the unity of Scripture was unstable, and the historicity of the biblical text was untrustworthy. According to Hans Frei, "The full force of the change in outlook and argument concerning the narrative biblical texts came in the eighteenth century."[16] Belief in the Bible's authority and unity had declined. Johann Semler (1725–1791), a major historical-critical scholar, believed that the Bible contained matters of religious interest but that "one can no longer believe in the equal inspiredness of all the books of the Bible."[17] Semler's view was quite representative. There had been a slow but steady shift toward a "historical interpretation" of the Bible in the works of Eichhorn, Gabler, Michaelis, and others, but Semler was the first German Protestant theologian to approach the Bible through the history of religions and to insist on a critical rather than dogmatic reading of it.[18] Then, by the end of the eighteenth century in Germany, "most Old Testament professors were either neologists (skeptical biblical scholars) or rationalists."[19]

Summary

During the Enlightenment, some major biblical-theological assumptions of premodern exegetes were questioned and suspended. The goal was to pursue meaning with an objective method, not allowing the biases of the interpreter to affect the interpretation of the biblical text. Human reason was elevated, and the divine inspiration and unity of Scripture were seen as impediments to understanding the real meaning of the text. In this philosophical environment, allegorical interpretation is a nonstarter, for this method depends on the very assumptions that were being suspended. Scholars imagined the Bible to be like any other piece of literature. But according to the Great Tradition, the Bible isn't like any other book, and interpreting the Bible is always done from a set of assumptions. There is no true objectivity, for every interpreter has a worldview, and that worldview impacts the understanding of the biblical text.

---

15. Iain Provan, *The Reformation and the Right Reading of Scripture* (Waco, TX: Baylor University Press, 2017), 391.
16. Frei, *Eclipse of Biblical Narrative*, 51.
17. Frei, *Eclipse of Biblical Narrative*, 111.
18. Craig G. Bartholomew, *Introducing Biblical Hermeneutics: A Comprehensive Framework for Hearing God in Scripture* (Grand Rapids: Baker Academic, 2015), 211.
19. Bartholomew, *Biblical Hermeneutics*, 211.

REFLECTION QUESTIONS

1. How did Thomas Hobbes and Baruch Spinoza approach biblical interpretation?

2. How should we respond to the notion of interpretive objectivity?

3. What role should human reason play in the task of interpretation?

4. How was allegorical interpretation affected by the elevation of human reason?

5. What did the Puritans think about allegorical interpretation?

How Was Allegory Practiced in the Late Modern Era?

Significant philosophical shifts in the Enlightenment were like seeds that grew into trees of skepticism and anti-supernaturalism, and in the late modern era (1800–1900) we tasted the fruit on the branches. Not all initial advocates of the historical-critical method had a distaste for the Bible's supernatural claims and events, but the pursuit of meaning behind the biblical text was a trajectory away from canonical exegesis into something that, in the end, diminished the Bible and scorned the Great Tradition.[1]

What to Do with the Old Testament

Whereas the unity of the Testaments grounded the practice of allegorical reading, the compartmentalization of the Testaments—and of individual books—destroyed this practice. A major issue for interpreters was what to do with the Old Testament. According to Ellen Davis, "Probably the most far-reaching issue separating traditional and modern (or postmodern) biblical interpretation is whether—and if so, how—to read the Old Testament as a witness to Jesus Christ."[2]

How could the Old Testament bear witness to Christ if the historicity of its teachings and events was in doubt? And if the New Testament referred to Old Testament people who didn't exist and events that didn't happen, then the New Testament must be viewed with suspicion rather than as an authoritative

---

1. It became popular to prioritize the deconstruction of texts, propose stages of composition, and explain away any supernatural elements in the accounts. If academic practice revealed priorities, then biblical "truth" was to be found not in the canonical form of the text but in the text's alleged precanonical history and in the reimagined context and community that eventually gave rise to the text(s).
2. Ellen F. Davis, "Teaching the Bible Confessionally in the Church," in *The Art of Reading Scripture*, eds. Ellen F. Davis and Richard B. Hays (Grand Rapids: Eerdmans, 2003), 18.

and trustworthy engagement of the Old Testament. If Adam never lived, if a garden never grew in Eden, if an ark never survived a flood, if the Red Sea never parted, if manna never rained from heaven, if Sinai never thundered with smoke and fire, if the tabernacle was never built—if all these things and more didn't happen as the text reports them, then what shall we do with the Old Testament? If Isaiah didn't write the book of Isaiah, and if the book of Daniel was written later than the events it prophesies, then what shall we do with the Old Testament?

The ironic effect of historical criticism—whether intended or not—was to deny what the Bible presented as historical and to equate criticism with skepticism. As Carl Braaten and Robert Jenson put it, "The historical-critical method was originally devised and welcomed as the great emancipator of the Bible from ecclesiastical dogma and blind faith. Some practitioners of the method now sense that the Bible may have meanwhile become its victim."[3]

Getting Behind the Myths

One scholar who stood "at the origin" of biblical criticism was Wilhelm de Wette (1780–1849). He believed that the biblical texts contain not reliable history but myth, and myths can contain "sublime ideas" that are worthy to observe and study.[4] For example, the stories in the Pentateuch, while of no value for the historian, were "a product of the religious poetry of the Israelite people, which reflects their spirit [*Geist*], a way of thought, love of the nation, philosophy of religion."[5] When Julius Wellhausen (1844–1918) came along, he speculated about nondivine origins of the Pentateuch, and his views—formulated in the Documentary Hypothesis—"became the virtual consensus" in Old Testament scholarship.[6] Wellhausen did not want philosophical concerns to impact biblical studies; in his view, "Old Testament research uncovers the facts, and philosophy can follow the facts but should not precede them!"[7] He expected research to be scientific, objective, and neutral.[8] When Heinrich Ewald (1803–1875) studied the Old Testament accounts, he wanted to know what *really* happened, not just what tradition handed down.[9] And by "tradition," Ewald means the biblical text! He believed, for example, that the value

---

3. Carl E. Braaten and Robert W. Jenson, eds., *Reclaiming the Bible for the Church* (Grand Rapids: Eerdmans, 1995), ix.
4. Craig G. Bartholomew, *Introducing Biblical Hermeneutics: A Comprehensive Framework for Hearing God in Scripture* (Grand Rapids: Baker Academic, 2015), 213–14.
5. Bartholomew, *Biblical Hermeneutics*, 215.
6. J. Rogerson, *W. M. L. de Wette, Founder of Modern Biblical Criticism: An Intellectual Biography*, Journal for the Study of the Old Testament Supplement 126 (Sheffield: Sheffield Academic, 1992), 55, quoted in Bartholomew, *Biblical Hermeneutics*, 220.
7. Bartholomew, *Biblical Hermeneutics*, 222.
8. Bartholomew, *Biblical Hermeneutics*, 223.
9. Iain Provan, *The Reformation and the Right Reading of Scripture* (Waco, TX: Baylor University Press, 2017), 412.

of the patriarchal narratives (or traditions) in Genesis were not reliable and must be doubted.[10]

In the area of New Testament studies, a significant historical-critical scholar was Ferdinand Christian Bauer (1792–1860). He applied an anti-supernatural approach to the New Testament, he denied that the Pauline Letters could be reconciled with the accounts in Acts, and he classified Acts as a second-century document that was historically untrustworthy.[11] S. J. Hafemann summarizes Bauer's impact: "Ever since Bauer all interpretations of the New Testament have had to pass the test of historical probability in a way not enforced prior to the nineteenth century, even for those who accept the reality of divine intervention and the authority of Scripture."[12] When David Strauss (1808–1874) rejected the miracles and divinity of Christ—and by implication rejected Christianity—he was working out in his scholarship the implications of the historical-critical assumptions. Strauss basically argues for the application of the category of myth to the New Testament.[13] He argues that Origen's allegorical method is an example of the mythological approach.[14] The image of a kernel and husk is helpful for Strauss. He believes the allegorical method extracts the rational idea (or kernel) from the text, while the husk of historical truth is discarded.[15] Benjamin Jowett (1817–1893) believed the interpreter should try to "get rid of interpretation,"[16] so that no system of thought outside the Bible would influence the interpreter. A key component of Jowett's hermeneutical approach is clear, in his own words: *"Interpret the Scripture like any other book."*[17]

Forsaking the Great Tradition

Despite how the premodern exegetes were viewed by some scholars in the nineteenth century, and despite attempts by Strauss to say that his mythologizing project was parallel to the method of Origen, at least four observations are in order. First, the view that Scripture should be read like any other book is in stark contrast with the Great Tradition. As Richard Muller and John Thompson state, "Precritical exegesis was not always correct in its assertions, nor certainly univocal in its views; but it was always concerned to locate

---

10. Provan, *Reformation and the Right Reading of Scripture*, 412.
11. Bartholomew, *Biblical Hermeneutics*, 219.
12. S. J. Hafemann, "Bauer F(erdinand) C(hristian) (1792–1860)," in *Historical Handbook of Major Biblical Interpreters*, ed. D. K. McKim (Downers Grove, IL: InterVarsity, 1998), 289.
13. Craig A. Carter, *Interpreting Scripture with the Great Tradition: Recovering the Genius of Premodern Exegesis* (Grand Rapids: Baker Academic, 2018), 117.
14. Carter, *Interpreting Scripture with the Great Tradition*, 117.
15. Carter, *Interpreting Scripture with the Great Tradition*, 118.
16. Benjamin Jowett, "On the Interpretation of Scripture," in *Essays and Reviews* (London: John W. Parker & Son, 1860), 384.
17. Jowett, "Interpretation of Scripture," 377 (emphasis original).

biblical exegesis within the community of those who valued the text as more than a curiosity, indeed, as inspired Scripture."[18]

Second, an interpreter's commitment to the historical-critical method will lead to conclusions undermining Christian convictions, such as God's divine authorship of Scripture and the unity of the Testaments. Andrew Louth is right: "Nothing like traditional Christianity can survive in such an environment, for such traditional Christianity claims that through certain specific events in the past God has revealed himself to men."[19] The practice of something like allegorical interpretation is excluded by the historical-critical method.

Third, Strauss's comparison of his own method to that of Origen's allegorizing is not a fair comparison. Origen believed in the divine inspiration and unity of Scripture; Strauss did not. Origen over and over affirmed the historicity of biblical persons and events; Strauss did not. When Origen did deviate from a historical reading and spoke only of a spiritual one, he believed the text compelled him to do so; Strauss was driven by his antisupernatural presuppositions. When Origen opened the Bible, he did not believe he was reading myths; Strauss did. According to Henri de Lubac,

> If one wants to find anything like veritable imitators of the ancient mythologists, the Cornutuses and Heraclituses, the Sallusts and Julians, the Procluses and Olympiodoruses, this is not to be achieved by turning to Origens or Gregories, Augustines, Bedes, or Ruperts. It would rather be among a certain number of scholars of the last century, who briskly turned into myths not only the narratives of Genesis but also those of the books of Judges and Kings, and sometimes even those of the Gospels. Such imitators included G. L. Bauer (1802), Lebrecht de Wette (1807), H. Ewald (1843), Th. Noldeke (1868), Ed. Schrader (1869), J. Wellhausen (1878), E. Stucken (1896), H. Winckler (1902). Such an imitator was D. Fr. Strauss (1835–36). For Bauer, for example, the majority of the alleged facts of the Bible had their parallels in the Greek or Roman fables; for de Wette, the key of myth naturally explained all the alleged miracles of the Bible; for Stucken, the Patriarchs were merely the stars, etc.[20]

18. Richard A. Muller and John L. Thompson, "The Significance of Precritical Exegesis: Retrospect and Prospect," in *Biblical Interpretation in the Era of the Reformation*, eds. Richard A. Muller and John L. Thompson (Grand Rapids: Eerdmans, 1996), 345.

19. Andrew Louth, *Discerning the Mystery: An Essay on the Nature of Theology* (Oxford: Clarendon, 1983), 16.

20. Henri de Lubac, *Medieval Exegesis: The Four Senses of Scripture*, vol. 2, trans. Mark Sebanc (Grand Rapids: Eerdmans, 2000), 18.

Fourth, to begin with an antisupernatural posture toward the biblical text is to leave the realm of neutrality. Moreover, no neutral position toward the Bible is possible. The objectivity of the scientific method cannot be seamlessly transferred to the task of reading Scripture. According to Peter Leithart, "The whole process is a ruse. No method is theologically neutral, and method often functions as a way of determining ahead of time what the text can and cannot be allowed to say."[21]

Summary

In the nineteenth century, allegorical interpretation was treated with a general distaste. The rise of the historical-critical method brought great damage to the interpreter's engagement with the text. Instead of scholars devoting themselves to the canonical text, they deviated into methods of deconstruction, all the while driven by an alleged neutrality of antisupernaturalism. They needed to get behind the text and see through the myths, in order to arrive at the true meaning of what the (human) authors intended. In Criag Carter's assessment, "Modern historical-critical study of the Bible is based on a false conception of created reality, a false conception of history, and a false conception of the Bible. The study of the Bible is not enhanced by historical criticism; it is only eroded and demeaned."[22]

REFLECTION QUESTIONS

1. What kind of assumptions about the Bible does the historical-critical method make?

2. Who were some higher-critical scholars in the nineteenth century?

3. According to higher-critical scholars, what is the value of the Old Testament if its narratives do not report historically reliable events?

4. Why did David Strauss justify his approach to the Bible using the allegorical interpretations of Origen?

5. Why is allegorical interpretation not possible in the higher-critical method?

---

21. Peter J. Leithart, "The Quadriga or Something Like It: A Biblical and Pastoral Defense," in *Ancient Faith for the Church's Future*, eds. Mark Husbands and Jeffrey P. Greenman (Downers Grove, IL: IVP Academic, 2008), 116.

22. Carter, *Interpreting Scripture with the Great Tradition*, 126.

How Was Allegory Practiced in the Postmodern Era?

The postmodern era (1900 to present day) has witnessed a retrieval of premodern exegesis. This retrieval has not been unanimously embraced, for the implications of the historical-critical method are still seen and practiced in scholarship. But the interest in premodern exegesis is being cultivated and provides a needed corrective to the antisupernatural presuppositions that have pervaded biblical scholarship for the last few centuries.

Looking for the Real Jesus

The first quest for the historical Jesus (1778–1906) began with the publication of H. S. Reimarus's book *The Wolfenbüttel Fragments*, in which he disputed the connection between the "Jesus of history" and the "Christ of faith." In the first decade of the twentieth century, this quest came to an end as publications sent Jesus scholars in different directions.[1] But a second quest began in 1954, led by Ernst Käsemann (1906–1998) and other students of Rudolf Bultmann, and they valued noncanonical "gospel" documents in the attempt to understand how Jesus was connected to early Christianity.[2] This second quest has not ended. A third quest began in approximately 1965, connected to G. B. Caird's publication of *Jesus and the Jewish Nation*, a book that—like the third quest—seeks to situate Jesus in the context of first-century Second Temple Judaism.[3]

---

1. Andreas J. Köstenberger, L. Scott Kellum, Charles L. Quarles, *The Cradle, the Cross, and the Crown: An Introduction to the New Testament*, 2nd ed. (Nashville: B&H Academic, 2016), 125–26.
2. Köstenberger, Kellum, Quarles, *Introduction to the New Testament*, 127.
3. Köstenberger, Kellum, Quarles, *Introduction to the New Testament*, 128.

If the search for the real Jesus begins with forging a split between a "Jesus of history" and "Christ of faith," then scholars have derailed already. Since all historical inquiry is done according to a worldview, any quest for the real Jesus is a quest anchored in presuppositions. While these modern quests entertain the notion of whether the Jesus of history is the Christ of faith, the premodern exegetes in the Great Tradition would have rejected this false dichotomy. The Jesus of history *is* the Christ of faith.

The modern quests for Jesus have implications for allegorical interpretation. If the canonical text—even with its supernatural elements—is not the locus of truth about Jesus, then the notion of divinely embedded meaning in the words and events of Scripture is a nonstarter. Much about these historical quests for Jesus do not foster an academic pursuit in continuity with the Great Tradition. But if we posit that the Jesus of history is the Christ of faith, if we read the Bible as God's inspired and authoritative Word to his church, if we recognize that the unity of the Bible was established by a divine author who has woven symbol and mystery into the text, then allegorical interpretation would not be considered an outlandish approach to sacred Scripture.

The Parables and Jülicher

When reading the parables in works of premodern exegetes, we will find that seeing symbolic and allegorical significance to the details was a common approach. A famous example is Augustine's interpretation of the good Samaritan in Luke 10:30–37. Augustine said the wounded man was Adam, the beating was enticement to sin, the Samaritan was Jesus, two denarii were the two commandments to love God and neighbor, the inn was the church, and so on.[4] Countering this approach was the work of Adolf Jülicher (1857–1938), who argued that the parables as originally told by Jesus were meant to highlight one point of comparison and that the allegorical elements were later additions made by the church.[5]

Rather than reading parables according to Jülicher's assumption, we should see the parables in the Gospels as accurately conveying the teaching of Christ, and that even the allegorical elements were intended by him. Good wisdom is in the following approach: "The parables of Jesus are neither simple stories teaching single morals nor pure allegories. In most parables, some details are symbolic and some are not. The key to proper interpretation is to distinguish the symbolic and non-symbolic elements and then determine the referents of each symbol."[6] This key does not mean that interpreting Jesus's parables is solely in the eye of the beholder, but it does mean that we should understand, in Craig Blomberg's words, that "the Gospel parables, with or

---

4. Köstenberger, Kellum, Quarles, *Introduction to the New Testament*, 209.
5. Köstenberger, Kellum, Quarles, *Introduction to the New Testament*, 209–10.
6. Köstenberger, Kellum, Quarles, *Introduction to the New Testament*, 210.

without the alleged additions and interpretations of later tradition, are allegories, and they probably teach several lessons apiece."[7]

Approaching the Song of Solomon

In the Great Tradition, the Song of Solomon was treated allegorically, until modern scholarship. Hans Boersma writes, "When we look at the way people read the Song of Solomon in the past, we notice a fairly radical break in about the mid-1800s in the way people understand the Song. . . . All this time, for the first 1,800 years of the Christian faith, people read this love song about Solomon and the Shulamite as an allegory, a picture of the relationship between Christ and his church."[8] And the shift in interpretive approach continued into the 1900s and into the twenty-first century as well. For example, one commentator writes that there is nothing in the Song of Solomon "that hints of a meaning different from the sexual meaning."[9]

Yet some commentaries in our postmodern era have been written that approach the Song of Solomon in a way reminiscent of premodern exegetes. For example, Christopher Mitchell wrote on the Song of Solomon and advocates many figurative and allegorical interpretations of the biblical book's details.[10] And James Hamilton wrote a commentary whose title is very transparent: *Song of Songs: A Biblical-Theological, Allegorical, Christological Interpretation.*[11] These recent works are part of a growing movement of exegesis that we could consider a return to premodern interpretation.

Returning to Premodern Interpretation

In 1980, David Steinmetz published an article called "The Superiority of Pre-Critical Exegesis."[12] He contends, "Only by confessing the multiple sense of Scripture is it possible for the church to make use of the Hebrew Bible at all or to recapture the various levels of significance in the unfolding story of creation and redemption."[13] But by no means does Steinmetz offer an endorsement of all the interpretations from premodern exegetes. He says, for example, that the "medieval exegetes made bad mistakes in the application of

7. Craig L. Blomberg, *Interpreting the Parables* (Downers Grove, IL: InterVarsity, 1990), 69.
8. Hans Boersma, *Sacramental Preaching: Sermons on the Hidden Presence of Christ* (Grand Rapids: Baker Academic, 2016), 43.
9. Tremper Longman III, *Song of Songs*, New International Commentary on the Old Testament (Grand Rapids: Eerdmans, 2001), 36.
10. Christopher W. Mitchell, *The Song of Songs*, Concordia Commentary (St. Louis: Concordia Publishing House, 2003).
11. James M. Hamilton Jr., *Song of Songs: A Biblical-Theological, Allegorical, Christological Interpretation*, Focus on the Bible (Fearn, Ross-shire, Scotland: Christian Focus, 2015).
12. David C. Steinmetz, "The Superiority of Pre-Critical Exegesis," *Theology Today* 37, no. 1 (April 1980): 27–38.
13. Steinmetz, "Superiority of Pre-Critical Exegesis," 32.

their theory, but they also scored notable and brilliant triumphs."[14] Steinmetz is rightly critical of the modernist assumptions that undermined the Great Tradition: "Until the historical-critical method becomes critical of its own theoretical foundations and develops a hermeneutical theory adequate to the nature of the text which it is interpreting, it will remain restricted—as it deserves to be—to the guild and the academy, where the question of truth can endlessly be deferred."[15]

In his book *Discerning the Mystery* (1983), Andrew Louth addresses some effects of the Enlightenment and makes a defense for allegorical exegesis.[16] During the 1990s and 2000s, a series of works were published that address parts or the whole of the Great Tradition. Frances Young wrote *Biblical Exegesis and the Formation of Christian Culture*, where (among other arguments) she countered the caricatures connected to the Alexandrian and Antiochene schools.[17] Henri de Lubac's series on *Medieval Exegesis* was published in English.[18] He delves not only into the vast realm of the Middle Ages and its many interpreters but also lays the foundation of patristic hermeneutics in order to demonstrate the continuity developing in the Great Tradition. Hans Boersma and Matthew Levering edited *Heaven on Earth? Theological Interpretation in Ecumenical Dialogue*, which contains essays like "'There's Fire in That Rain': On Reading the Letter and Reading Allegorically" by Lewis Ayres and "Origen against History? Reconsidering the Critique of Allegory" by Peter Martens.[19]

In 2017–2018, Baker Academic published three important books: *Scripture as Real Presence* by Hans Boersma,[20] *Interpreting Scripture with the Great Tradition* by Craig Carter,[21] and *The Letter and Spirit of Biblical Interpretation* by Keith Stanglin.[22] These books encourage the understanding and implementation of premodern interpretation that is rooted in assumptions like the divine authorship and inspiration of Scripture, the unity of the

---

14. Steinmetz, "Superiority of Pre-Critical Exegesis," 38.
15. Steinmetz, "Superiority of Pre-Critical Exegesis," 38.
16. Andrew Louth, *Discerning the Mystery: An Essay on the Nature of Theology* (Oxford: Clarendon, 1983).
17. Frances M. Young, *Biblical Exegesis and the Formation of Christian Culture* (Grand Rapids: Baker Academic, 1997).
18. Henri de Lubac, *Medieval Exegesis: The Four Senses of Scripture*, 3 vols., trans. Mark Sebanc (Grand Rapids: Eerdmans, 1998–2009).
19. Hans Boersma and Matthew Levering, eds., *Heaven on Earth? Theological Interpretation in Ecumenical Dialogue* (Hoboken, NJ: Wiley-Blackwell, 2013).
20. Hans Boersma, *Scripture as Real Presence: Sacramental Exegesis in the Early Church* (Grand Rapids: Baker Academic, 2017).
21. Craig A. Carter, *Interpreting Scripture with the Great Tradition: Recovering the Genius of Premodern Exegesis* (Grand Rapids: Baker Academic, 2018).
22. Keith D. Stanglin, *The Letter and Spirit of Biblical Interpretation: From the Early Church to Modern Practice* (Grand Rapids: Baker Academic, 2018).

Testaments, and the christological reading of the Old Testament. While the authors of these three books do not endorse all the interpretations of premodern exegetes, they heartily commend a posture toward sacred Scripture that is consistent with the Great Tradition rather than the historical-critical method.

Summary

Our postmodern era has witnessed a recovery—even a rediscovery—of premodern exegesis in academic circles. Various articles and books in the 1900s and 2000s have addressed the Great Tradition with the goal of countering caricatures, providing nuance and clarification, and tracing the development and direction of the literal and spiritual senses of Scripture. Some commentaries have even employed allegorical interpretations. The revived interest in premodern exegesis is not unanimous, for scholarship is still mixed with those who study the Old and New Testaments with little or no interest in holding the interpretive convictions of the Great Tradition. But for those who believe the Bible is the Word of God for the people of God, the Great Tradition will continue to be a source of wisdom and guidance.

REFLECTION QUESTIONS

1. How did so-called quests for the historical Jesus impact the practice of allegorical interpretation?

2. Do Jesus's parables have allegorical elements?

3. What shifted in the interpretation of the Song of Solomon in the 1800s?

4. What does David Steinmetz think about the historical-critical method and premodern exegesis?

5. How were the 1990s and 2000s significant for understanding premodern exegesis?

Identifying Allegories

How Should We Practice Allegorical Interpretation?

We should practice allegorical interpretation only if we can make a textual and canonical case for our conclusions. The previous sentence makes at least three assumptions: good arguments are vital, allegorical interpretations are not automatically erroneous, and the meaning of a text is clearest in light of the whole canon.

The Literal Sense and More

Paying attention to the literal sense of a biblical text, we must consider whether there are literary reasons to move beyond what we see there. For example, are we reading a parable or a prophetic vision? Those may have allegorical elements that are built into the passage itself. In fact, sometimes an allegorical interpretation is even supplied in a subsequent biblical text, such as when Jesus explains what he meant in a parable or when a prophetic vision is unpacked by God, an angel, or the prophet himself.

In narratives, allegorical interpretation might be done when elements in the passage seem connected to other parts of the biblical revelation. The interpreter must be cautious with narratives, though, for allegorizing them will surpass not only what the initial audience may have understood but also what the human author may have intended. The reason that allegorizing narratives could be valid, however, is the divine authorship of Scripture. The two testaments are interconnected in hundreds of places, all of which the Lord has superintended by the Spirit and for the benefit of readers.

In the early church, interpreters embraced literal and spiritual senses of Scripture. Thus a passage would have levels of both *historia* and *allegoria*. Origen divided the spiritual sense into the Scripture's soul and spirit. John Cassian—and the medieval interpreters that followed him—divided the

senses of Scripture fourfold: the literal, allegorical, tropological, and anagogical senses. The last three senses comprised the spiritual sense. Medieval
interpreters like Aquinas, along with the Reformers who came later, wanted
to press heavily on the literal sense and to root any other meaning in that
literal (or "plain") sense. By majoring so strongly in the literal sense, these
interpreters considered spiritual meaning to be an extension or application
of—and not departure from—the literal sense.

So how should we classify allegorical interpretation as twenty-first century readers? Allegorical interpretation is a kind of spiritual reading that
needs to be warranted by and grounded in the literal or plain sense of the
text as viewed through a canonical lens. Allegorical interpretation should
not be motivated by a desire to diminish the historical accounts in Scripture
or to circumvent the supernatural elements in Scripture. There ought to be
sound literary reasons—textual arguments—for an allegorical reading. For
example, if the parable of the prodigal son (see Luke 15:11–32) should be
read allegorically, then the interpreter should be able to defend those exegetical conclusions by pointing to the context, other parables, other clear
teachings of Jesus, or allusions to the Old Testament in order to vindicate a
deeper reading of Jesus's words. Or if the actions of a Bible character should
be understood allegorically, such as Rahab's hanging a scarlet cord from
a window, then the interpreter should be able to defend that position by
pointing to surrounding passages or literary features that bolster a deeper
reading of that character's action.

Learning from Allegorical Excesses

When present-day interpreters consider the notion of allegorical interpretation, a common objection is the observation of excesses. And if we can
point to previous interpreters who took the text too far, what is to keep us
from doing the same? Couldn't allegorizing texts simply be a risk too great
to take? Consider, first, that whenever we interpret a passage of Scripture (no
matter the method), we do so as uninspired interpreters who are engaging
the inspired text. There is an inherent "risk" in this task, since the certainty of
interpretations could be on a spectrum ranging from most probable to most
improbable. Second, the historical-critical method has embraced its own kind
of speculation. Stanglin explains:

> Ironically, one of the common criticisms leveled by moderns
> against allegorical interpretation is that it leads to specula-
> tion far removed from the text at hand and that it serves as
> a means to show off the creativity of the interpreter. Yet the
> historical-critical method, as generally practiced, includes
> no less speculation, albeit of a different flavor. Unrestrained,

premodern spiritual speculation has been traded in for unrestrained, modern historical speculation.[1]

The answer to unbridled allegorical interpretation is not to abandon allegorical interpretation but to bridle it. One reason allegorical excesses have occurred is insufficient textual warrant. An interpreter may object to an allegorical reading by insisting that there is no textual reason to affirm such a reading. This is a valid objection because we should avoid readings that have no other defense than the subjective instinct of the allegorizer. A second reason allegorical excesses have occurred is the desire to find meaning in too many details. If an allegorical interpretation tries to account for every detail in a passage, the credibility of the method becomes strained by overzealous readings. Not every detail of a passage has to be allegorized in order for an allegorical interpretation of a passage to be valid. A third reason allegorical excesses have occurred is the failure to allow the literal sense to shape or inform any further meaning in the passage. The literal sense is crucial, as the Great Tradition will attest. Yet attending to the literal meaning of the text "does not necessitate ruling out a spiritual meaning that can be described as a *sensus plenior* or the spiritual or christological sense of the text."[2] In fact, the literal sense refers to the *meaning* of the biblical text, "whether that meaning is conveyed through literal statements or through some sort of figural language and whether that meaning is what the human author consciously intended or is an extension of the human author's intention implanted in the text by the Holy Spirit through inspiration."[3]

Searching for Controls

Because the divine plan of redemption was integral to God's purpose in creation, the characters and events of the Old Testament had a significance greater and deeper than could be understood at the time. But as God's progressive revelation unfolded in Scripture, the interconnected nature of salvation history became clear. The divine author, who has knitted us together in our mother's wombs, has knitted together a grand epic in the womb—or canon—of Holy Scripture. The pieces cohere because a divine mind has superintended the process from beginning to end.

As interpreters in the Great Tradition engaged the Word of God, they were aware that the Bible's human authors did not see everything clearly and that only in light of the whole canon could a text's fullest meaning be

---

1. Keith D. Stanglin, *The Letter and Spirit of Biblical Interpretation: From the Early Church to Modern Practice* (Grand Rapids: Baker Academic, 2018), 200.
2. Craig A. Carter, *Interpreting Scripture with the Great Tradition: Recovering the Genius of Premodern Exegesis* (Grand Rapids: Baker Academic, 2018), 164.
3. Carter, *Interpreting Scripture with the Great Tradition*, 166–67.

discerned. Multiple controls existed for allegorical interpretation in order to restrain subjective nonsense from being attributed to the Word of God. After all, "the primary concern of those who oppose the spiritual sense, as we have seen, is that there are no limits or controls to what one can find in Scripture."[4] The spiritual sense was never intended to be a slippery slope into nonsensical interpretations. Rather, "it is clear that early Christian interpreters, especially since the time of Irenaeus, have advocated the use of proper limits on the spiritual sense."[5]

First, an allegorical reading needed to be rooted in the plain sense of the text, thus cohering with the rule of Scripture. Calvin criticized allegorical interpretation that wasn't based in the plain sense of the text.[6] Allegorical readings needed to grow out of the "plain sense." The reader should pay attention to words, grammar, context, and organic development that may transpire across the canon. Premodern interpreters cared about such things, and so should we.

Second, an allegorical reading should not contradict other clear passages of Scripture. This means that interpreters must apply the "rule of Scripture." As Aquinas put it, an interpreter should not embrace a spiritual interpretation from a text that is not taught elsewhere in the literal sense.[7] Calvin, who had strong words to say about the allegorical practice, wrote, "Allegories ought not to go beyond the limits set by the rule of Scripture, let alone suffice as the foundation for any doctrines."[8]

Third, not only did allegorical interpretation need to be based in the literal sense and not violate the rule of Scripture, it needed to honor the rule of faith. With Augustine, Calvin, and others, we should insist that allegorical readings not be the foundation of Christian doctrine, yet allegorical readings must not be permitted to contradict the teaching of Christ's church either. The rule of faith is, essentially, Jesus Christ as the scope of Scripture, with the Apostles' Creed serving as a litmus test for exposing anti-Christian interpretations. "For premodern interpreters who emphasized spiritual interpretation, the content of Christian faith was always understood as being a necessary boundary."[9]

Fourth, the unity of the Testaments was a control, for the Great Tradition has recognized that the Old Testament sets up what is fulfilled—or at least inaugurated—in the New Testament. Therefore, we need the New Testament to understand the Old, and we need the Old Testament to understand the New.

---

4.   Stanglin, *Letter and Spirit of Biblical Interpretation*, 205.
5.   Stanglin, *Letter and Spirit of Biblical Interpretation*, 205.
6.   Carter, *Interpreting Scripture with the Great Tradition*, 186.
7.   Stanglin, *Letter and Spirit of Biblical Interpretation*, 206.
8.   John Calvin, *Institutes of the Christian Religion*, eds. John T. McNeill, trans. Ford Lewis Battles, 2 vols., Library of Christian Classics (Philadelphia: Westminster, 1960), 2.5.19 (339).
9.   Stanglin, *Letter and Spirit of Biblical Interpretation*, 206.

If someone seeks a meaning in an Old Testament passage while ignoring what the New Testament has to say on the matter, an interpretive misstep is taking place. "The point is that any interpretation of a part must fit the whole—the whole canon of Scripture and the whole rule of faith."[10]

Creating Space for Christ

Allegorical interpretation sees the Bible as a collection of divinely inspired writings that make space for Jesus. As Chad Ashby puts it, "The Old Testament is as much about narrating salvation history as it is about creating recognizable motifs, narrative cycles, and literary structures in the collective memory of God's people. As the central figure of salvation history, Jesus Christ is an infinitely faceted character. He cannot waltz onto the stage of history until there is actually a *stage* to waltz onto."[11] Allegorical interpretation is saying that such a stage exists, that the central figure of salvation history has come, and that we as interpreters can discern where and how space has been made for his arrival.

The canonical sweep of Scripture helps us to see that the entire Old Testament set the stage for Christ's coming, and so allegorical interpretation is pursued from the conviction that God embedded in that earlier Scripture the Savior who is Christ Jesus the Lord. Ashby writes:

> Allegory is not so much about ignoring the immediate context of a narrative as it is about recognizing its greater canonical context. Each passage of Scripture is received by a people necessarily shaped by the context created by the motifs of God's Word. . . . Good allegorical interpretation does not seek to erase a narrative in its immediate context. Rather, it treasures the narrative for the context it creates for Christ.[12]

Summary

Those who advocate the legitimacy of allegorical interpretation from the perspective of premodern exegesis must, in the same breath, insist that this is not turning over Scripture to the subjective whims of the interpreter. It is not an "anything goes" method of reading the Bible. Rather, an interpreter should approach Holy Scripture with premodern convictions and controls. Allegorical excesses are real, and plenty of examples can be found in history. But by attending to the literal sense of the text, and by making textual arguments for any spiritual reading that we propose, we will be poised to avoid

10. Stanglin, *Letter and Spirit of Biblical Interpretation*, 207.
11. Chad Ashby, "On Canonical Reading, Context, and Collective Biblical Consciousness," blogpost from chadashby.com, posted on April 27, 2015.
12. Ashby, "On Canonical Reading."

the exegetical fancies that—understandably—have fueled frustration toward allegorical interpretation. Through allegorical interpretation, we see how the Scripture created context and space for the Son of God to come. He is wrapped in the swaddling cloths of the Law, Prophets, and Writings.

REFLECTION QUESTIONS

1. Can allegorical interpretation, rightly done, dispense with textual arguments?

2. For an allegorical interpretation, what is the role of a text's literal sense?

3. What are some reasons that allegorical excesses have occurred in the history of interpretation?

4. Why is the rule of faith important as a "control" for allegorizing biblical texts?

5. Why is the unity of the testaments an important "control" for allegorizing biblical texts?

Are There Allegories in Genesis through Deuteronomy?

The Bible's patterns and symbols, its figures and shadows, all begin in the Pentateuch. The biblical authors in the Old Testament wrote about things beyond their ability to understand fully, because the significance of their writings had not yet reached the redemptive climax in Christ. With the coming of Christ, dawning light shines upon the shadows of the Old Testament. Once our eyes adjust to focus on the epic story that God is telling, we can say—with the Great Tradition before us—that the Testaments are testifying together about the Word who was in the beginning with God and became flesh in the fullness of time.

Genesis

Adam and Eden

Violating the command of God, Adam and Eve left the garden of Eden in exile (Gen. 3:24). They faced judgment and the curse, their only hope being a future seed who would bring victory (see Gen. 3:15).[1] The historical story about Adam is also significant on multiple levels, and these levels are established because the two testaments are true and united. Adam is Israel and Israel is Adam, for the Israelites violated the commands of God in their history and were exiled from their sacred place because of God's judgment and curse (2 Kings 25).[2] In the fullness of God's Word, the story of Israel is

---

1. About Genesis 3:15, Benjamin Keach writes, "The first promise of the Gospel and the whole mystery of redemption to come, is proposed by God himself in this allegory" (*Preaching from the Types and Metaphors of the Bible* [1855; repr., Grand Rapids: Kregel, 1972], 192).
2. See Seth D. Postell, *Adam as Israel: Genesis 1–3 as the Introduction to the Torah and Tanakh* (Eugene, OR: Pickwick, 2011).

foreshadowed by Adam. But we are also Adam. In him we have sinned (Rom. 5:12) and fallen short of God's glory (Rom. 3:23). We are in spiritual exile outside Eden, and our only hope is Eve's promised son. Like Adam, God covers our shame. God calls us out of hiding and provides the garments of Christ's righteousness. Ultimately, Christ is Adam *and* Eve's promised son. The Lord Jesus bore the curse for us and now leads us back to Eden. His cross has become our covering. Now, instead of God's curse in Adam, we have every spiritual blessing in Christ in the heavenly places (Eph. 1:3).

Cain and Abel

Cain hated and opposed his righteous brother Abel. This opposition led to murder and injustice (Gen. 4:8–11). Cain was the template for future opponents of God's people. The seed of the serpent would be at enmity with the seed of the woman (Gen. 3:15). "Within the overall context of Genesis the 'seed of the woman' refers to those who are righteous, whereas the 'seed of the serpent' denotes those who are wicked."[3] We should not be Cain, who murdered his brother, for God is love (1 John 3:12; 4:8). The saints are Abel, who loves the Lord but whose devotion provokes hatred. They both offered sacrifices, but God was only pleased with Abel. The religious leadership in Jesus's day was Cain, for they dishonored God despite their outward conformance to sacrificial laws (Matt. 15:8–9). The story of Cain and Abel tells us about false and true worship and about unbelievers and believers. But Jesus is also Abel, who faces persecution and death as a result of the hatred levied against him. Being Cain's brother, Abel was with his own family—yet his own received him not (John 1:11). The historical account of Cain and Abel contains every story of rivalry that follows it.[4]

Abraham, His Wives, and Their Sons

Abraham was married to Sarah, and at Sarah's recommendation, he took Hagar as a wife in order to have a son like God had promised (Gen. 16). But the line of promise would not come through Abraham and Hagar's child. Instead, God opened Sarah's womb and enabled her to conceive with the patriarch, and Isaac—the promised son—was born (Gen. 21). The situation with Hagar and Ishmael was the result of natural human fleshly striving and scheming, whereas the birth of Isaac through Sarah showed the effect of God's power and the faithfulness of God's word. Within the lives of Abraham and

---

3. T. D. Alexander, *The Servant King: The Bible's Portrait of the Messiah* (Leicester: Inter-Varsity, 1998), 18.

4. According to James Hamilton, "The seed conflict that runs through Genesis and into the rest of the Bible takes both an individual and a collective shape. . . . In the symbolic world Genesis gives its readers, people are either seed of the serpent, on the side of the snake in the garden, or seed of the woman, on the side of God and trusting in his promises" (*God's Glory in Salvation through Judgment: A Biblical Theology* [Wheaton, IL: Crossway, 2010], 82, 84).

his wives and their sons, we see a trajectory that is set: not everyone from Abraham is a son of promise. The work of God is paramount over the work of the flesh. Paul argues that, in the Old Testament, these lines have covenantal significance.[5] The wives are two covenants, one bearing children for slavery and the other bearing children for freedom (Gal. 4:24–26). Unbelievers need to know that they are Ishmael, born according to the flesh only and thus not children of promise or heirs (4:25, 30–31). Believers need to know that they are Isaac, children of promise and born by the Spirit (4:28–29).

Joseph and His Brothers
The ultimate purpose of the story of Joseph and his brothers is to reveal the Savior who was rejected and then vindicated.[6] When Joseph descended into the pit, was sold to Midianite traders, was falsely accused by Potiphar's wife, and was imprisoned before being raised up to a position of power (Gen. 37–41), these terrible events are carving gospel lines that will look like Jesus when the promised Redeemer comes. When we see Joseph reveal himself to his brothers, let us marvel at the Savior who revealed his risen and glorified state to his fearful disciples (Gen. 45:3; John 20:19–29). As Joseph forgives his brothers and reconciles with them, do you hear the pardoning words of the risen Christ for sinners whom he has reconciled to God (Gen. 45:14–15; 50:19–21; Mark 2:5)? Joseph, the beloved son, became the person of hope and goodwill for the hungry. The stories about Joseph and his brothers (Gen. 37–50) have a greater meaning. The claim of the brothers—"You have saved our lives" (47:25)—digs to the place of our deepest need. The story of Joseph becomes, and was always meant to be, the story of our deliverance in Christ.

Exodus

Out of Egypt and through the Sea
In the fullness of the biblical canon, the point of Egyptian captivity was our spiritual subjugation to sin and death. Our new Moses, the Lord Jesus, brought redemption through shed blood. The Passover taught Israel about a substitute being slain in their place, and thus God was teaching them about the cross of Christ (Exod. 12; 1 Cor. 5:7; 1 Peter 1:19). The victory of Christ means the exodus from Egypt is not less significant, but more! According to Paul, God led the people through the Red Sea for their baptism and then gave them food and drink to demonstrate his provision

---

5. See Matthew Y. Emerson, "Arbitrary Allegory, Typical Typology, or Intertextual Interpretation? Paul's Use of the Pentateuch in Galatians 4:21–31," *Biblical Theology Bulletin* 43, no. 1 (February 2013): 14–22.
6. Samuel Cyrus Emadi, "Covenant, Typology, and the Story of Joseph," (PhD diss., Southern Baptist Theological Seminary, 2016).

and care (1 Cor. 10:1–4). The Christian story has Old Testament roots and exodus imagery. The Red Sea stood between sinners and their Creator, yet the one who made the water can also part the water. Because of our union with Christ through faith, his victory is ours. We are an exodus people who have left our slavery, and the cloud of his presence is with us, even to the end of the age (Matt. 28:20).

Manna and Water

Allegorical interpretation shows continuity between former and latter times of salvation history. As the Israelites journeyed from Egypt to Sinai, God provided them food and drink to sustain them. But we see in the New Testament that the manna and water was always about Christ (John 6:48–51; 1 Cor. 10:4). If the people did not eat the bread, they would perish. And if we refuse to take Christ by faith, we will perish. Life comes only through eating his flesh and drinking his blood (John 6:53). To feed on his bread means everlasting life (6:58). To receive his water means everlasting life (4:13–14). During Israel's journey, the real manna and the real water were about a real Redeemer.

Tabernacle Furniture

The tabernacle was God's portable dwelling place, built according to the instructions given to Moses (Exod. 25–31; 35–40). But in God's plan, the tabernacle was about Jesus.[7] We need Christ's sacrifice, so an altar for sacrifice was the first piece of furniture visible as you entered the courtyard (Exod. 40:6). We need the cleansing that the cross would accomplish for unclean sinners, so a laver of water stood in front of the tabernacle for the priests to wash away their filth before entering the large room known as the Holy Place (Exod. 40:7). We need Christ's light of life, so a lampstand was put on the south side of the Holy Place (Exod. 40:4). We need the bread and drink that only Christ can supply, so a table of bread was set up on the north side of the Holy Place (Exod. 40:4). We need the intercessory and high priestly work of Christ, so an altar of incense stood right in front of the veil that concealed the Most Holy Place (Exod. 40:5). And we need Christ's atoning work that we might dwell in God's very presence, so behind the veil was the ark of the covenant, which symbolized the holy and glorious presence of God (Exod. 40:3). The tabernacle was built at the bottom of Mount Sinai, and it was already connected to Mount Calvary. When Jesus died, the veil was ripped from top to bottom, for his body was a veil torn for us, that he might be the way to God (Mark 15:38; John 14:6).

---

7.   See Philip Graham Ryken, *Exodus: Saved for God's Glory*, Preaching the Word (Wheaton, IL: Crossway, 2015), 1055–73.

Leviticus–Deuteronomy

The Sacrificial System

The offering of animals was a practice shouting *substitution*. The whole sacrificial system, all of its burnt offerings and sin offerings, all of its peace offerings and grain offerings, were about Jesus (see Lev. 1–7).[8] "In Augustine's notion of language, the Levitical details—animals, blood, grain, oil, and the rest—are 'real sounds,' within a continuum of meaning in which Jesus is the final sound or word by which God indicates himself."[9] Jesus was the Great High Priest who offered himself, doing a greater work than Aaron or any priest of Levi's tribe had ever done (Lev. 16). The annual Day of Atonement was established for the sake of Christ. The annual remembrance of Passover was for the sake of our unblemished Savior who was slain. The consequences for defilement he would bear for us, and the blessings of obedience would be imputed to us. When we meditate upon the sacrificial system of the Old Testament, we see the good news of the cross embedded ahead of time, so that when our High Priest said, "It is finished" (John 19:30), we will realize no other priest could have ever said those words and meant them.

The Arrangement of the Camp

In the years following the exodus, Israel was a camping nation. They built the tabernacle and, setting out from Sinai, encamped around the tabernacle when they stopped (Exod. 40:36–38; Num. 10). Three tribes were stationed on each of the tabernacle's four sides (Num. 2). The portable dwelling place was the center of the camp, and this placement had a theological point: God was to be the center of Israel's life. If Israel followed God's word, they would be a God-centered people. "The desert war camp formed a hollow square, with the tabernacle of the divine Presence in the middle. He was the Source of strength, the 'nuclear reactor.' God's people were not islands of destiny but a community under God, with each individual and every subgroup fully accountable to him."[10] Aaron and the tribe of Judah encamped on the east side, which was the entrance to the courtyard and tabernacle (Num. 2:3; 3:38). This placement also has meaning, for one must pass through a royal and priestly presence in order to approach God. The Lord Jesus—the perfect king and priest—reconciles us to God. And as we follow the word of God, we will be a Christ-centered people (1 Cor. 10:31; Col. 3:17).

---

8. See T. D. Alexander, *From Paradise to the Promised Land: An Introduction to the Pentateuch*, 2nd ed. (Grand Rapids: Baker Academic, 2002), 225–26.
9. Ephraim Radner, *Leviticus*, Brazos Theological Commentary on the Bible (Grand Rapids: Brazos, 2008), 296.
10. Roy Gane, *Leviticus, Numbers*, NIV Application Commentary (Grand Rapids: Zondervan, 2004), 506.

The Wilderness Journey

Israel was redeemed out of Egypt and bound for the Promised Land. That's the story of the Christian life. The new exodus in Christ has aimed us toward heaven and the new creation. But we are not there yet. Like Israel, we are in the wilderness, journeying between deliverance and inheritance. Along the way are temptations and trials, doubts and fears. But the message of Immanuel is true—we have God with us (Matt. 1:23; 28:20). We are elect exiles (1 Peter 1:1) and sojourners who will die before receiving the things promised (Heb. 11:13). Israel journeyed in the wilderness between Egypt and Sinai and between Sinai and Canaan. Their experience is important for us to consider, since we have not yet entered into that "rest" that God has prepared (Heb. 4:9–11).[11]

Summary

The stories in the Pentateuch are full of spiritual significance for the coming of Christ and for the Christian life. In the previous ten examples, we have only scratched the surface in making meaningful connections between earlier and later biblical passages. God's dealings with the patriarchs and the story of Israel, in canonical perspective, form large templates and allegories for new covenant realities. God's design is that these historical characters and events have deeper meanings. The understanding of the early biblical authors does not limit the meaning of these passages. Rather, the divine author, through the progressive revelation of Holy Scripture, threads together the ways in which the Pentateuch finds its greatest significance in Christ and his people.

REFLECTION QUESTIONS

1. In what ways is the story of Adam about more than the story of Adam?

2. How did Paul understand the narratives about Abraham and his wives and their respective children?

3. What deeper significance is there to the furniture in the tabernacle?

4. What can we learn about the arrangement of Israel's tribes around the tabernacle?

5. How can the wilderness journey of Israel serve as a template for the Christian life?

---

11. See Alexander, *Paradise to the Promised Land*, 251–52.

Are There Allegories in Joshua through Esther?

The historical narratives of Scripture continue with the books of Joshua through Esther. And as these stories report what happens with the people of Israel, God continues to put advanced glimpses of the gospel into these accounts. During these books, the biblical authors record the entrance into the Promised Land and eventual exile from it.

Joshua–Ruth

Conquering the Land

Beginning with Jericho, Joshua—the new Moses—led the people of God to inhabit the territories of the Canaanites (Josh. 6). A new Joshua arises in the New Testament, whose name in Greek is Jesus (Matt. 1:21). And Jesus conquers the land as well, performing signs and wonders and exercising dominion. He overcomes demons and disease and death (Mark 5). He saves sinners by conquering souls, bringing liberation from darkness and idolatry. When Joshua and the Israelites conquer northern and southern kings (Josh. 10–12), we see a preview of God's glory that will fill the earth and transform what is fallen and cursed.[1] In union with Christ, believers have a global mission not qualified by any geographical boundaries (Matt. 28:19–20; Acts 1:8). Making disciples of all nations—the Great Commission—is the conquest of the church. Fitted with the armor of God, we wrestle not merely against flesh and blood but against spiritual powers and principalities (Eph. 6:10–20).

---

1. See James M. Hamilton Jr., *God's Glory in Salvation through Judgment: A Biblical Theology* (Wheaton, IL: Crossway, 2010), 148, where he writes, "With Yahweh in their midst, Israel has recaptured something of the Edenic experience. As they cross into the land, Israel moves in the direction of the reversal of the curse."

Sanctification is conquest, subduing the desires of the flesh to the desires of the Spirit (Gal. 5:16–25). We must mortify the deeds of the sinful nature (Rom. 8:13). We persevere from a position of victory in Christ. Nothing can separate us from God's love for us in Christ, and we are more than conquerors through him (Rom. 8:37). Though conquerors, we will die; and like Christ, we will rise to inherit the earth.

The Scarlet Cord

Passover was first kept by putting lamb's blood on the doorposts (Exod. 12), and the story about Rahab reminds the reader of that scene. Rahab was told to do something to her home so that judgment would pass over (Josh. 2:14–18). The scarlet cord was a symbol of her obedience to the spies and a pledge of her devotion to Yahweh. She confessed Yahweh to be God in the heavens and earth (Josh. 2:11). The thing that ultimately delivers sinners is the cross, so the cross is the deepest meaning of the scarlet cord. Rahab is every sinner who is willing to confess the Lord in faith. There is now no condemnation for anyone in Christ (Rom. 8:1).

A Famine in the Land

The book of Ruth operates on multiple levels. By setting the book of Ruth in the period of Judges, the reader can see that the lack of food and lack of spiritual leadership are related (Ruth 1:1). The Israelites are a people in need, and the famine indicates that all is not well.[2] Then come reports of death, and suddenly Naomi has a famine of family too (Ruth 1:3). The reader's concern for Naomi is mirrored in concern for Israel: Will blessing fill the need in the land during the dark period when the judges rule? But the hope for Naomi becomes hope for Israel. God brings blessing to Naomi's line through Ruth and Boaz and the birth of their son, Obed (Ruth 4:15). Obed is an ancestor of King David, so the story of restoration in the book is about God's plan for the nation to get a king (Ruth 4:18–22). The arc of the book is from famine to fullness. That arc also describes the effects of sin and the future new heavens and earth. Christ takes us from famine to fullness. He brings peace to our chaos and joy to our mourning. Sin empties us out, leaving our souls barren and destitute. But Christ comes to nourish and fill (John 6:35). He comes to redeem us and make us whole. And he won't stop this work until death is defeated through our resurrection. He always finishes what he starts.

---

2. See Peter J. Leithart, *A House for My Name: A Survey of the Old Testament* (Moscow, ID: Canon, 2000), 119–22.

1 Samuel–2 Chronicles

David and Goliath

In the story of David versus Goliath, we are previewing the promised king who triumphs while all the odds seem stacked against him. Young David takes on the enemies of God, and their representative is Goliath (1 Sam. 17:4). The motif of God's enemies takes us beyond Goliath to Satan and his demonic host. The stone is the cross, and the wound on Goliath's forehead is the serpent's head finally crushed (Gen. 3:15; 1 Sam. 17:49). When read within the whole canon, the victory of David over Goliath has messianic tones for those with ears to hear.[3] And in our union with Christ, the victory of David is ours as well. Through the strength of Christ, we overcome temptations and persevere through trials.[4] If God is for us, who can be against us?

The Rebuke from Nathan

King David took Bathsheba and arranged the murder of her husband Uriah. So God sent Nathan to David, and Nathan had a story (2 Sam. 12). There was a rich man and a poor man, and the rich man had many flocks while the poor man had just a little lamb. The poor man raised the lamb, cared for it, and fed it from his own food and cup (2 Sam. 12:2–3). But then, said Nathan, when the rich man had a guest and was unwilling to prepare a meal from his own flock, the rich man took the lamb from the poor man and prepared it for the guest (2 Sam. 12:4). David was angered and said, "The man who has done this deserves to die" (2 Sam. 12:5), and Nathan said, "*You are the man!*" (12:7). Nathan's story was an allegory about David. Not every detail of the story needs an interpretation. But David was the rich man who had much but who took from the poor man. Though Bathsheba belonged to Uriah, David wanted her for himself. He exploited his position and authority, and Nathan rebuked him through the allegory.

---

3. See Peter J. Leithart, "The Quadriga or Something Like It: A Biblical and Pastoral Defense," in *Ancient Faith for the Church's Future*, eds. Mark Husbands and Jeffrey P. Greenman (Downers Grove, IL: IVP Academic, 2008), 122–24.

4. Leithart writes, "The allegory of conquest leads into a tropology, and at this point all the homiletical flourishes on this passage come to the foreground. With all the odds against him, David trusted Yahweh to deliver him; so should you. David defended Yahweh's honor; so should you. The story is about crisis management and teaches that we should confront the Goliaths that surround us with the faith of David. The God who defeated Goliath through David is the God who raised Jesus from the dead, and he can raise you from your personal Sheol. Notice that, operating by the quadriga, these exhortations to confidence, faith and courage are not generalized moral encouragements but, because they grow out of an allegorical reading of the story, are specific forms of imitation of Christ, the greater David" ("Quadriga or Something Like It," 124).

Building the Temple

Solomon (the son of David) builds God's temple (1 Kings 6), and Jesus (the Son of David) builds God's temple, too (John 2:19). Though Solomon's accomplishment was destroyed, nothing will prevail against Christ's temple—the church (Matt. 16:18). The grand and glorious temple complex in 1 Kings is surpassed by the multiethnic church of the redeemed in Revelation (Rev. 7:9). With the favor of Christ shining on us, we reflect more brightly than all the temple's metals and stones. And when Christ returns to raise the dead unto immortal life, we will shine like the stars forever (Dan. 12:3). Just as the materials and vessels of the temple reflected God's beauty and glory, the resurrection of the righteous will be the glorification of God's dwelling place. As Solomon builds the temple in 1 Kings, the deepest meaning of that construction is the glorification of the church and the transformation of creation.

Exile and Return

When Israel is exiled out of the Promised Land (2 Kings 25), it is Adam and Eve leaving the garden of Eden all over again (Gen. 3:24). Israel—a national Adam—goes to the east under judgment. The nation's physical exile was the result of their spiritual exile. At the end of 2 Kings, thousands of Israelites are deported, the temple is destroyed, and the city of Jerusalem is ravaged. The nation experienced a corporate death through the curse of exile. But the return was resurrection from the dead. From the tomb of Babylon, the Israelites emerged and returned to the Promised Land. The national Adam was reentering Eden. On the cross, Jesus bore the curse of our spiritual exile, and on the third day he rose from physical death. The victory of Christ is a story of exile and return. And because of our union with Christ, it is also the story of the Christian life: we are no longer spiritual exiles and have been freed from our captivity in order to inherit God's promises. As children of Abraham who are united to the seed of Abraham, we are coheirs with Christ and true Israelites (Gal. 3:29; 4:6–7).

Ezra–Esther

Rebuilding the Walls

After the exile ended and Israelites returned to the promised land, their plans to rebuild had a spiritual significance. Rebuilding the physical temple and walls would suggest a readiness to renew sacrifice and worship according to the law of Moses. But when the process of rebuilding stalled, this pause suggested something spiritually negative (Ezra 3–4). And even though the temple was eventually rebuilt, the walls of Jerusalem remained in ruins (Neh. 1–2). Nehemiah came to rebuild the walls and, in doing so, build up the people too.[5] The hope for sinners is that God is a rebuilder. He takes our ruins and brings restoration. Inwardly, we are being renewed day by day (2 Cor. 4:16).

The Hanging of Haman

In the book of Esther, wicked Haman prepared gallows to hang his nemesis Mordecai (Esther 5:14). But in a reversal of expectations, Haman faces the fate he had planned for Mordecai. If someone was hanged, it was an act of judgment. In Esther 7, Haman is the one hanging on the gallows under judgment. Such a public death showed dishonor and shame upon the guilty. This judgment on God's enemy is an installment of God's victory over all his enemies. The plot against Mordecai—even against the Jews in the book, or against God's Son and the church—comes back onto the one who hates the Lord. The wicked fall into the trap they set for others.[6]

Summary

Life in the Promised Land, followed by exile and return, is chronicled in historical narratives that have a deeper meaning than their literal sense may first suggest. The books of Joshua through Esther were inspired by the divine author with the whole canon in mind, so that the individual characters and events find their greatest significance in new covenant realities. Proper allegorical reading is a fuller or thicker reading of biblical texts in light of the biblical canon. In this type of reading, things like scarlet cords and rebuilt walls, and people like David and Haman, are about something and Someone more.

REFLECTION QUESTIONS

1. What is an allegorical reading of the scarlet cord in the book of Joshua?

2. How does the book of Ruth operate on multiple levels?

3. What is an allegorical reading of the battle between David and Goliath?

4. In the fullness of the canon, what is the meaning of Solomon's temple?

5. In the fullness of the canon, how can we understand Nehemiah's rebuilding of the walls?

---

5. See Leithart, *House for My Name*, 236–37.
6. See Leithart, *House for My Name*, 228–29.

Are There Allegories in Job through Song of Solomon?

The books traditionally known as wisdom literature—Job, Psalms, Proverbs, Ecclesiastes, and the Song of Solomon—are filled with poetic writing. Poetry makes use of imagery, symbols, and metaphors, and allegorical interpretation can identify deeper significance to the biblical passages in these books.

Job–Psalms

The Story of Job

The deepest meaning of Job's story is the story of Jesus. The account of Job—a man who suffered the loss of family and animals and who faced the ridicule and accusations of his "friends" (Job 1–3)—is part of a larger story taking us to the righteous sufferer, the Lord Jesus, who faced betrayal and suffering and death. The story about Job also reminds us that those who fear the Lord can face unjust suffering at the hands of others. In the hardness of life, believers may find themselves in a darkness and despair where the book of Job takes on fresh significance. Job is Jesus, and Job is us. We see in his story the agenda of Satan against us, and we read the false accusations of those who think they know our motives and why things happen to us. But Job's story tells us that God has the last word (Job 38–41). His power can bring vindication and renewal, despite the suffering and the heartache his people experience (Job 42).[1] Leviathan seemed an untamable adversary, but God is supreme over this creature (Job 41). Leviathan is Satan, the one who opposed Job at the

---

1. See Toby J. Sumpter, *A Son for Glory: Job through New Eyes* (Monroe, LA: Athanasius, 2012), 184–85.

beginning of the book (Job 1–2), but also the one whose every move is under the eye of our sovereign God. No man can tame Leviathan, but God can.

Beholding God's Face

In Psalm 17, David ends his song by saying, "As for me, I shall behold your face in righteousness; when I awake, I shall be satisfied with your likeness" (Ps. 17:15). In the psalm, he calls upon God to hear his cry so that vindication may come (Ps. 17:1–2). He prays for shelter in the shadow of divine wings (17:8–9). He hopes the Lord will confront and subdue those seeking David's destruction (17:13–14). The confidence to awake and see God's face is a hope to be found in the right. But the deepest significance of this hope is the resurrection of the body and the beatific vision (to see God). The pure in heart shall see God (Matt. 5:8). Though the righteous sleep in death, they will awake again through the power of resurrection (Phil. 3:10–11).[2] Our bodies will reflect the glorious body of the risen Christ (Phil. 3:21). While David hoped to be delivered from trouble, the fullest sense of his words is glorification in Christ. At the return of Christ, we shall be raised and shall behold him.

The King with Long Life

In Psalm 72, Solomon—the son of David—calls for God to give to the king, among other things, "dominion from sea to sea" (72:8), for the king's enemies to "lick the dust" (72:9), and for his life to be long (72:15). The best application of this psalm is to Christ, for he truly has all dominion in heaven and earth, he will reign until he has put all enemies under his feet, and he will reign for days unending.[3] In 72:17, Solomon says, "May his name endure forever, his fame continue as long as the sun! May people be blessed in him, all nations call him blessed!" Jesus is Abraham's seed, in whom all the families of the earth will be blessed (Gen. 12:2–3; Gal. 3:16). When we read Psalm 72, we can see the truth in Jesus's words that the Psalms testify of him and must be fulfilled (Luke 24:44).

Ravaging the Vine

In Psalm 80, the judgment of God against his people is depicted allegorically. The psalmist says, "You brought a vine out of Egypt; you drove out the nations and planted it. You cleared the ground for it; it took deep root and filled the land" (Ps. 80:8–9). This refers to God delivering the Israelites out of Egyptian captivity, bringing them into the Promised Land through conquest, and allowing them to occupy the territories that had been allotted for them.

---

2. See Derek Kidner, *Psalms 1–72*, Tyndale Old Testament Commentaries, vol. 14a (Downers Grove, IL: InterVarsity, 1973), 89–90.

3. See Richard P. Belcher Jr., *The Messiah and the Psalms: Preaching Christ from All the Psalms* (Fearn, Ross-shire, Scotland: Mentor, 2006), 137–39, 203.

Then, "the mountains were covered with its shade, the mighty cedars with its branches. It sent out its branches to the sea and its shoots to the River" (80:10–11). The might of Israel increased, and the boundaries of the land expanded under David and Solomon. This planted vine was now an extraordinary sight! But, the psalmist asks, "Why then have you broken down its walls, so that all who pass along the way pluck its fruit? The boar from the forest ravages it, and all that move in the field feed on it" (80:12–13). God brought judgment to the land of Israel through raising up a foreign adversary. Then came invasion, subjugation, and exile. Poetically and allegorically, the psalmist tells of how Israel came into the land, prospered, and then faced the curses of the broken covenant.[4]

Proverbs–Ecclesiastes

The Call of Wisdom
One of the most recognizable literary features of the book of Proverbs is the personification of wisdom as a lady who calls to the simple and foolish. Lady Wisdom beckons the hearers to come to her for knowledge in order to avoid the disaster that comes with a life of folly (Prov. 1:20–33). The deepest meaning of Wisdom's call is the good news of Christ Jesus. Sinners need to heed the gospel through repentance and trust and then live in a way that conforms to the gospel they profess (Matt. 7:24–27; Gal. 2:14). The voice of Wisdom is the voice of Christ, whose words of invitation and warning will lead to life for those with ears to hear. The disciples of Jesus are disciples of Wisdom.

Bread upon the Waters
When the author of Ecclesiastes says to "cast your bread upon the waters, for you will find it after many days. Give a portion to seven, or even to eight, for you know not what disaster may happen on earth" (Eccl. 11:1–2), he is not talking about actual bread.[5] He is urging the reader to take chances, to risk, to diversify, even if not all the factors are controlled nor the outcome guaranteed. Fear of the future can paralyze people from making decisions. The call to "cast" is a call to act. The "bread" represents an investment, a seizing of opportunity. Sometimes life can seem like trial and error, a series of attempts and midcourse corrections and eventual arrivals. The meaning of the writer's wisdom is that though we don't know the future, we should act (Eccl. 11:3–6).

---

4. See Peter J. Leithart, *A House for My Name: A Survey of the Old Testament* (Moscow, ID: Canon Press, 2000), 199–200.
5. See Benjamin Keach, *Preaching from the Types and Metaphors of the Bible* (1855; repr., Grand Rapids: Kregel, 1972), 195.

A Body Breaking Down

Near the end of Ecclesiastes, the writer describes a body breaking down, though at first the meaning may be ambiguous.[6] In Ecclesiastes 12:3, the housekeepers tremble, the strong men bend, the grinders (which are left) cease, and those who see through the windows are dimmed. In the next verse, the doors on the street are shut, sound is decreased, and daughters of song are brought low (12:4). Ultimately the silver cord snaps, causing the golden bowl to break and the pitcher to shatter (12:6). All this different imagery is clarified by 12:7: "the dust returns to the earth as it was, and the spirit returns to God who gave it." Using many metaphors, the author describes the physical deterioration of the human body.[7] The hands tremble, legs bend, teeth stop working, sight dims, ears can't hear as well (if at all), the voice lowers and is soft, and eventually the cord of life itself is severed at the last exhale. While the author could have spoken directly about the different parts of the body, he deemed an allegory more fitting. With an allegorical interpretation of Ecclesiastes 12, we are witnessing the end of life as the human spirit returns to God.

Song of Solomon

The Locked Garden

In a poetic passage depicting the consummation of the couple in the Song of Solomon, the husband speaks of "a garden fountain, a well of living water, and flowing streams from Lebanon" (Song 4:15). And in 4:16, the bride invites him to come to her garden and let its spices flow. But the language about the garden and water is not about a garden and water. The garden is the body of the bride! The context bears out this allegorical reading: "A garden locked is my sister, my bride, a spring locked, a fountain sealed" (4:12). The heavily metaphorical nature of the Song of Solomon prepares the reader for allegorical readings deep and wide.[8] There are metaphors that refer to their engagement, their wedding, their consummation, their bodies, and more. When we interpret these many figurative descriptions, we are automatically engaging in an allegorical reading.

The Husband and Wife in Covenant

The Song of Solomon is not about just any husband and wife. It is not about just any wedding. It is not just any love story. The poetry in the Song of

---

6. See Sidney Greidanus, *Preaching Christ from Ecclesiastes* (Grand Rapids: Eerdmans, 2010), 276, 290–94; Zack Eswine, *Recovering Eden: The Gospel according to Ecclesiastes* (Phillipsburg, NJ: P&R, 2014), 98–99.
7. See Keach, *Types and Metaphors of the Bible*, 194.
8. See James M. Hamilton Jr., *Song of Songs: A Biblical-Theological, Allegorical, Christological Interpretation*, Focus on the Bible (Fearn, Ross-shire, Scotland: Christian Focus, 2015), 28–33.

Solomon is anchored in the biblical canon, which testifies to God's Son, who laid down his life for the church, his bride.[9] In the Old Testament, God's relationship with Israel was covenantal (see Exod. 24). Abandoning Yahweh was tantamount to spiritual adultery (Hos. 2:2). The Song was written by the son of David (Song 1:1), and so a Davidic dimension of the book appears in the opening verse. Throughout the history of the Christian church, interpreters have seen the relationship in the Song as referring ultimately to God's communion with his people in Christ. Paul confirms the use of such a biblical metaphor when he says human marriage is a profound mystery about Christ and the church (Eph. 5:32). An allegorical reading of the Song of Solomon not only connects with the Great Tradition but is coherent within the storyline and canon of Scripture. The couple knows the strength of divine love and its unquenchable nature (Song 8:6–7). Nothing can separate us from the love of God that is in Christ Jesus our Lord (Rom. 8:39).

Summary

The poetic sections of Scripture are friendly to allegorical reading because the nature of the language is filled with images and metaphors that invite the interpreter beneath the surface of the text. From the experiences of Job to the marriage in the Song of Solomon, the christological purpose of Scripture shapes and informs what comes before Christ. The characters and events are, in the canonical scheme of things, called to testify on the stand. And when we listen to their testimony, they speak of Christ and his people. Their testimony converges in perfect harmony, and they speak what is trustworthy and true. The suffering of Job, the lyrics of the psalmists, the voice of Lady Wisdom, the dying body in Ecclesiastes, the garden in the Song of Solomon—these and many more examples call the reader to reflect on the Old Testament as Christian Scripture, and to see in those texts the Christ who is there, the Savior in the shadows ready to come forth.

REFLECTION QUESTIONS

1. How does an allegorical interpretation affect the book of Job?

2. In addition to the ones mentioned in this chapter, are there other parts of Psalms that call out for a deeper, spiritual reading in light of the whole canon?

3. How can Ecclesiastes benefit from allegorical interpretation?

---

9. See Keach, *Types and Metaphors of the Bible*, 194; Hamilton, *Song of Songs*, 33.

4. Why should interpreters consider an allegorical approach to the Song of Solomon?

5. What evidence within the Song of Solomon can suggest that allegorical interpretation is crucial to the meaning of the book?

Are There Allegories in Isaiah through Malachi?

The Old Testament prophets ministered God's word to the people of Israel. They ministered during a fractured kingdom and amid the drumbeats of future disaster. Their words and actions had deeper meanings for the listeners and readers, and sometimes these deeper meanings were provided in the prophet's text. The books of these prophets are filled with visions that require, again and again, allegorical interpretation to be understood. The reason for this requirement is the widespread occurrence of images and symbols in these visions.

Isaiah–Ezekiel

The Mountain above the Mountains

The prophet Isaiah saw that the mountain of God's house would one day be raised above the tallest mountain, lifted up above the hills, and all nations would come to it (Isa. 2:2). The temple—God's house—was the most important place in Jerusalem, and Jerusalem was the most important city in the world. So the elevation of the temple meant its global prominence, and this position would be compelling to the nations who would stream to it (Isa. 2:2). Isaiah's vision would be partly completed by Christ, the Word who tabernacled among the nations (John 1:14). Jesus said that when he was high and lifted up, he would draw the nations to himself (John 12:32). Isaiah's vision is coming to pass through the advance of the gospel in the world, as the elect from every tribe and tongue are streaming to Christ through faith. The vision will be completely fulfilled in the new heavens and new earth, when everyone walks according to God's word and when peace reigns in the global city of God (Isa. 2:3–5).

Destroying the Vineyard

In Isaiah 5, God had a beloved vineyard that he planted. He dug its place, moved any stones, and built a watchtower to look over it (Isa. 5:1–2). God looked for the vines to produce grapes, but they produced wild grapes instead (5:2). In response to the fruit that God saw, he removed the hedge of the vineyard so that it would be devoured and trampled, making room for thorns to grow on an area no longer pruned or cultivated (5:5–6). Israel is the vineyard, and the bad fruit was Israel's disobedience.[1] God's response was the enaction of covenant curses, which culminated in a foreign adversary trampling the land in judgment. He removed his hedge of protection that spared Israel from destruction.

Spoiling the Loincloth

God told the prophet Jeremiah to buy a linen loincloth, wear it around his waist, and not dip it in any water (Jer. 13:1). Jeremiah obeyed the Lord's word, bought the loincloth, and wore it. And God's word came again to the prophet: take the loincloth and hide it in a cleft of the rock (13:4). Jeremiah followed this instruction too. And when the Lord told Jeremiah to retrieve the loincloth, Jeremiah found it spoiled and good for nothing (13:6–7). The meaning of God's instructions and Jeremiah's activity was about Israel. Judah's pride was the linen loincloth, and God would spoil it, for they refused his words and followed their own hearts and went after idols (13:9–10). Israel was supposed to cling to God like the loincloth clung to the prophet, but they worshiped other gods and so became good for nothing (13:10–11).

Good Figs and Bad Figs

The Lord gave Jeremiah a vision of two baskets of figs: one basket had good figs, the other had bad figs (Jer. 24:1–2). The second basket of figs was so bad that they could not be eaten. We learn that these fig baskets are the Israelites. The good figs are the exiles from Judah that went to Babylon in captivity (24:5).[2] God's plans for them are good, for he will plant them and build them up and be their God (24:5–7). But the basket of bad figs, which cannot be eaten, are people like King Zedekiah, his officials, the remnant of Jerusalem who remained in the land, and those who dwelled in Egypt (24:8). God would make this "basket" of people a horror and a reproach, a curse in the places they dwell (24:9). The end for this second basket is destruction (24:10).

---

1. See Peter J. Leithart, *A House for My Name: A Survey of the Old Testament* (Moscow, ID: Canon, 2000), 199, where he writes about a parallel notion in Jeremiah 1:5 and 1:10, "Israel is pictured as a garden or a vineyard that the Lord has planted in the land (cf. Psalm 80; Isaiah 5), hoping she will produce fruit for His delight. Judah has no fruit, so the Lord is threatening to uproot her."
2. Leithart, *House for My Name*, 207–8.

A Tale of Two Sisters

The Lord told Ezekiel about two women. These women were sisters and lived in immorality. The older sister was named Oholah, and the younger sister was named Oholibah (Ezek. 23:4). But these sisters became the Lord's, and they had children. Oholah represented Samaria, and Oholibah represented Jerusalem—which means the two sisters stood for the land of Israel.[3] Though Oholah belonged to the Lord, this sister "played the whore" and went after her lovers, the Assyrians (23:5). As a consequence, Oholah fell into their hands for judgment (23:9). The other sister, Oholibah, was worse than Oholah and went after other lovers, the Babylonians (23:14–17). Oholibah's lusts would be her undoing (23:20–23). She would be exposed and humiliated, uncovered and defiled (23:28–30). The meaning of the allegory is that God had judged the northern kingdom of Israel, and now he would judge the southern kingdom of Judah, for the whole land of Israel had been defiled in their pursuit of idols and immorality. Their actions were spiritually adulterous, and the time for judgment had come.

The Death of Ezekiel's Wife

In Ezekiel 24, the prophet experiences the death of his wife. But her death means something deeper. Earlier in the chapter, Jerusalem falls to the Babylonians (Ezek. 24:2, 14), which was the corporate death of the nation. And then Ezekiel's wife dies (Ezek. 24:18). These corporate and individual deaths are connected. Ezekiel represents God, and each of them experiences loss. The death of Ezekiel's wife represents the loss of the Israelites, the people of God in the Promised Land. "The death of Ezekiel's wife is symbolic of the fall of the sanctuary. The Lord uses the same words to describe Ezekiel's love for his wife ('the desire of your eyes,' 24:16) and his concern for the sanctuary ('the desire of your eyes, the delight of your soul,' 24:21)."[4] The juxtaposition of these corporate and individual deaths suggests that they have an interpretive relationship.

Dry Bones in a Valley

In a vision to the prophet in Ezekiel 37, there is a valley of dry bones. God tells Ezekiel to prophesy over them, calling them to hear and obey (37:4). The bones come together, sinews and flesh cover them, and skin stretches over them (37:7–8). At last, breath enters the bodies, and the formerly dry bones rise in the valley to form a great army (37:9–10). The valley of bones represented the Israelites in exile, for the Babylonian judgment had caused the

---

3. See Benjamin Keach, *Preaching from the Types and Metaphors of the Bible* (1855; repr., Grand Rapids: Kregel, 1972), 195.
4. Leithart, *House for My Name*, 218.

corporate death of the nation.[5] What Ezekiel saw, however, meant the rise and return of Israel. God would bring the nation out of its Babylonian graveyard, and they would reenter the Promised Land (37:12).

Daniel

The Dream of an Image

Nebuchadnezzar, the king of Babylon, has a dream of an image made of different materials. The head is gold, the chest and arms are silver, the middle and thighs are bronze, and the legs and feet are made of iron and clay (Dan. 2:32–34). In the dream, a stone struck the image and then became a mountain that filled the whole earth (2:35). Daniel explains that the head of gold is Nebuchadnezzar, and that the other metals are kingdoms that follow Babylon (2:37–40). Eventually a stone will come that represents an everlasting kingdom (2:44–45). If the head of gold is Nebuchadnezzar and Babylon, we can confirm historically that the subsequent kingdoms are Persia, Greece, and Rome.[6] As Nebuchadnezzar's dream foresaw, a stone would arrive during the fourth empire. Jesus, the Stone, was born during the reign of Caesar Augustus (Luke 2:1–7). And as the Son of David, he established the everlasting kingdom of God.

The Ram and the Goat

The prophet Daniel had a vision of a ram that trampled everything in its path (Dan. 8:3–4). Then a goat arose and challenged the ram, rushing at it in wrath and defeating it (8:5–7). This description in Daniel's vision needed an interpretation, so an angel explained its meaning (8:16–17). The ram represented the Medo-Persians, and the goat represented the Greeks (8:20–21). When Daniel saw the goat overcome the ram, he was seeing the defeat of the Medo-Persians by the Greeks. In historical hindsight, we can identify other parts of Daniel's vision as well. The mighty goat had a single horn that became broken and was replaced by four other horns (8:8, 22). This great horn was Alexander the Great who led the Greeks in victory over Medo-Persia, yet after Alexander's death his empire was divided among four generals.[7]

---

5. See Leithart, *House for My Name*, 219, where he says that the vision in Ezekiel 37 is "about a resurrection from the death of exile."
6. Mitchell L. Chase, "Daniel," in *ESV Expository Commentary*, vol. 7, *Daniel–Malachi* (Wheaton, IL: Crossway, 2018), 43–45.
7. Chase, "Daniel," 114.

Hosea–Malachi

The Names of Hosea's Children
There is a deeper meaning to the names of Hosea's children. He named one Jezreel, another Lo-ruhama, and a third Lo-ammi (Hos. 1:4–11). The names, respectively, mean God Will Scatter, No Mercy, and Not My People.[8] Hosea's historical family had a theological purpose. His family was testifying to God's righteous indignation against the Israelites, for the rebellion of the Israelites had aligned themselves against the Lord. Therefore, God treated them as his enemies, who would not receive mercy and who were not his people. He would scatter them in exile. The names, however, would be reversed after a period of judgment ended. God would allure the Israelites (Hos. 2:14). God would bring in the scattered people and sow them in the Promised Land once more (2:22). Those who were Not My People would be called "my people," for those who received No Mercy would be given mercy (2:23).[9]

The Rebellion and Deliverance of Jonah
The prophet Jonah fled from God's instruction, that he might go to Tarshish by boat instead of going to preach in Nineveh (Jonah 1:2–3). Adding to Jonah's disregard for the inhabitants of Nineveh, he did not show concern for the people on the boat who became endangered by his presence on it (1:4–10). Instead of repenting and agreeing to go to Nineveh, Jonah told the sailors that the storm would stop if they threw him overboard (1:11–12). Into the water he went, and he began to drown. Swallowed by a fish, Jonah's life was spared, and after three days, the fish vomited the prophet onto dry land (1:17; 2:10). The mindset of Jonah was shared by others. He was a prophet from the northern kingdom of Israel (2 Kings 14:25), and his mindset was their mindset. The northern kingdom was failing to be a light to the nations, represented in the prophet Jonah. Nineveh, which was in Assyria, had a god that was part fish, so Jonah's time in the belly of a fish foreshadowed the coming invasion of Israel by Assyria. The Assyrians would consume the northern kingdom—but eventually God would bring the Israelites home.[10] They would return from the belly of the adversary, entering the dry Promised Land.

---

8. See George W. Schwab Sr., "Hosea," in *ESV Expository Commentary*, vol. 7, *Daniel–Malachi* (Wheaton, IL: Crossway, 2018), 182–84.
9. According to Schwab, "In the light of Pentecost and the subsequent unfolding of the history of the church, in which God sent his Spirit into the hearts of non-Jews, a whole new vista of meaning opened up for Paul. Those of whom it was said 'not my people' are now declared to be 'Children of the living God' (cf. Hos. 1:10; Rom. 9:22–26). This refers to Gentiles. Paul sees in this a prophecy of the Gentiles' coming to faith through Jesus" (Schwab, "Hosea," 184–85).
10. See Leithart, *House for My Name*, 184.

Summary

The words, actions, and visions of God's prophets are full of spiritual significance, and allegorical reading exposes this significance for the interpreter. Sometimes the meaning is evident in the immediate context or is explained later in the biblical passage. The sheer volume of images and symbols means that allegorical reading is not only appropriate but essential to discerning the meaning of many texts. The eleven examples in this chapter, while not exhaustive, are sufficient to show that the prophetic literature contains layers of meaning designed by God. Interpreters cannot adopt an "anything goes" approach but, rather, must be sensitive to the immediate and canonical text of the biblical passage, while also factoring in later historical fulfillments that could clarify a prophetic passage in hindsight.

REFLECTION QUESTIONS

1. How does a spiritual reading clarify Isaiah's vision about a mountain rising above all other mountains and the nations flocking to it?

2. What is the allegorical meaning of Ezekiel's vision about dry bones coming to life in a valley?

3. When King Nebuchadnezzar dreamed of an image made of various metals, how does Daniel's interpretation—and our historical hindsight—identify what the king saw?

4. Why did God choose specific names for Hosea's children?

5. How do the mindset and actions of the prophet Jonah represent larger truths about the northern kingdom of Israel?

Are There Allegories in Matthew through Acts?

In the New Testament, the realities of the new covenant are inaugurated as the promised Messiah lays his life down for his bride. The biblical authors write of the life and ministry of Christ, and of the ministry of his apostles, which followed his ascension. Their new covenant quills drip with Old Testament ink. The biblical authors, inspired by the Holy Spirit, provide authoritative interpretations of the Old Testament, and they depict the words and actions of Christ and his apostles with layers of significance ready for the reader to see and explore.

Matthew–John

The Gifts of the Magi

When the Magi learn that the baby Jesus is in Bethlehem, they bring him gifts. After falling before him in worship, they present their treasures of gold, frankincense, and myrrh (Matt. 2:11). The reader may remember that the queen of Sheba brought gold and spices to Solomon (1 Kings 10:2) and that a royal psalm spoke of gifts being brought to God's king (Ps. 72:10–11, 15). Furthermore, the items of gold, frankincense, and myrrh were all associated with the tabernacle (Exod. 25–30). At last, the Word became flesh and tabernacled among sinners (John 1:14), being the promised Son of David who was worthy of devotion and exaltation. And the gifts of the Magi certainly communicated worship and devotion. These were gifts fit for a king! The gifts should provoke interpreters to consider their own heart's response to the Christ. The reader of the Bible should fall before him and worship. When we ponder the gifts of the Magi, are we ready to take up our cross and follow Jesus, since he is the king of infinite worth? Imitating the gifts of the Magi is not the point. Beneath the surface, however, we are exhorted to esteem the Christ. We should love him with all our heart, soul, mind, and strength.

The Diet of John the Baptist

John the Baptist was dressed like Elijah, wearing a garment of camel's hair and a leather belt around his waist (Matt. 3:4; see 2 Kings 1:8). But what was the point of the diet—the locusts and wild honey? These are not extraneous details for the reader. Not only does John's dress tap into the Old Testament; his food taps into it as well. Locusts were an example of God's judgment. God sent locusts upon Egypt (Exod. 10:1–20), God warned of locusts upon Israel (Deut. 28:42), and locusts are an image of judgment in the prophets (Joel 1:4–7). Honey, however, is a picture of God's blessing. God would rescue Israel out of Egypt and take them to a land flowing with milk and honey (Exod. 3:8). The sweetness of honey applied to delight in God's word (Ps. 19:10). So when John the Baptist is eating locusts and honey, the meaning is about the message he's proclaiming in the region around the Jordan River.[1] He's proclaiming repentance and forgiveness for those who come to confess their sins and be baptized. His message, like honey, is sweet to those who receive it. But to those who reject it, his message, like locusts, is a judgment and curse. The food going into his mouth represents the message coming out of his mouth.

Laying Down Nets

Jesus came to fishermen and said, "Follow me, and I will make you fishers of men," so they laid down their nets and followed him (Matt. 4:19–20). Being fishermen was their livelihood, so following Jesus meant a reorientation of life. The priority was Jesus. This doesn't mean, of course, that the men never held a net in their hands again, but the initial abandonment of their nets is a pivotal moment where a shift in allegiance is clear. The act of laying down nets, therefore, means surrendering to Christ, ready to follow him wherever he goes. Later he teaches that if others want to come after him, they must deny themselves, take up their cross, and follow him (Mark 8:34). Discipleship (pictured by the nets and the cross) means that we follow Jesus with all that we are, denying whatever else would vie for centrality. The nets are our lives. We may not be fishermen, but Jesus wants us to lay down our nets and take up our cross.[2]

---

1. According to Andrew T. Le Peau, "Locusts suggest John is eating off the land, which Israel did when foreign armies came in judgment to invade and devastate the land (see Isa 7:14–25, esp. 15 and 22)—an ironic contrast to the Promised Land with its abundance of 'milk and honey.' Honey continues the wilderness theme ('wild honey'). Ezekiel 3:3 also compares how the scroll of God's word tasted to the prophet to something as sweet as honey. All this emphasizes the role of the prophets (and so of John) to bring the people God's word both of promise and of judgment" (*Mark through Old Testament Eyes* [Grand Rapids: Kregel Academic, 2017], 35).

2. See Le Peau, *Mark through Old Testament Eyes*, 42–43.

The Woman and the Well

When Jesus goes to a well in Samaria, a woman arrives, and they have a conversation that operates on more than one level. First they're talking about physical water. And then Jesus starts talking about spiritual water. The spiritual meaning in the passage is vital to understanding Jesus's words to the woman. Jacob's well will leave you thirsty again, Jesus explains (John 4:13). Not so with the well Jesus has and *is*. The water from Jesus is the greatest kind of living water, welling up to eternal life (4:14). The woman, however, did not perceive the transition in their conversation (4:15). The woman sees him but doesn't really *see* him. But when they are finished talking, she has learned he is the Messiah (4:26), and she goes back to her town to proclaim it (4:29, 41–42). The water that Jesus offered her is the water he offers us. Jacob's well is whatever we rely on other than Christ to sustain us spiritually. Yet the soul's thirst is never quenched by worldly wells. In the story of the Samaritan woman, Jesus is calling us to drink from him, to learn that he is the Christ, and to proclaim that truth to others that they may drink too.

Calming a Storm

On a boat traveling across the Sea of Galilee, the disciples encounter a violent storm (Mark 4:35–37). But they have Jesus with them. They wake him and cry out in distress (4:38). In contrast to his disciples, Jesus exhibited a great calm in his heart and commanded a great calm upon the sea. He asked the disciples why they were afraid (4:40), and they asked who this could be, whose words the wind and sea obey (4:41). The presence and power of Christ is a remedy for our fears. He is not physically with us on a boat, but he is present in our lives. And through all the storms we face, he calls us to be people of faith rather than people debilitated by fear. If the wind and sea obey the words of Christ, then nothing we face is beyond his authority and sovereignty. When the unexpected happens, when we realize that we can't control our lives or the lives of those around us, when our boats are filling with the water of overwhelming circumstances and internal doubts, we can cry out to Christ, who is with us always and is an ever-present help in our trouble. In this boat we will have trouble, but take heart: he has overcome the wind and the sea.

Healing a Paralytic

Friends of a paralytic brought him to Jesus, and Jesus said to the man, "Take heart, my son; your sins are forgiven" (Matt. 9:2). Then, to demonstrate his authority to forgive sins, Jesus spoke to the man's physical condition: "Rise, pick up your bed and go home" (9:6). The man left healed, physically and spiritually. If the man went home walking but unforgiven, he would die in his sins. The greater healing was the forgiveness Jesus bestowed. Yet the need for physical healings suggests the degree of sin's effects in this world. We are not just inwardly broken, we are outwardly wasting away. By making the lame to walk, Jesus is affirming the value of the physical, created world and reversing tangible effects of the curse (see Isa. 35:6). The physical miracles are displays of Christ's power, but they are also signs pointing to the spiritual condition of us all. The physical inability of the lame man points to the spiritual inability of the same man and of every sinner as well. Only Jesus can raise us out of the deadness of our transgressions. We're so paralyzed that we have to be brought to Jesus through the gospel words of others who carry us to the Great Physician.

The Miraculous Feedings

Jesus fed thousands of people with a small amount of bread and fish. He did this for a crowd of five thousand and later with a crowd of four thousand (Mark 6:30–44; 8:1–10). In those hillside meals, Jesus was the messianic host, the one feeding the multitudes of Jews and Gentiles.[3] Everyone who ate was satisfied, and there was food left over! The grace of Jesus went overboard in a blessed way. In John's account of the first feeding, Jesus claimed, "I am the bread of life" (John 6:48). This identification showed what was true beneath the surface of the loaves. Jesus was giving himself. He was the bread, and he would be broken and dispensed through faith to Jews and Gentiles who would receive him. When Jesus fed the thousands, he was showing them truths about the salvation he came to bring. He said, "The bread that I will give for the life of the world is my flesh" (John 6:51). For those with ears to hear and eyes to see, the miraculous meals revealed the Bread of Life who had come down from heaven in order to feed sinners by giving them *himself.*

Healing a Blind Man

On the road out of Jericho, there was a blind beggar named Bartimaeus who heard that Jesus was passing by (Mark 10:46–47). He called Jesus the "Son of David" and cried out for mercy (10:48). When Jesus called Bartimaeus to him, the blind man went to Jesus and asked for his sight (10:51). Jesus assured him that "your faith has made you well" (10:52). The man gained his sight and followed Jesus. His physical sight revealed his spiritual sight.[4] Bartimaeus followed Jesus because he trusted in him. The man's wellness was not just physical; above all, and most importantly, it was spiritual. When we come to understand who Jesus is, our sight has been restored. Jesus's physical miracles are digging beneath the surface of things. Apart from the work of the Spirit, every sinner is blind Bartimaeus. We need the voice of Christ to beckon us

---

3. See Leroy A. Huizenga, *Loosing the Lion: Proclaiming the Gospel of Mark* (Steubenville, OH: Emmaus Road, 2017), 165–66; Le Peau, *Mark through Old Testament Eyes,* 143–44.
4. See Le Peau, *Mark through Old Testament Eyes,* 192–94.

and restore us, to give us eyes to see him that we may follow him as a disciple.[5] Every disciple must understand that the reason Bartimaeus followed Jesus is the same reason any of us follow Jesus: mercy.

The Parable of the Sower

The nature of parables showed who was on the inside and who was on the outside in terms of understanding the mysteries of the kingdom. Jesus told parables in order to cloak and conceal. This is why the disciples would ask him, "What did you mean by what you said?" The meaning of Jesus's parables wasn't self-evident. For instance, Jesus once told a parable about a sower who scattered seed along the path, on rocky ground, among thorns, and on good soil (Mark 4:3–8). But then Jesus called for a true hearing of his words (4:9), hearing that meant *understanding*. Plenty of people heard him without understanding him. He explained to his disciples that the seed is the word, and that the soils are kinds of people. Some people receive the word, but it is snatched like seed sown along the path (4:15). Some people receive the word, but when suffering comes on account of the word, they fall away like seed that has no root because of rocky ground (4:16–17). Some people receive the word, but worldliness captivates them and the seed is unfruitful, like seed sown among thorns, which choke the growth (4:18–19). Some people receive the word and bear fruit, and this is like seed sown on good soil (4:20). This parable, like other parables Jesus told, contains allegorical elements that must be pondered and interpreted.[6] Sometimes Jesus provides the interpretation, while at other times the context of the parable, or the incorporation of similar parables, can clarify the meaning of Jesus's words. In Mark 4:1–20, Jesus is the sower who has come to sow the word of the kingdom, but not every listener responds the same way. The reason people need a certain kind of hearing for parables is because they need a certain kind of hearing for Jesus.

The Good Shepherd

Jesus spoke about people who enter the sheepfold the wrong way—not by the gate but by climbing in like a thief (John 10:1). A stranger's voice won't compel the sheep to follow (10:5). Unlike strangers who don't care for the sheep and who are thieves and robbers coming only to steal and kill and destroy, Jesus is the Good Shepherd who lays down his life for the sheep (10:8–11). The language about strangers and false shepherds is an indictment against Israel's leaders who have led the people wayward. Jesus is the Good

---

5. In speaking about Mark's Gospel as a whole, Leroy Huizenga writes, "In the story, characters are to literally follow Jesus on the way of discipleship, like the no-longer-blind Bartimaeus in Mark 10:52, who then become metaphorical, allegorical exemplars of discipleship" (*Loosing the Lion*, 46–47).

6. See Le Peau, *Mark through Old Testament Eyes*, 87–96; Matthew Black, "The Parables as Allegory," *Bulletin of the John Rylands Library* 42, no. 2 (1960): 273–87.

Shepherd whose voice the sheep will hear and follow. The sheep are the elect from the nations. Jesus lays down his life for his sheep by going to the cross, and through death he saves and secures his flock.

Cursing a Fig Tree

On Monday of Jesus's passion week, he journeyed toward Jerusalem and cursed a fig tree along the way (Mark 11:12–14). This word of judgment against the tree—"May no one ever eat fruit from you again" (11:14)—was not really about the fig tree. Jesus's words were about Israel and the temple. In the Old Testament, the Israelites were compared to various plants, including a fig tree (see Hos. 9:10). And though Israel was to bear the fruit of obedience, they were like a fig tree with no fruit. The deeper meaning to Jesus's action in Mark 11 is confirmed by the arrival of Jesus in Jerusalem, where he enters the temple and turns over tables and drives out buyers and sellers and moneychangers (11:15–19). The cursing of the fig tree was about the judgment that was coming.[7] Showing unrighteous fruit, the leaders of Israel would call for the crucifixion of the Son of David before that week was over.

Washing Feet

With the hour of arrest drawing near, Jesus washed the feet of his disciples (John 13:1, 3–5). The foot washing was the surface act that he performed, but it meant something far more important. The disciples just couldn't see it yet. When Jesus came to Peter, the disciple said, "Lord, do you wash my feet?" (13:6). Jesus told him, "What I am doing you do not understand now, but afterward you will understand." Jesus was symbolizing that he had come to wash the disciples through his death. He said, "If I do not wash you, you have no share with me" (13:8). The washing by Jesus would lead to sharing with Jesus. The Son of Man had come not to be served but to serve, to give his life as a ransom (Mark 10:45). Jesus humbled himself to death on a cross, in order to cleanse the unclean by his precious blood. Peter watched what Jesus did with the towel that cleaned their feet, yet at the same time he did not see the real meaning. After the cross and resurrection of Christ, however, these acts in his earthly ministry would be seen and understood in a clearer light and with clearer sight.

The Bread and the Cup

At the Last Supper with his disciples on Thursday evening of passion week, Jesus took in his hand the bread and then the cup (Mark 14:22–23). Centuries of Passovers had unfolded before that night, and it was customary for the head of the family to interpret what the elements of the meal meant (Exod. 12:26–27). But Jesus did not focus on an exodus and a covenant in

---

7. See Huizenga, *Loosing the Lion*, 239–50; Le Peau, *Mark through Old Testament Eyes*, 203–5.

the past; he focused on a new exodus and a new covenant in the *future* (Luke 22:20). He said the bread was his body and the cup his blood, ready to be broken and poured out for sinners (Mark 14:22–24).[8] The deepest meaning of the Passover was the cross. Just as he dispensed bread to his disciples and shared the cup, his death would mean life for the world (John 6:35). Before Jesus had begun his public ministry, John the Baptist had declared the truth behind all the lambs that had ever been offered: "Behold, the Lamb of God, who takes away the sin of the world!" (John 1:29). In the upper room with his disciples, Jesus taught that his body and blood would be broken and slain, for he knew he was the Lamb set apart for this atoning work.

Acts

Healing the Lame Beggar

The apostles Peter and John were on their way to the temple when they came across a lame man begging for alms (Acts 3:1–3). Peter said that while he had no silver and gold, "what I do have I give to you. In the name of Jesus Christ of Nazareth, rise up and walk!" (3:6). Just as Isaiah had foreseen, the lame were leaping (3:8; Isa. 35:6). The Spirit of God worked through the apostles of Christ, and these apostles performed many of the same kinds of miracles that their Master did. The healed man left worshiping God (Acts 3:8), which suggests that deliverance had entered his heart and not just his limbs. The miracle confirmed the authority of Christ's apostles and the power of Christ's name. Through these ambassadors of the Lord, the effects of sin and the curse were overcome. Sinners need inward restoration, and the story about the lame man in Acts 3 is a testimony that restoration has come in the name of Christ. Peter had taken the lame man by the hand and raised him up (Acts 3:7), and the hand of Peter was the hand of Christ. Our restoration comes when Christ's hand grasps us and pulls us from the darkness of sin and sets us upright for a life of worship. How much greater than silver or gold is everlasting life!

The Vision of a Great Sheet

The apostle Peter saw a vision while on a housetop (Acts 10:9). He had become hungry, but before he went to eat, he saw a vision of a great sheet descending from heaven (10:9–11). The sheet was covered with all kinds of animals, reptiles, and birds, and a voice said, "Rise, Peter; kill and eat" (10:12–13). Peter was reluctant, because the implications overturned the dietary laws between clean and unclean food. But God declared the end of those dietary laws (10:15). Though Peter did not understand all that the vision meant, suddenly Gentiles arrived at the house. It became clear that the barriers between

---

8. See Le Peau, *Mark through Old Testament Eyes*, 260–61.

clean foods/people and unclean foods/people were no longer in force. The vision of the animal-covered sheet was applying the new covenant realities that Christ had accomplished. Our one Savior has one people. He has taken believing Jews and Gentiles and made them, in himself, a new man and one body (Eph. 2:14–16).

Summary

It was common for Jesus to speak and act in multilevel ways. When we consider the Four Gospels and the book of Acts, the usefulness of allegorical reading is evident due to the abounding number of symbols, parables, miracles, and teachings that beckon interpreters beneath the surface of what is said and done. Yet interpreters must read carefully and canonically, offering spiritual readings that can be textually defended and are canonically coherent. Jesus himself engaged in allegorical teaching, especially when he connected his ministry to the Old Testament hopes he had come to fulfill.

REFLECTION QUESTIONS

1. What is the meaning of John the Baptist's diet of locusts and honey?

2. What would an allegorical reading conclude about the miraculous feedings that Jesus performed with bread?

3. Why is an allegorical approach important for understanding Jesus's parables, such as the parable of the sower?

4. Is there a deeper meaning to Jesus's cursing of the fig tree on Monday of passion week?

5. When Jesus cleaned the feet of his disciples, what was the deeper significance that they would eventually understand?

Are There Allegories in Romans through Revelation?

In the letters of Christ's apostles, interpreters will notice allegorical readings of the Old Testament as well as the description of figures that an allegorical reading will make clearer. The book of Revelation, in particular, requires allegorical readings in many places due to the nature of apocalyptic literature. The following examples will complete our noncomprehensive investigation of allegories in the Bible.

Romans–Philemon

Not Muzzling an Ox

Part of Paul's message to the Corinthians was about how an apostle can forego his rights. One of these rights is to receive compensation for labor. To ground his point, he appeals to what the law of Moses teaches: "You shall not muzzle an ox when it treads out the grain" (1 Cor. 9:9, quoting Deut. 25:4). A muzzled ox can't benefit from the work it is doing.[1] Paul brings up this verse about an ox in order to talk about apostles. Since the apostle works for Christ, he has the privilege of benefiting financially from his ministry labors. When Paul cites Deuteronomy 25:4, he asks, "Is it for oxen that God is concerned?" The answer seems to be yes, for the context in the law is addressing oxen. But Paul writes about God's words in the law: "Does he not speak entirely for our sake? It was written for our sake, because the plowman should plow in hope and the thresher thresh in hope of sharing in the crop. If we have sown

---

1. See Jan L. Verbruggen, "Of Muzzles and Oxen: Deuteronomy 25:4 and 1 Corinthians 9:9," *Journal of the Evangelical Theological Society* 49, no. 4 (December 2006): 699–711. Though Verbruggen doesn't believe Paul is reading Deuteronomy 25:4 allegorically, she provides a helpful survey of the issues and possible interpretations.

spiritual things among you, is it too much if we reap material things from you?" (1 Cor. 9:10–11). The deeper and truer significance of a worker benefiting from labor is not the oxen who treads but the preacher who proclaims. Paul says the words about the oxen were "written for our sake."

Foreshadowing the Ordinances

The experiences of Israel in the Old Testament were shadows of the New Testament church. In the new covenant community, Christ has decreed the ordinances of baptism and the Lord's Supper. But there is a measure of continuity between the Israelites and the Corinthians to whom Paul wrote. He says, "All were baptized into Moses in the cloud and in the sea, and all ate the same spiritual food, and all drank the same spiritual drink. For they drank from the spiritual Rock that followed them, and the Rock was Christ" (1 Cor. 10:2–4). Israel's journey through the Red Sea and their subsequent meals of manna were an appropriate background for the new covenant realities that are symbolized in baptism and the Lord's Supper. Paul offers a fuller reading of Israel's experiences. He also mentions that "with most of them God was not pleased" (10:5), so the Corinthians should not presume upon grace and live in unrepentance or idolatry. The events in Israel's history "happened to them as an example, but they were written down for our instruction, on whom the end of the ages has come" (10:11). Through new covenant lenses, Christians read the Old Testament as their own history and as written for them.

Freedom and Slavery in Abraham's Family

The most famous New Testament example of allegorical interpretation is Galatians 4:24–31, where Paul reflects on the family of Abraham and says that "this may be interpreted allegorically" (Gal. 4:24).[2] Paul's readers in Galatia were being tempted to ways of living that seemed enlightened but that would actually enslave them. Works of the law could not justify sinners. In order to reveal the beauty of God's promise in Christ Jesus, Paul pointed to the wives and children of Abraham. Only one son—Isaac—was the son of promise. The other son—Ishmael—was also from Abraham but was not a son of promise. Ishmael represented the striving of the flesh, for his birth was the result of Abraham and Hagar's relationship. Ishmael and Hagar were exiled from Abraham's home, and Ishmael was separated from the covenantal scope of God's promises to Abraham. Hagar, then, bears "children for slavery" (Gal. 4:24), and enslavement is the spiritual status of everyone seeking to earn their righteousness by works of the law. But if people come to Christ through faith and trust his sufficient work on their behalf, they are children of promise

---

2. See Matthew Y. Emerson, "Arbitrary Allegory, Typical Typology, or Intertextual Interpretation? Paul's Use of the Pentateuch in Galatians 4:21–31," *Biblical Theology Bulletin* 43, no. 1 (February 2013): 14–22.

like Isaac. Sarah and her promised son represent freedom, and freedom is the spiritual status of everyone in Christ (4:31). Paul's allegorical reading of Abraham's family does not minimize the historicity of those relationships and events, but it does indicate that epic truths were unfolding through the respective women and children in that family.

Hebrews–Revelation

Outside the Camp with Christ

The letter to the Hebrews sanctions a christological hermeneutic for the Old Testament. Near the end of the letter, the writer calls the reader to follow Christ, even if it means suffering for him. The imagery of this command evokes the Israelite encampment of the Old Testament, which served as a boundary marking those inside the camp from those outside the camp. Being outside the camp was exile, a place of reproach and uncleanness. That is why it is significant that Christ's crucifixion occurred outside the city of Jerusalem: Christ was sent outside the camp to bear reproach. Now we bear a different reproach. The writer says, "Therefore let us go to him outside the camp and bear the reproach he endured" (Heb. 13:13). While Christ bore our sins, the "reproach" in the verse is primarily referring to the suffering he endured at the hands of his opponents. In following Christ, we will face opposition as well, and so we join him outside the camp.[3] We must be willing to bear reproach for the name of Christ. We must be willing to live as exiles in this world of those who are not yet in the lasting City.

The Word That Remains Forever

In Peter's first letter, he reminded his readers that they were born again through "the living and abiding word of God" (1 Peter 1:23), and then he anchored his point in an Old Testament passage from Isaiah: "All flesh is like grass and all its glory like the flower of grass. The grass withers, and the flower falls, but the word of the Lord remains forever" (1 Peter 1:24–25; see Isa. 40:6, 8). In the context of Isaiah 40, a speaker is crying out "Comfort!" for the people, and the abiding word of the Lord is contrasted with the people whose flesh fades like flowers and grass at the breath of the Lord. And then the speaker is told to ascend a mountain and declare "good news" for the cities of Judah: God is coming with his delivering might (Isa. 40:9–10). It is this context that shapes Peter's message to his readers. The delivering might of God has been consummately shown in Christ Jesus, whose death and resurrection are the good news to be proclaimed. Sinners are born again through the abiding good news. When Peter reads Isaiah 40, he rightly sees that the

---

3. Dennis E. Johnson, "Hebrews," in *ESV Expository Commentary*, vol. 12, *Hebrews–Revelation* (Wheaton, IL: Crossway, 2018), 209.

gospel of Christ is what will endure forever. After referring to Isaiah's "word" that "remains forever," Peter writes that "this word is the good news that was preached to you" (1 Peter 1:25). Peter sees that the gospel is the deepest meaning of the living and abiding "word" in Isaiah 40. The greatest message of comfort, the most precious news to be shouted from the mountaintop, is the good news of the cross.

The Woman and the Dragon

In a well-known scene in the book of Revelation, a pregnant woman encounters a great dragon who wants to devour her child (Rev. 12:1–4). The child is born despite the dragon's murderous intent, and the child is the promised king who will rule the nations with a rod of iron (12:5). The place of the son's rule is the throne of God (12:5). The woman flees into the wilderness where God sustains her during the time of persecution (12:6, 14–17). The short story is full of messianic hope.[4] The child is the Christ, the Son of God from Psalm 2 who would rule the nations. The incarnation occurred amid warfare, for the dragon—namely, Satan—despised the child. The satanic plans of Herod the Great were for the child's death (see Matt. 2:16–18). But Satan cannot stop God's Anointed One, so the dragon pursues God's people. The woman is the remnant of God's people, for Jesus was born from the nation of Israel. The woman is also Mary who was God's chosen instrument for the Messiah's birth, and the woman is Eve as well, since the promise of God was that an offspring of Eve would defeat the serpent (Gen. 3:15). Jesus Christ— the seed of Eve, Messiah of Israel, and son of Mary—was born to reign, and reign he does at the right hand of God in heaven.

Summary

In the books of Romans through Revelation, one way the biblical authors communicate to their readers is with allegorical interpretation. This strategy was not motivated by a rejection of the historicity of previous characters or events. Rather, these biblical authors read earlier texts with eyes illumined by the new covenant realities of Christ and his church. Whether Paul or Peter or John or the author of Hebrews, these authors are helping their first readers— and helping us by extension—to see and savor the good news. And since this good news is living and abiding and everlasting, don't you want to imitate these authors and delight in it with your whole heart?

---

4.   Thomas R. Schreiner, "Revelation," in *ESV Expository Commentary*, 12:658–60.

REFLECTION QUESTIONS

1. When Paul quotes from the law of Moses about not muzzling an ox when it is treading the grain, how does he understand its meaning?

2. How does Paul tie the ordinances of baptism and the Lord's Supper to the experiences of Old Testament Israelites?

3. How does Paul see Abraham's wives and children as revealing greater truths about freedom in Christ and slavery under the law of Moses?

4. How does an allegorical reading explain the enmity between the woman and the dragon?

5. Can you think of other passages in Revelation that an allegorical reading can clarify?

PART 4

Reflecting on Typology and Allegory

Why Should Interpreters Care about Typology and Allegory?

O ur last question in this biblical and historical study is why you should care at all about the topics in the previous chapters. We need to reflect on why typology and allegory matter. They are not subjects exclusive to academic conversations or church history enthusiasts. These subjects matter because they pertain to the Bible, and the Bible is the most important book in the world. A crucial task for believers is to be a faithful student and interpreter of Scripture, so we need to ask why typological and allegorical interpretation helps with this task.

The Testimony of Christ

The words of Jesus should make us care about typology and allegory. He taught that the Old Testament contained "the things concerning himself" (Luke 24:27). He came to fulfill the Law, the Prophets, and the Writings (24:44). Jesus claimed that Moses "wrote of me" (John 5:46) and that the Scriptures as a whole "bear witness about me" (5:39). He wanted his disciples to know how the Old Testament testified to him, so he opened their minds to understand it (Luke 24:45). Suddenly the shadowy rooms of messianic hope in the Old Testament were filled with light. The ancient prophets did not fully grasp what the Spirit showed them, but they knew they were serving believers beyond their day (1 Peter 1:10–12).

Now if the Lord Jesus insisted that the Old Testament prepared his way, then typological and allegorical interpretation are ways to read that earlier Scripture in light of his claim. Typological and allegorical interpretation demonstrate the truthfulness of Christ's testimony. These reading strategies show *how* the Scripture testifies to Christ. These strategies take seriously the Lord's use of the Old Testament, the way he taught his disciples to interpret it, and the value of imitating the biblical authors in their engagement with it.

Christian Scripture doesn't begin with the time of fulfillment; it begins with the time of promise. The whole Old Testament is Christian Scripture, reaching back to Genesis 1:1 when God created the heavens and the earth. Every subsequent verse, every genealogy and journey, every covenant and deliverance, was preparing the way for the Lord. Let us affirm Keith Stanglin's words:

> There is no book of the Old Testament, no matter how intimately tied to its ancient Near Eastern context, that is not finally about Christ. Such readings are not Christocentric to the exclusion of the Father and the Holy Spirit or to the subversion of the narrative at hand. But the narratives, laws, psalms, wisdom, and prophecies all point to the revelation of God in Christ and testify to the reconciliation that God brings his people in Christ.[1]

The Interconnectedness of Scripture

Not only does the New Testament use the Old Testament; the Old Testament uses the Old Testament. A careful reader of Scripture will notice how interconnected the biblical passages are across the canon. Given this interconnectedness, we need the reading strategies of typology and allegory because they can clarify what a biblical author is doing with an earlier passage and what the meaning of that passage is in its canonical context.

The interconnectedness of Scripture is not the work of mere humans. The sixty-six canonical books, which tell one epic story and bear witness to our Redeemer, are themselves a united testimony of divine authorship. The biblical authors were writing *God's* Word. Typological and allegorical interpretation strengthen the veracity of this divine authorship because the careful interpreter peruses the nuance and genius throughout the many genres and stories of the Bible. This attention by the interpreter can serve an apologetic purpose too, for diligent Bible study can reveal the self-authenticating glory of Scripture.

Typological and allegorical reading proves the well-known claim of Augustine: "The New is in the Old concealed, the Old is in the New revealed."[2] The veiled glories in the Old Testament are made known and uncovered in the New. The Old Testament is transfigured in the New. Kevin Vanhoozer states,

> As the transfiguration displays the glory of the Son in and through his flesh, so "transfigural" interpretation discovers

---

1. Keith D. Stanglin, *The Letter and Spirit of Biblical Interpretation: From the Early Church to Modern Practice* (Grand Rapids: Baker Academic, 2018), 43.
2. Augustine, "Questions on the Heptateuch 2.73," as quoted in Michael Cameron, *Christ Meets Me Everywhere: Augustine's Early Figurative Exegesis* (New York: Oxford University Press, 2012), 248.

the glory of the prophetic word in the "body" of its text. De Lubac has it right: "the Old Testament lives on, transfigured, in the New." Spiritual interpretation is ultimately a matter of *transfigural* reading that discerns the mystery of God's glory in the body of the text, the earthiness of history.[3]

Practices in the Great Tradition

Every reader of the Bible is an interpreter, and every interpreter approaches the Bible from a worldview which shapes his or her interpretation. The question of worldview, then, is paramount. Typological and allegorical interpretation rely on premodern presuppositions, which help us critique and step outside of those aspects of our postmodern worldview that are contrary to the Christian faith. If interpreters will study the practices of the Great Tradition, we will see that the faithful figures of church history may not have all agreed on conclusions about this or that text, but they engaged Scripture with a posture of faith and believed that the divine author's intent and design were effectively written throughout the centuries of progressive revelation.

Typological and allegorical reading beckon us into the Great Tradition, where interpreters held to the unity of the two Testaments and sought to read Scripture accordingly. If we hope to read God's Word in concert with the community of saints before us, we must consider the role of typological and allegorical reading. And we must read the works of these ancient interpreters. Richard Muller and John Thompson say, "The time has come, therefore, to move beyond the 'chronological snobbery' so often displayed by modern exegesis toward its own forebears. Indeed, many of the modern histories of precritical exegesis have themselves spent far more time vilifying these earlier interpreters than understanding them."[4]

By considering the interpretive practices of the Great Tradition, we are by no means indebted to the conclusions they reached about certain narratives, prophecies, or images. Rather, by engaging in typological and allegorical reading, we are engaging the larger exegetical conversation about how to faithfully read the Word of God. The Reformers certainly modeled this. Muller and Thompson point out that "the Reformers shared with earlier eras a vision of interpretation that was communal in nature, insofar as it drew on the 'cloud of witnesses' comprised of the church and its exegetes throughout the ages."[5]

---

3. Kevin J. Vanhoozer, "Ascending the Mountain, Singing the Rock: Biblical Interpretation Earthed, Typed, and Transfigured," in *Heaven on Earth? Theological Interpretation in Ecumenical Dialogue*, eds. Hans Boersma and Matthew Levering (Oxford: Blackwell, 2013), 222 (emphasis original).

4. Richard A. Muller and John L. Thompson, "The Significance of Precritical Exegesis: Retrospect and Prospect," in *Biblical Interpretation in the Era of the Reformation*, eds. Richard A. Muller and John L. Thompson (Grand Rapids: Eerdmans, 1996), 336.

5. Muller and Thompson, "Significance of Precritical Exegesis," 342.

The cloud of interpretive witnesses matters because interpreting Scripture is always done in conversation with someone before us, whether that "someone" is a preacher we grew up hearing or an early church father whose treatises impacted us. Because of people who shape us, we may be reluctant to see certain types in the Old Testament, or we may even be resistant to consider the value of allegorical readings in general. And interpretive abuses in our present day—and throughout history, for that matter—do not alleviate instinctive concerns we feel. If anything, examples of bad exegesis can leave us wary of promoting typological or allegorical readings at all!

The hermeneutical practices of the Great Tradition can give us a needed perspective. We are reminded that many who have gone before us have made interpretive errors, and so will we. Not everyone thought Origen was right about everything, not everyone agreed with Augustine's writings, and not everyone sided with all of Luther's views. And what more shall I say? For time would fail me to tell of Irenaeus, Chrysostom, Basil, Cassian, Gregory the Great, Bonaventure, Bede the Venerable, Aquinas, Calvin, Spurgeon, and Clowney. The practices of the Great Tradition come from a cloud of witnesses whose line is not complete. Let us join them!

The High Task of Preaching

Sunday is always coming, so the preacher must be ready to speak from God's Word. The task of preaching warrants typological and allegorical readings of Scripture because these readings edify the church, treating Scripture as the Word of God for the people of God. If we affirm the unity of the Testaments given by a divine author, and thus believe in the inspiration and authority of the Bible, then the high task of preaching is inviting the congregation to feast with the preacher upon the Word of God. Or, to switch metaphors, preaching is lifting the lid of the chest that all might behold treasures and glories together.

Stanglin writes, "In the case of Scripture, the assumption of early Christians is that it must be edifying to the church morally and spiritually. One reads Scripture for moral and spiritual transformation, to draw nearer to God. For Christians, then, Scripture instructs in love and morals, but it also instructs in the faith and doctrine."[6] With typological and allegorical interpretation, the preacher shows the faithfulness of God, the surety of his promises, the patience in his character, the majesty of redemption, and the consummation of his purposes in Christ.

The whole church needs the whole counsel of God. They need the narratives but also the laws, the letters but also the prophecies, the psalms but also the sacrifices. Through typological and allegorical interpretations, preachers are tasked with proclaiming that God will—and has already begun to—sum up all things in Christ.

---

6.   Stanglin, *Letter and Spirit of Biblical Interpretation*, 75.

The Blessing for the Reader

There is a beatitude we need to believe: blessed are the typological and allegorical interpreters, for they shall see Christ in the Scriptures. And when we behold Christ, we are changed. We are encouraged, convicted, exhorted, reoriented. We are blessed. This experience is the testimony of many believers who see certain passages set, for the first time, in their canonical and christological context. These readers say, "I never understood this passage before until now," or "I never realized why this was important."

An Old Testament example of this kind of blessing is Israel's laws and ordinances for the sacrificial system. No doubt, parts of Exodus and Leviticus are challenging reading when it comes to the details of what Israel was to offer and when and how to offer it. But J. C. Ryle is right: "Let it be a rule with us, in the reading of our Bibles, to study the types and ordinances of the Mosaic law with prayerful attention. They are all full of Christit. . . . Those who neglect to study the Jewish ordinances, as dark, dull, and uninteresting parts of the Bible, only show their own ignorance, and miss great advantages."[7] The ceremony of Passover proves Ryle's point. Jesus is our Passover lamb (1 Cor. 5:7; John 1:29), and his sacrifice put a period at the end of the long sentence that was the sacrificial system (Heb. 10:12). Reading about these Old Testament ceremonies can be a great blessing to the Christian interpreter because they were designed to point to Christ! "Those who examine them with Christ as the key to their meaning, will find them full of Gospel light and comfortable truth."[8]

The reader will be enriched by seeing the characters and events in the Old Testament as shadows of Christ's person and his past or future work. The stories of the patriarchs, the suffering of the righteous, and the lives of the prophets carve out christological contours that Jesus fills. Through typological and allegorical interpretation, the reader can be edified by seeing, with Melito of Sardis, that

> This is the one who was murdered in Abel,
> tied up in Isaac,
> exiled in Jacob,
> sold in Joseph,
> exposed in Moses,
> slaughtered in the lamb,
> hunted down in David,
> dishonored in the prophets.[9]

---

7. J. C. Ryle, *Mark: Expository Thoughts on the Gospels* (Carlisle, PA: Banner of Truth Trust, 1994), 305.
8. Ryle, *Mark*, 306.
9. Melito of Sardis, *On Pascha* (Yonkers, NY: St. Vladimir's Seminary Press, 2001), 56.

It is a happy experience for an interpreter to be drawn into the riches of Scripture, and typological and allegorical readings will pull the reader into these riches. The spiritual depth exemplified by the Great Tradition demonstrates the profundity and inexhaustibility of God's Word. As we exult in the Christ-revealing glory of God's Word, our taste for Scripture will sweeten and our love for Scripture will deepen.

Summary

Given the testimony of Jesus, the interconnectedness of Scripture, the practices of the Great Tradition, the high task of preaching, and the blessing for the Bible reader, these are sufficient reasons why we should care about typological and allegorical interpretation. The Bible's big story is ready to be read and embraced with faith, hope, and love, and God will use it to make us people of stronger faith, hope, and love. We read Scripture now as exiles waiting for that lasting City. One day we will dwell there, and God himself will be our God. With tears wiped away and death gone forever, faith will be sight, hope will be fulfilled, and love will remain forever.

REFLECTION QUESTIONS

1. How do typological and allegorical interpretation relate to Christ's words about the Old Testament's testimony?

2. How does the interconnectedness of Scripture justify typological and allegorical interpretation?

3. How should the practices in the Great Tradition influence our interpretation today?

4. Why would typological and allegorical interpretation be important for the task of preaching?

5. How do typological and allegorical interpretation bring blessing to the Bible reader?

Select Bibliography

Barrett, Matthew. *Canon, Covenant and Christology: Rethinking Jesus and the Scriptures of Israel.* New Studies in Biblical Theology. Vol. 51. Downers Grove, IL: IVP Academic, 2020.

Beale, G. K. *Handbook on the New Testament Use of the Old Testament: Exegesis and Interpretation.* Grand Rapids: Baker Academic, 2012.

Boersma, Hans. *Scripture as Real Presence: Sacramental Exegesis in the Early Church.* Grand Rapids: Baker Academic, 2017.

Boersma, Hans, and Matthew Levering, eds. *Heaven on Earth? Theological Interpretation in Ecumenical Dialogue.* Oxford: Blackwell, 2013.

Carter, Craig A. *Interpreting Scripture with the Great Tradition: Recovering the Genius of Premodern Exegesis.* Grand Rapids: Baker Academic, 2018.

Clowney, Edmund P. *The Unfolding Mystery: Discovering Christ in the Old Testament.* Phillipsburg, NJ: P&R, 1988.

Danielou, Jean. *From Shadows to Reality: Studies in the Biblical Typology of the Fathers.* Translated by Dom Wulstan Hibberd. London: Burns & Oates, 1960.

Davidson, Richard M. *Typology in Scripture: A Study of Hermeneutical TUPOS Structures.* Berrien Springs, MI: Andrews University Press, 1981.

De Lubac, Henri. *Medieval Exegesis: The Four Senses of Scripture.* 3 volumes. Translated by Mark Sebanc. Grand Rapids: Eerdmans, 1998–2009.

Fairbairn, Patrick. *The Typology of Scripture: Viewed in connection with the Whole Series of the Divine Dispensations.* 2 volumes. 6th edition. Edinburgh: T&T Clark, 1876.

Frei, Hans W. *The Eclipse of Biblical Narrative: A Study in Eighteenth and Nineteenth Century Hermeneutics*. New Haven, CT: Yale University Press, 1974.

Froehlich, Karlfried. *Biblical Interpretation in the Early Church*. Sources of Early Christian Thought. Philadelphia: Fortress, 1984.

Goppelt, Leonhard. *TYPOS: The Typological Interpretation of the Old Testament in the New*. Grand Rapids: Eerdmans, 1982.

Hamilton, James. M., Jr. *God's Glory in Salvation through Judgment: A Biblical Theology*. Wheaton, IL: Crossway, 2010.

————. *What Is Biblical Theology? A Guide to the Bible's Story, Symbolism, and Patterns*. Wheaton, IL: Crossway, 2014.

Johnson, Dennis E. *Walking with Jesus through His Word: Discovering Christ in All the Scriptures*. Phillipsburg, NJ: P&R, 2015.

Legaspi, Michael C. *The Death of Scripture and the Rise of Biblical Studies*. New York: Oxford University Press, 2010.

Leithart, Peter J. *Deep Exegesis: The Mystery of Reading Scripture*. Waco, TX: Baylor University Press, 2009.

————. "The Quadriga or Something Like It: A Biblical and Pastoral Defense." In *Ancient Faith for the Church's Future*. Edited by Mark Husbands and Jeffrey P. Greenman, 110–25. Downers Grove, IL: IVP Academic, 2008.

Levy, Ian Christopher. *Introducing Medieval Biblical Interpretation: The Senses of Scripture in Premodern Exegesis*. Grand Rapids: Baker Academic, 2018.

Louth, Andrew. *Discerning the Mystery: An Essay on the Nature of Theology*. Oxford: Clarendon, 1983.

Muller, Richard A., and John L. Thompson, eds. *Biblical Interpretation in the Era of the Reformation*. Grand Rapids: Eerdmans, 1996.

Ninow, Friedbert. *Indicators of Typology within the Old Testament: The Exodus Motif*. Frankfurt: Peter Lang, 2001.

O'Keefe, John J., and R. R. Reno. *Sanctified Vision: An Introduction to Early Christian Interpretation of the Bible.* Baltimore: Johns Hopkins University Press, 2005.

Schrock, David. "From Beelines to Plotlines: Typology That Follows the Covenantal Typography of Scripture." *Southern Baptist Journal of Theology* 21, no. 1 (Spring 2017): 35–56.

Stanglin, Keith D. *The Letter and Spirit of Biblical Interpretation: From the Early Church to Modern Practice.* Grand Rapids: Baker Academic, 2018.

Vos, Geerhardus. *Biblical Theology.* Carlisle, PA: Banner of Truth, 1948.

Young, Frances M. *Biblical Exegesis and the Formation of Christian Culture.* Grand Rapids: Baker Academic, 1997.

Scripture Index

Genesis

Reference	Pages
1	60, 123, 124, 141
1:1	123, 296
1:26–28	124
1:28	55, 124, 129
1–2	18, 209
1–11	17
2	141
2:7	222
2:8	124
2:9	126
2:9–10	124
2:15	74, 124
2:16	126
2:16–17	74
2:17	126
2:23	125
2–3	74
3	18
3:2–6	126
3:6	55, 125
3:7–8	126
3:7–10	55
3:15	18, 20, 127, 128, 161, 182, 255, 256, 263, 290
3:17–19	55
3:19	29
3:21	126
3:22	126
3:24	124, 126, 130, 142, 168, 255, 264
4	18
4:1–2	127
4:7	30
4:8–11	256
4:10	127
4:25	127
4:26	127
5	67
5:3	128
5:22–24	128
5:29	128
6:5	18
6:9	128
6:18	129
6–8	18
6–9	73
9	18
9:1	55, 120
9:7	129
9:9–17	129
9:20	55
9:20–21	55
9:22–24	55
11	18
11:30	132
12	18
12:1	129
12:1–3	17, 74
12:2–3	18, 129, 268
12:7	130
12:10	29
12:15	29
12:16	29
12:17–19	29
12:20	29
14:1–17	130
14:18–20	130
14:20	130
15	18
15:5–8	129
15:18	131
16	256
16:15	132
17:5	18
17:11	131
17:14	131
18:10	132
18:22–33	131
18–19	29
19	132
19:24	131
19:25	132

19:28.. 131
21...18, 256
21:1–7 132
21:9–10 132
21:12.. 132
22:1–3 132
22:2.. 132
22:11–13 132
23... 25
25...18, 132
25:29–34 133
29:35.. 134
29–30 18
32... 133
32:24.. 133
32:28.......................................18, 133
32:30.. 133
35:11.. 133
37... 18
37:7–10 133
37:12–28 133
37:26–27 134
37–41.. 257
37–50.. 257
39:13–20 133
41:43–46 133
41–47.. 29
42:3.. 134
42:7–8 133
43:9.. 134
44:33.. 134
45... 18
45:1–15 133
45:3.. 257
45:14–15 257
46–47.. 18
47:25.. 257
49:10......................................17, 31, 134
50... 18
50:19–21 257
50:20.. 133

Exodus

1... 18
1:8–14 29
1:22–2:10 137
2... 19
2:14.. 137
3... 19
3:8...138, 280
3:14–16 146
4:22...61, 138

4:30.. 146
6:6.. 157
7:14–8:19 146
7–12.............................. 19, 29, 137, 138
9:6.. 30
9:9.. 30
10:1–20 280
12......................31, 84, 97, 167, 257, 262
12:1–28 72
12:21–22 31
12:21–23 138
12:23.. 154
12:24–27 139
12:26–27 284
12:28.. 138
12:35–41 29
12–17.. 184
13–14.. 138
14... 19
14:9–10 139
14:13.. 139
14:22.. 139
14–15.. 29
15... 19
15–17.. 138
16..19, 38
16:9–10 146
16:22–26 139
16:35.. 139
17............................... 19, 84, 140, 171
17:6.. 140
17:10.. 140
17:11–12 140
19–23.. 19
19–24.......................................138, 181
20... 141
20:8–11 141
23:15.. 141
23:16.. 141
24..19, 125, 271
25:8.. 142
25:10–15 142
25:18–20 143
25–30.. 279
25–31.. 258
25–40.......................................19, 25
26:31–34 147
28... 202
28:1.. 146
35–40.. 258
40:3.. 258

40:4 258
40:5 258
40:6 258
40:7 258
40:12–15 143
40:36–38 259

Leviticus
1:3 145
1–7 .... 19, 259
8 146
9 146
16 .... 147, 259
16:11–17 147
16:14–15 147
16:21 147
23:15–22 141
23:33–44 141
25 .... 148, 157
25:10 148
26 .... 29, 181
26:33 151

Numbers
2:3 259
3:5–39 143
3:38 259
10 .... 19, 259
13 19
13:31–32 148
14 19
14:2 146
14:32–34 148
16:1–3 149
16:30–33 149
20:24–28 146
21:4–9 85
21:5 149
21:6 149
21:8 149
25:1 150
25:2–3 150
25:4–5 150
25:7–8 150
25:11 150
25:11–13 150
27:15–18 153

Deuteronomy
1–3 19
4–6 19
13–26 19
18:15 150

18:18 150
25:4 .... 27, 287
28 .... 29, 181
28:64 151
28–30 19
31 120

Joshua
1 .... 19, 120
1:7 153
1:14–15 155
1–3 184
2:9–11 154
2:11 262
2:13 154
2:14–18 262
2:18 154
3 19
3:7 120
3:14–17 154
6 .... 19, 261
7–12 19
10–12 .... 155, 261
13–22 19
23–24 20
24 153

Judges
1–2 20
6:15 156
6:16 156
6:30 156
6:34 156
6:36 156
7:6–8 156
7:19–25 156
8:30–31 156
13:3 156
13:5 156
13:24 156
16:19–21 156
16:22 156
16:29–30 156
16:30 156
17:6 155
18:1 155
19:1 155
21:25 .... 20, 155

Ruth
1:1 .... 158, 262
1:3 262
1:3–5 158

2:15–16 157
3:10–11 157
3:13 157
3:14 157
3:15 157
4 67
4:9–10 157
4:14–15 158
4:15 .... 158, 262
4:18–22 .... 20, 262
4:22 158

1 Samuel
1:20 159
2:35 .... 159, 160
3:1–18 159
3:19 160
3:20 159
5:4 160
5:9 160
5:12 160
6:11–15 160
7:15 159
15 171
16:11 160
16:13 160
17 89
17:4 263
17:42–43 161
17:45–47 161
17:49 .... 161, 263

2 Samuel
5 20
5:6–7 161
5:9 161
5–6 20
6:2–4 161
6:7 143
6:16–17 161
7:12–13 .... 20, 54, 162, 168
11:1–5 160
12 263
12:2–3 263
12:4 263
12:5 263
12:7 263

1 Kings
3:12 162
3–4 74
4:29–30 162
4:33 162

4:34 162
5–8 .... 20, 162, 163
6 264
6–8 .... 161, 184
10:2 279
12 20
17 163
18 163
19 164

2 Kings
1:8 .... 27, 164, 280
2 163
2:9 164
2:12–14 164
4:18–37 164
4:40–41 164
4:42–44 164
13:21 164
14:25 277
17:14 181
20:1 164
20:5–6 164
24:11–12 165
24:13 165
24:15 165
25 .... 161, 184, 255, 264
25:27–28 165
25:29–30 165

1 Chronicles
1 67

2 Chronicles
34:1–2 165
34:8 165
34:15 165
34:19 165
34:21 165
34:31 165
35:1 165
35:16–17 165
36:22 166
36:23 166

Ezra
1:2–3 167
2:1–2 168
3:2 168
3:10–11 168
3–4 264
7 21
7:8–9 168
7:10 168

9:2–3 168
9:6–15 168

Nehemiah
1:3–5 169
1–2 264
2:1–8 169
4–6 169
6:15 .... 21, 170
13 169

Esther
2 21
3:1 171
3:2–6 170
3:6 171
3:13 171
4:14 170
4:16 170
4–5 21
5:1 170
5:1–8 170
5:14 .... 170, 265
6:10 170
6:11 171
7 265
7:1–6 170
7:10 171
8–9 171
9 171
10:3 171

Job
1:1 173
1:21 173
1–2 268
1–3 267
2:7–10 173
2:11–13 173
3–31 173
19:25–27 173
38–41 267
41 .... 67, 267
42 267
42:10 174
42:12 174

Psalms
2 .... 28, 49, 290
2:1–6 171
2:4 149
2:7 28
3 174
3:1–2 174

4 222
6:2–3 174
6:10 175
11:7 175
16 49
17 268
17:1–2 268
17:8–9 268
17:13–14 268
17:15 268
19:10 280
22:1 .... 174, 175
22:18 .... 72, 175
23:1 30
23:6 175
24:1 41
24:7 175
42:1 30
69:21 175
72 268
72:8 .... 175, 268
72:9 268
72:10–11 279
72:11 175
72:15 .... 268, 279
72:17 268
80 .... 38, 268, 274
80:8–9 268
80:10–11 269
80:12–13 269
95 149
95:7–11 149
106:7–12 29
110 .... 49, 130
110:1 .... 130, 140
110:2 130
110:4 130

Proverbs
1:8–9 175
1:20–33 269
1:22 30
2:4 176
8 176
8:23–24 176
8:25–26 176
8:27–29 176
8:30–31 176
8:35 176
9:17 31
22:20–21 213

Ecclesiastes
3:20 29
11:1–2 269
11:3–6 269
11:9 177
12 270
12:1 177
12:3 270
12:4 270
12:6 270
12:7 270
12:12 177
12:13 177

Song of Songs
1:1 .... 178, 271
1:6 177
1:7 177
2:1 177
2:8 177
2:10–14 177
3:9–11 178
3:16 178
4:1–5:1 178
4:1–15 178
4:11 178
4:12 270
4:12–15 178
4:15 270
4:16 270
5:1 178
8:6 178
8:6–7 .... 178, 271

Isaiah
1:10 29
2:2 273
2:3–5 273
5 .... 193, 274
5:1–2 .... 184, 274
5:2 274
5:5–6 274
5:7 193
7 182
7:1–2 182
7:3–4 182
7:7 182
7:11–12 182
7:14 182
7:14–16 182
7:14–25 280
12 92
35:6 .... 282, 285

40 289
40:6–8 289
40:9–10 289
40–66 92
42 28
42:1 28
53 49
55 49
65:17 123

Jeremiah
1:5 274
1:6 .... 150, 183
1:10 274
3:12 183
5 183
13:1 274
13:4 274
13:6–7 274
13:9–10 274
13:10–11 274
20 183
22:5 183
24:1–2 274
24:5 274
24:5–7 274
24:8 274
24:9 274
24:10 274
31 183
31:31–34 27
38:1–13 183
43 183

Lamentations
1:2 183
1:8 183
2:2 183

Ezekiel
3:3 280
14:14 29
16 125
23:4 275
23:5 275
23:9 275
23:14–17 275
23:28–30 275
24 275
24:2 275
24:14 275
24:16 275
24:18 275

24:21 275
37 ...... 167, 275
37:4 275
37:7–8 275
37:9–10 275
37:12 276

Daniel
1:1–4 184
1:8 184
1:20 185
1:20–21 185
2:32–34 276
2:35 276
2:37–40 276
2:44–45 276
2:48–49 185
3:4–7 185
3:13–18 185
3:19–21 185
3:25 185
3:27 185
5 166
5:29 185
6:1–5 186
6:6–9 186
6:10–11 186
6:14–16 186
6:17 186
6:19–23 186
6:24 186
6:28 185
8:3–4 276
8:5–7 276
8:8 276
8:16–17 276
8:20–21 276
8:22 276
9:20–27 148
9:24 148
9:26–27 148
12:3 264

Hosea
1 125
1:2 186
1:4–11 276
1:10 277
2:2 271
2:14 277
2:14–23 186
2:22 277
2:23 277

3:1 186
3:2–3 186
9:10 284
11 61
11:1 61
11:5 61
11:10–11 61

Joel
1:4–7 280
3:4 187
3:7–8 187
3:19 187

Amos
1:2–2:3 187

Jonah
1:1–4 187
1:2–3 277
1:4–6 187
1:4–10 277
1:11–12 277
1:15 187
1:17 ...... 187, 277
2:10 ...... 187, 277

Micah
5:2 61

Habakkuk
1 49

Haggai
1:4–8 188
2:9 188
2:23 168

Malachi
4:5 164

Matthew
1 67
1:1 ...... 22, 119, 132, 162
1:1–17 ...... 131, 161
1:5 158
1:14 67
1:21 ...... 153, 182
1:22–23 182
1:23 260
1–2 156
2 61
2:1 61
2:6 61
2:11 279
2:13–18 137

2:15..61
2:16–18 290
2:23..61
3:4...280
3:16–17 161
3:17..28
4:1–11 ....138, 185
4:19–20 280
5:8...268
5:17....................157, 165, 169, 184
5:34–35 31
7:24...177
7:24–27 269
8:11...166
9:2...281
9:6...281
10:29...41
11:14..164
11:23...65
11:24..132
11:28..141
11:39–40 65
12:6......................................163, 184
12:28–29 155
12:38...35
12:39–40 187
12:40...35
12:40–41 119
12:41..................................35, 37, 188
12:42..................119, 163, 177, 185
13:44...30
15:8–9 256
16:18....................................168, 264
17:5...150
21:9...162
21:25...31
23:37..169
23:37–38 183
24:37–39 65
24:38–39 129
25:31–32 187
25:31–34 185
25:34....................................124, 151
25:41..151
26...133
27:46..175
27:51..147
27:59–66 186
28...134
28:18....................................140, 171

28:19–20 261
28:20....................................258, 260

Mark
1:6.......................................27, 164
1:11....................................132, 165
1:15....................................177, 183
1:27–28 163
1:40–45 164
1–3..155
2:5...257
2:23–28 141
3:1–6 141
3:6.....................................137, 169
3:20–21 133
3:27...161
3:32...133
4..177
4:1–20 283
4:3–8 283
4:9...283
4:15...283
4:16–17 283
4:18–19 283
4:20...283
4:35–37 281
4:38...281
4:40...281
4:41...281
5...155, 261
5:38–43 164
6:19–25 164
6:30–44 282
7:24–8:10 158
8:1–10 282
8:31.....................................133, 174
8:34...280
10:45...............134, 157, 169, 187, 284
10:46–47 282
10:48..282
10:51..282
10:52....................................282, 283
11...284
11:1...169
11:12–14 284
11:14..284
11:15–19 284
11–12 177
12:32..177
12:36..140
12:37....................................163, 177
13...183

14:1–2 ....139, 185
14:6.. 137
14:22–23 284
14:22–24 285
14:25.. 166
14–15 183
15:1–15 186
15:15.. 186
15:16–20 171
15:24.. 72
15:38.. 258

Luke
1:35...132, 159
1–2... 156
2:1–7..160, 276
2:4–7... 158
2:40...160, 176
2:47.. 176
2:52...160, 176
3... 67
4:16–24 166
7:11–17 164
9:31..27, 167
10:30–35 196
10:30–37 242
14:26... 30
15:11–32 250
22:20...138, 187, 284
23:34.. 127
24:16.. 48
24:27...44, 48, 295
24:32.. 48
24:44...44, 268, 295
24:45...49, 295
24:46–47 49

John
1:1–3.. 176
1:4... 176
1:11..132, 256
1:14.. 54, 142, 181, 273
1:29......................72, 119, 139, 146, 285, 299
1:46.. 156
2:19...163, 184, 264
2:19–21 170
2:19–22 .... 54, 188
2:20.. 184
2:21.. 163
3:14–15 149
3:16..126, 132
3:16–17 170
3:29.. 178

3:30.. 164
4:13.. 281
4:13–14 258
4:14...140, 281
4:15.. 281
4:26.. 281
4:29.. 281
4:41–42 281
5... 47
5:18... 47
5:19...161, 176
5:19–20 47
5:36...47, 137
5:38... 48
5:39...44, 48, 295
5:45... 48
5:46...44, 48, 295
5:46–47 48
6:1–15 164
6:32... 38
6:32–33 140
6:35...262, 285
6:48.. 282
6:48–51 258
6:51...119, 282
6:53.. 258
6:58.. 258
7:5... 133
7:37–39 142
8:12.. 142
8:29.. 176
10:1.. 283
10:5.. 283
10:8–11 283
10:14.. 178
10:16.. 178
10:17.. 134
11:38–44 164
12:31.. 161
12:32.. 273
13:1.. 284
13:3–5 284
13:6.. 284
13:8.. 284
14:6.. 258
14:26... 43
15:1..38, 184
15:26... 43
16:7... 43
16:8–11 43
16:13–14 43

16:33.. 174
17:1.. 161
17:8...................................146, 161, 181
19:24.. 175
19:28.. 175
19:30...................................147, 183, 259
19:41.. 143
20:1–10 160
20:11–12 143
20:19–29 257
20:25... 35
20:30–31 26
20–21 134

Acts
1:3.. 49
1:8...22, 261
1:14.. 133
2:1.. 142
2:25–28 49
2:34–35 49
3:1–3.. 285
3:6.. 285
3:7.. 285
3:8.. 285
3:22...119, 150
3:26.. 150
4:25–26 49
7:43–44 35
7:44... 36
7:52.. 182
7:52–53 181
8:30.. 49
8:31.. 49
8:32–35 49
9:4–5... 149
10:9.. 285
10:9–11 285
10:12–13 285
10:15... 285
13:14.. 49
13:22.. 160
13:27.. 49
13:33–41 49
17:2–3 49
23:25... 35

Romans
1:3.. 162
1:5.. 135
2:28–29 131
3:23.. 256
4:13.. 130

5...66, 73, 74, 83
5:12.. 127
5:12–21 66
5:14.......................35, 36, 73, 119, 120, 125
5:20.. 74
6:3–5... 129
6:17.. 35
8:1..185, 262
8:13.. 262
8:18–21 123
8:20–22 170
8:21–23 124
8:31–34 172
8:31–39 ....125, 178
8:37.. 262
8:39.. 271
9:22–26 277
16:20... 171

1 Corinthians
1:30.. 176
5:7.......................... 31, 165, 257, 299
6:19.................................54, 163, 188
9:9...27, 287
9:10–11 288
10:1–4 ....201, 258
10:1–5 65
10:1–11 208
10:2–4 288
10:4.................................119, 140, 258
10:5.. 288
10:6.................................... 35, 36, 65
10:11... 288
10:31... 259
11:25–26 172
15:4.. 165
15:20.................... 128, 142, 165, 172
15:23... 124
15:25...............................128, 155, 171
15:25–26 125
15:26... 124
15:45...74, 125

2 Corinthians
3:14–16 55
4:16.. 265
4:17.. 174
11:2.. 125
11:3.. 125

Galatians
2:14.. 269
3:13.. 157

3:16.........................54, 132, 138, 268
3:29.....................................54, 264
4..208, 224
4:1–7..54
4:6–7..264
4:24..200, 288
4:24–26 257
4:24–31 288
4:25...257
4:28–29 257
4:30–31 257
4:31...289
5:16–25 262
6:15...131

Ephesians
1:3...256
1:10...43
1:11...41
2:14–16 286
5:25–27 178
5:32..........................125, 177, 271
6:10–20 261

Philippians
1:6...187
1:21...174
2:8...133
2:9–11 ....134, 171
2:10–11 175
3:9...126
3:10–11 268
3:17...35
3:18–19 187
3:21...268

Colossians
1:15...125
1:15–16 44
1:16–17 176
1:17...41
2:3...176
2:9...160
2:11...131
2:16–17 142
2:17...37
3:17...259

1 Thessalonians
1:7...35

2 Thessalonians
1:10...187
3:9...35

1 Timothy
2:5–6...143
4:12...35

Titus
2:7...35

Hebrews
1:1–2......................................150, 182
1:3...........................125, 164, 175
3:7–11 149
3:12...149
4:8...154
4:9...141
4:9–11 260
5:1–6...146
7..131
7:7...131
7:9–10 131
7:23–25 146
7:24...143
7:26...119
7:26–27 146
7:27...146
8:1–2...38
8:4...36
8:5.....................................35, 36, 37
8:8–12 27
9:4...143
9:7...146
9:11...56
9:11–28 37
9:12...147
9:21–22 37
9:23...37
9:24......................37, 38, 49, 56, 143, 175
9–10...49
10:1...37, 49
10:4...145
10:10...146
10:12......................................146, 299
10:20...147
10:31...149
11:4...127
11:5...128
11:7...128
11:8–9 129
11:10......................................130, 162
11:13......................................130, 260
11:13–16 54
11:14...130

11:16...130, 154
12:22..162
12:24..127
13:13..289

1 Peter
1:10–11 43
1:10–12 295
1:12..43
1:19...173, 257
1:23..289
1:24–25 289
1:25..290
2:4–5...188
2:5...163, 168
2:9..166
2:21..173
3:19..160
3:20–22 129
3:21..37
3:22..160
5:3..35

2 Peter
1:21..42
2:4–10 149
2:6..132
3:7..129
3:13..171

1 John
1:5..30
3:12..256
4:8..256

Jude
14–15 128

Revelation
1..22
2–3...22
5:5..162
7:9...133, 264
7:9–14 ....158, 165
12:1–4 290
12:5..290
12:6..290
12:14–17 290
19:9..125
19:16..162
20..23
20:2–3 155
21..23
21:1..123
21:2...126, 162, 184
21:4...123, 162
21:8..183
21:27..124
21–22 124
22..60
22:1–2 124
22:3..124

40 QUESTIONS SERIES

40 Questions About Angels, Demons, and Spiritual Warfare
John R. Gilhooly

40 Questions About Arminianism
J. Matthew Pinson

40 Questions About Baptism and the Lord's Supper
John S. Hammett

40 Questions About Biblical Theology
Jason S. DeRouchie

40 Questions About Calvinism
Shawn D. Wright

40 Questions About Christians and Biblical Law
Thomas R. Schreiner

40 Questions About Church Membership and Discipline
Jeremy M. Kimble

40 Questions About Creation and Evolution
Kenneth D. Keathley, Mark F. Rooker

40 Questions About Elders and Deacons
Benjamin L. Merkle

40 Questions About the End Times
Eckhard Schnabel

40 Questions About the Great Commission
Daniel L. Akin, Benjamin L. Merkle, George G. Robinson

40 QUESTIONS SERIES

40 Questions About Heaven and Hell
Alan W. Gomes

40 Questions About the Historical Jesus
C. Marvin Pate

40 Questions About Interpreting the Bible, 2nd ed.
Robert L. Plummer

40 Questions About Islam
Matthew Aaron Bennett

40 Questions About Pastoral Ministry
Phil A. Newton

40 Questions About Prayer
Joseph C. Harrod

40 Questions About Roman Catholocism
Gregg R. Allison

40 Questions About Salvation
Matthew Barrett

40 Questions About Typology and Allegory
Mitchell L. Chase